Eternal & Present:
40 Days unto The Spirit

by B.R. MØRK

Published by:
Valley Springs Institute
http://www.valleyspringsinstitute.com

Quotations from the Bible are from the King James Version, public
domain.

Cover photography and artwork by the authors.
Back Cover "Valley Springs Institute" artwork by Booker Atkins.

Dedicated to:
The Friends of the Bridegroom

John 3:29

Table of Contents

*For encouragement or prayer along the way, please contact us at
eternalandpresent.author@gmail.com.*

Eternal and Present: Purpose, Design and Method

"That though mightest know the certainty of those things, wherein thou hast been instructed."
Luke 1:4

Long ago and in diverse ways, God revealed Himself to His children. In those desert days, He heaped up water, set blazing pillars of fire in the midst of the camp, rained down bread from heaven, and brought forth surging water from the Rock. Though His people had turned away and danced to idols of their own making – in Him there is no shadow of turning (James 1:17b).

Though His people still turn this way and that before the idols of our time, He draws them forth unto Himself through water and the fire of the Holy Spirit. By the power of Jesus' death and resurrection, are we led from merely walking in the world – to walking upheld by the leading hand of the Holy Spirit as ambassadors of the Kingdom of God (Isaiah 41:13; 2 Corinthians 5:20). Though there is confusion in our culture; God is not silent and man is not alone.

Jesus, the Author and Perfecter of our Faith, entered into His ministry via Baptism, then was drawn by the Spirit unto walking 40 days in the desert (Matthew 4:1-ff.). We believe that Jesus Himself is leading you forward in your spiritual walk toward a fuller relationship with Him and a Spirit-led ministry to others...and that you are being drawn, as we were, and as Christ was...into a desert encounter.

This book is written for all who long to experience the leading hand of the Holy Spirit and see the power of God bring deliverance and life in the midst of the 24/7 press of the daily grind. Though the world has changed the Rock pouring forth rivers of Living Water has not! Indeed, "The word of the Lord endureth for ever" (1 Peter 1:25a) and the Name of the Word of the Lord is Jesus Christ (John 1).

We believe the LORD is who He declares Himself to be. As we set out, we testify that God is the Creator who is Eternal, Triune, Almighty and Holy; and our Heavenly Father who sent His Son Jesus Christ as the Savior of the world. Jesus is Bridegroom, Redeemer, Messiah, Good Shepherd and Friend; and through the Holy Spirit who is with us forever, we experience the daily presence of God as Paraclete, Counselor, Advocate, Teacher, Healer and Comforter....we are surely not orphaned or alone as we walk this side of heaven!

Our God is with us and calls each one of His own by name. And since God has known you before you were knit together in your mother's womb, these words are nothing but a mere witness to what is already true before the High King of Heaven. This book empties itself of any promise that it is a pathway to God or that it can bring you closer to Him....for Jesus declares Himself as the only way to the Father (John 14:6).

This book alone cannot lead you to victory in the circumstances of your life; yet it testifies that Jesus can and will. For in Christ, the victory over the enemy and over the world is sure. For those "who did not love their life, even unto death" overcome "by the blood of the Lamb, and by the word of their testimony" (Revelation 12:11). The Bible is explicit that those who believe in Jesus as the Son of God overcome the world (1 John 5:5b)! And this devotional journey takes the Word of God for His word, by simply drawing upon what is written.

While there are many reliable translations of scripture, we have perceived that a fresh encounter with God's Spirit often follows hearing a familiar passage in a new way. We are led of the Spirit to refer to the King James Version of the Bible for the sole reason that its language and semantic categories press past our current use of English. Even in our own study, we have experienced breakthroughs of God's Spirit as we have heard the Word afresh as it has been unhinged from modern categories of thought. If the King James Version is familiar to you, consider picking up the Geneva Bible or another translation rooted in or prior to the Reformation era.

Eternal and Present is a devotional work, covered in prayer, undergird with sound scriptural study, worked out in life and experienced by the authors as a pathway through which we encountered the touch of God's Spirit. As you pray through each day, we encourage you to linger in the King James for awhile to see what God's Spirit may do. We also encourage you to take up whatever device or translation you prefer and reference cross-translation as the Spirit leads. For God alone knows what you need and will light your path according to His perfect knowledge and will for your life. If you are new to scriptural study, fear not! All direct references to scripture are parenthetically included without abbreviation for your convenience.

This devotional is organized around six-day weeks under the impulse of Exodus 34:21, "Six days thou shalt work, but on the seventh day thou shalt rest: in earing time and in harvest thou shalt rest." As we have endeavored in the Lord through this work, the Holy Spirit continually appointed the seventh day as a day of fruit-filled rest. Wherever we went, the Lord wove together the words of this devotional with our Sabbath worship, to deeply root us in and grow us up in Christ (Colossians 2:7). We pray that your journey will be so blessed; and encourage you to walk through this book as the Spirit leads. If the Lord leads you to linger on a day, or change the order of the week; the Holy Spirit, not this book – is our Captain.

Even if some of the scriptural progression in this book may not, at first, make sense to the mind; we pray that you might press on and see where God leads your spiritual sense. For we have found that God has led us past even our own understandings as we have released ourselves into the flowing river of the Spirit's leading counsel. May He establish His word in your lives: "Nevertheless, I [God] am continually with thee: thou has holden

9

me by my right hand. Thou shalt guide me with thy counsel, and afterward receive me to glory" (Psalm 73:22-24).

This book is written as a love-offering unto the Lord. As such, each day is designed as a sacrifice of praise! The head scripture unfolds into a spiritual walk that begins in week one with a twenty-minute devotion, then becomes more robust week by week; culminating in days 37- 40 being designed for an hour or so of purposed consideration. It is our understanding and experience that the step-by-step progression of these *40 Days* will be used of God to strengthen the inner man.

The devotional content of *Eternal and Present* was given during hours of prayer and study in the last watches of the night and into the early light of morning. We perceive that as you are led by the Spirit, the Almighty will provide you with the commitment of time and sustenance to complete this journey; even as He made it possible for us in to walk in ways and means beyond ourselves.

- If you believe in Jesus the Son of God, and strain to hear His voice...
- If you love His Name, His Word, and pursue His Righteousness...
- If you call upon Him to guide your foot into the path of Life by the leading of the Holy Spirit...
- If you yearn to experience the victory of His cross in the doings of the day...

- If you are ready to take a stand with your life and declare that God is not silent...

- ...as you pray through *Eternal and Present,* we are believing that like us, you will experience the miraculous power of God.

For Jesus has promised, "I will not leave you comfortless: I will come to you" (John 14:18). He has given you a Spirit of Adoption "whereby we cry, Abba! Father!" (Romans 8:15). You are covered in the power-filled calling and the love of Christ for Jesus says, "...as my Father hath sent me, even so send I you" (John 20:21). "And I have declared unto them thy name, and will declare it: that the love wherewith thou hast loved me may be in them, and I in them" (John 17:26).

Under the banner of this Divine Presence, Calling, and Love, Jesus says the Holy Spirit will "teach you all things, and bring all things to your remembrance, whatsoever I have said unto you" (John 14:26) and "will guide you into all truth" (John 16:13b). Whatever God speaks, He fulfills (Numbers 23:19)! And this not out of human striving, education, pedigree, or by any other natural work – save by the power of His Spirit Alone. For it is "Not by might, nor by power, but by my spirit, saith the LORD of hosts" (Zechariah 4:6). Alleluia and Amen!

May God bless you and draw you nearer to Him according to this Promise:

For thus saith the high and lofty One that inhabiteth eternity, whose name is Holy; I dwell in the high and holy place, with him also that is of a contrite and humble spirit, to revive the spirit of the humble, and to revive the heart of the contrite ones.

Isaiah 57:15

May it be so through your lives and ours to the Praise of His Glorious Grace.

TO THE KING!

B.R. MØRK

Week One, Day One – Blessing of the Walk

"Fear not, little flock; for it is your Father's good pleasure
to give you the kingdom."
Luke 12:32

The beginning of walking in the Spirit, of leaving behind the shore of this world and setting one's feet upon the Way, is receiving God's Word as God gives His Word to you. The disciple or student of Jesus learns to delight in the instruction of the Lord through scripture. While Mary sat at the feet of Jesus and chose the One thing that would not be taken from her; so in like manner, Jesus' own sit at the feet of scripture and begin to learn what the voice of God sounds like (Luke 10:39-42).

Those who choose to be planted at the feet of God's self-revelation, which is God's own declaration of who He is and what He has done, begin to be trained in knowing the voice of the Father whose Word pours forth (Psalm 19:2). Those choosing to meditate on the Word are pictured as trees, deeply rooted near streams of water and drawing upon the flowing river for life (Psalm 1:3). So it is when the one who loves Jesus draws from the deep well-spring of God's Holy Word – the Bible.

A tree near a river simply plunges its roots into the source of life-giving nourishment in the ground where it is planted. To walk in the counsel of God is to accept Scripture as pure water and pure nourishment; that is, as God's self-revelation poured out to you through the faithful vessels of those who have gone before. This revelation is substantial and separate, for it is from God (2 Timothy 3:16). This revelation is unchanging, for God's Word is not removed from His Being; for "In the beginning was the Word, and the Word was with God, and the Word was God" (John 1:1).

When a person receives Christ as Lord and Savior, when they embrace the gift of faith of Jesus, they declare agreement with God's revealed Word-made-Flesh. Deep in their spirit, the root of faith begins to grow and in-that-moment, they receive the ability to know God and apprehend Him through the Holy Spirit. God cannot be known by human striving nor by the powers of intellect or logic but is "revealed from faith to faith" (Romans 1:17).

Indeed, many well-meaning people are taught to read the book of scripture apart from faith, and to divide it word by word by human intellect alone. With the mind, they believe they have found God; then move to declare what the Bible says and means to say and how interpretation and application of that word is to take shape. Yet the thoughts of a busy mind are not necessarily the thoughts of God (Isaiah 55:8) as the meaning of scripture is secured forever in the counsel of God (Isaiah 40:8, 46:10). The Holy Spirit, who is the Counselor – reveals the things of God to the people of God (1 Corinthians 2:10; John 15:26).

Fear not, little flock; for it is the Father's good pleasure to give you the Kingdom! Revelation of the Kingdom of God is not taken, nor apprehended, nor interpreted by human means; but is received as a gift of the Father's good pleasure! As we embark

14

together on this devotional journey, will you join us as listening sheep settled at the feet of the Good Shepherd (John 10:27)? Will you drink deeply of the stream of living water? Will you release yourself to pursue the One thing necessary, cease from mindful striving and sit as Mary sat under Jesus' instruction (Luke 10:39-42)? Will you be "taught of God" (John 6:45)?

For the Word of God carries the meaning God intends as, "The counsel of the LORD standeth for ever, the thoughts of his heart to all generations" (Psalm 33:11). As we pursue the unchanging and durable thoughts of the King's heart, will you allow the Holy Spirit to lead you as if by the hand, into the ever-deepening water of God's Word (1 Corinthians 2:10)?

Thankfully, knowing God is more than receiving some cognitive understanding or logical argument derived from a book. As a follower of Jesus, you are brought into proximal relationship with Immanuel – our God-with-us. This gift was received when you said in your own way, "Come into my heart, Lord Jesus!" He did come. He lives there now by the Holy Spirit in you – in the tent of your clay pot (1 Corinthians 6:19). He in you, and you in Him (John 17:22-23, 26).

And the water Jesus has given "shall be...a well of water springing up into everlasting life" (John 4:14b). Your prayer is caught up in Jesus' own words:

> Now they have known that all things whatsoever that thou hast given me are of thee. For I have **given unto them the words which thou gavest me**...and they have believed.

And the glory which thou gavest me I have given them; that they may be one, even as we are one: I in them, and thou in me…

John 17:7, 8b, 22-23a (emphasis ours)

Fear not dear friend, and receive what God declares has been given (Mark 5:36)! In receiving Jesus, you are brought to new life; as a tree planted, rooted and growing up into Him, no longer "tossed to and fro, and carried about with every wind of doctrine, by the sleight of men, *and* cunning craftiness" (Colossians 2:7; Ephesians 4:14-15). If you be not so rooted, confess Jesus now in your heart and with your lips as your Lord and Savior – and wherever you are – you become a sure sapling of God (Romans 10:9).

Rejoice dear brother or sister, for the Father *has* given you the Kingdom! Jesus, the King of Glory, tabernacles in you through the Holy Spirit. And where the King is; surely, there also is His Kingdom! In receiving King Jesus, may you receive the Bible as the enduring, pure counsel of God, and affirm by the power of the Holy Spirit: "Thus saith the LORD, thy Redeemer, the Holy One of Israel; I am the LORD thy God which teacheth thee to profit, which leadeth thee by the way that thou shouldest go" (Isaiah 48:17). May you rejoice in God's leading by saying, "This *is* the way, I will walk in it! The way of walking in the Spirit…Alleluia and Amen!"

Prayer of Response: Blessing of the Walk

Please pray aloud with us...

As we end each devotional reading, would you join your prayers with our own and pray aloud? Though it may be challenging to pray aloud, we will later unravel the importance of doing so, that we together may:

> ...take the helmet of salvation, and the sword of the Spirit, which is the word of God: Praying always with all prayer and supplication in the Spirit and watching thereunto with all perseverance and supplication for all saints.
>
> Ephesians 6:17-18

At the conclusion of each written prayer, please continue on in the Spirit as you are led. For though we walk together in the Holy Spirit, the Lord brings each of us to Him according to His boundless love.

Heavenly Father, I confess that in You, there is no shadow of turning. I rejoice in knowing that the counsel of Your heart stands even unto this moment. I rejoice in the revelation that it is Your good pleasure to give me the Kingdom. Release my heart, mind and soul from any understanding, fear or striving that is not of You. Open the eyes and ears of my spirit to receive Your Spirit alone, by Your Word alone, through Christ alone; that I may see and hear Your Counsel and walk in the way You are leading me to go – unto Your Glory alone! Thank you, Father. In Jesus' Name. Amen.

Week One, Day Two – It Is Possible

*"And Jesus looking upon them saith, 'With men it is impossible, but
not with God: for with God all things are possible.'"*
Mark 10:27

Upon accepting Jesus as Lord and Savior of your life, the
seemingly impossible happened; you were born again of God
through water and the Spirit. For Jesus says, "Verily, verily, I say
unto thee, except a man be born again, he cannot see the kingdom
of God. That which is born of the flesh is flesh; and that which is
born of the Spirit is spirit" (John 3:5-6). By this second birth, you
receive more than your father's eyes or your mother's smile. You
receive a spirit of adoption into the Kingdom of God and are made
a living son or daughter of the Most High God (Romans 8:15).

For to "...as many as received him [Jesus], to them gave He
power to become the sons of God...which were born, not of
blood...nor of the will of man, but of God" (John 1:12-13). God
Himself places a new heart within you, a new spiritual organ. For
through Jesus, your Father gathered you, sprinkled you clean and
declared, "A new heart also will I give you...I will take away the
stony heart...I will put my spirit within you" (Ezekiel 36:25-27).

What is it like to receive the Kingdom of God through this
new birth? As Jerusalem has many gates set within the walls, so
you stand as gate and watchman of your own walled city – your
God-given soul, mind, heart and body. When you freely choose to

confess belief in Jesus, you open the gate to your city and welcome the King of Glory to enter in as your King and your God!

In this moment, the gate of your stony heart rolls away and the dead spirit-of-man is forever restored! For the Spirit of God quickens you to life and takes up residence in the tabernacle of your supernatural new heart wherein God places His Spirit. Just as the Holiest of Holies is pictured within the Jerusalem Temple as the footstool of the Most High; so for the Believer, the Lord now tabernacles deep within. He knocked at your door and you invited this treasure into your clay jar. "Know ye not that ye are the temple of God, and that the Spirit of God dwelleth in you" (1 Corinthians 3:16)?

This new heart or spirit is ever more real than any natural attribute of the mind or body. For it is not a natural gift from man, nor a work of righteousness, but is a supernatural regeneration by the renewing work of the Holy Spirit (Titus 3:5). This new spirit can be likened to the Mercy Seat in the Temple. By this new spiritual organ, the spirit of a man encounters the Holy Spirit of God.

In this secret place, the Holy Spirit bears witness with your spirit that you are a child of God and joint-heir with Christ (Romans 8:16). In this deep inner chamber, you abide in the shadow of the Almighty (Psalm 91) even as you share your secret prayers with the Father and receive the consolations of the Spirit. In your hidden heart, Jesus loves you with an everlasting love, "...that the love wherewith thou [the Father] hast loved me may be

19

in them, and I in them" (John 17:26). The endless depths of the love of God are hidden within you; not as metaphor, copy or even as feeling, but as the actual fullness of God's Spirit. Faith alone receives this impossible gift-made-possible by God (Galatians 3:2, 14).

Anything of the natural flesh fades, but the spiritual carries the attribute of eternity. "Being born again, not of corruptible seed, but of incorruptible by the word of God, which liveth and abideth forever" (1 Peter 1:23). How impossible this new birth seems to the modern man. How impossible to natural logic is the declaration of scripture that our spirit meets directly with the Holy Spirit for conversation! *And Jesus looking upon them saith, 'With men it is impossible, but not with God: for with God all things are possible.'*

At this the mind-of-the-watchman rises up within many a Believer and enquiries ensue under its gate-arch: Does the Holy Spirit *really* talk with me personally? How can it be exactly that God pours a new spirit into *me*? What does it mean that the Immanuel *abides in me* and I in Him? Do *I hear Him* speaking between my ears, or myself, or another spirit? What *does* Jesus sound like? How do *I know* He is who He says He is and where He says He is? Why don't *I feel* the relational love, peace and joy that Jesus promises? Why don't *I experience* the power of God in *my* life?

Doubt rises up and the professionals are called in to settle the truth about what is really possible. The study books are opened,

20

the ink is spilled and the repetitive and ongoing questions press forward as from the beginning. The walled city of the mind, still insisting on being captained by the training of the world, places a bushel over the new spirit deep within "until" a sufficient answer can be found to the world-felling query - "Did God *really say...?"*

The whispers of the Spirit of God are choked by the cares of the world...yet the incorruptible seed does not die. For "...To day if ye will hear his voice, harden not your hearts, as in the provocation" (Hebrews 3:15). Are you longing to experience God? Are you longing to hear Him? If you will hear Him, then let Him past the interrogation gate-arch. For it is written...

> That [Jesus] was the true Light, which lighteth every man, that cometh into the world. He was in the world, and the world was made by him, and the world knew him not. He came unto his own, and his own received him not. But as many as received him, to them gave he power to become the sons of God, even to them that believe on his name.
>
> John 1:9-12

Watchman, will you receive His Light today? By belief on His Name, according to God's self-revelation in scripture, will you allow the bushel basket of darkening doubts to be overcome by Light (John 1:5)? He will not withhold Himself from you...for Jesus has already called you by name. He has already died to rescue you; and you are now a son or daughter of the Kingdom. God has already demonstrated His power deep within you; thereby proving that nothing – including making Himself personally know to you – is impossible for Him.

Prayer of Response: It Is Possible

Please pray aloud with us...

Heavenly Father, Thank You that Your Mercy Seat is no longer on the Temple Mount or upon some other holy hill. Thank You for my new heart and for the new spirit that You place within me. According to scriptures, I believe that Your Holy Spirit testifies to my spirit that I am Your child. I confess that I receive Your Name in my spirit, and hereby open the gate of my soul, mind and body to be led by You as my King and my God. Please release me from a spirit of doubt and any spirit of worldly wisdom. Please open the eyes and ears of my spirit to receive the words of Your Spirit alone, by Your Word alone, through Christ alone. In Jesus' Name, Amen.

Week One, Day Three – Set Apart

"Many there be which say of my soul, there is no help for him in God. But thou, O LORD, art a shield for me; my glory, and the lifter up of mine head."

"I will not be afraid of ten thousands of people, that have set themselves against me round about."
Psalm 3:2-3,6

King David, for all his flaws, was a man after God's "own heart" (Acts 13:22). Though he loved God, he departed from the God he loved by exercising his own counsel and helping himself to Bathsheba. As a result of this sin against God, the sword did not leave his house (2 Samuel 12:10). Psalm 3 is written as David flees for his life – from his own son.

Are you a man or woman after God's own heart? If so, do you take counsel from God alone through His Scripture alone, by Faith alone, under Grace alone through Christ alone? Or do you believe the prevailing culture's wisdom that self-help comes via self-reflection, self-direction, personal growth, accomplishment, or service?

Perhaps expectations within family, church, work or social relationships press hard upon your soul. As the clock ticks and the day passes, you mark your time and keep your head above water by crossing off the tasking list those things which are completed or "done" for others. You may be in survival-mode. In such a sink-

or-swim world, walking in the counsel of God's Spirit may seem impossibly impractical and time-consuming.

Yet whenever we turn to any authority other than God to guide, help or counsel; whenever we accept the priorities, patterns and teachings of this world as our master, we are in a dangerous way. Like David, we are attracted to what we see around us. We are drawn by those things that compete for the devotion of our heart and may even seem on the surface to fit into a pursuit of God.

Does God counsel His son or daughter to set personal goals, get the grade, grab the promotion, throw yourself into your work, get plugged in, be purpose driven, pull yourself up by your boot straps, learn the love languages or be happy, successful and passionate in all you do? Have you considered the subtle message of these compassing words?

Just as in David's day, so today; *"Many there be which say of my soul, there is no help for him in God."* Common wisdom declares that real help comes by personal striving or by changing the situation – that by just learning the right method and trying harder, success in all its forms will follow on. Many of God's sons and daughters have given over their lives to this attractive worldly counsel; yet "Know ye not, that to whom ye yield yourselves servants to obey, his servants ye are to whom you obey...?" (Romans 6:16)

Like David, *"ten thousands...have set themselves against me round about."* These forces press-hard against you and tell you who you must be and what you must do to be a responsible and

24

happy citizen of this world. These counselors may even sound overtly "Christian" as they seek to captivate your heart into achieving, by your own effort and self-improvement, apparently godly ends.

As David was tempted to be a man after the world, instead of a man after God – so too was Jesus. Satan winsomely presented attractive ends designed to allure Jesus from the perfect counsel and will of the Father. Jesus responds to this noisy foe with the Holy Word alone saying, "...it is written, Thou shalt worship the Lord thy God, and him only shalt thou serve" (Luke 4:8). In the face of the one who commands the armies of hell, Jesus demonstrated the line we are to hold in receiving counsel and standing without fear before our enemies. Jesus spoke the word of God from scripture. Satan departed. And ministers from heaven came to provide (Luke 4:1-13).

Jesus improved nothing that His Father had given. He applied no natural method of striving or earthly tactic for interpersonal confrontation. He set no other authority alongside the Father's teaching. His counsel came from God alone and carried the authority and power of the Almighty (John 5:19, 12:49).

What then of David? We may rejoice, for though he strayed into self-direction, the New Testament confirms that He is yet reckoned as a man after God's own heart who fulfilled God's will (Acts 13:22)! As David repents, then turns and returns his heart unto God alone; the LORD Himself does not waver as his Help, his Shield, and the One who lifts-up-his-head! For "The

LORD *is* merciful and gracious, slow to anger, and plenteous in mercy" (Psalm 103:8).

Will you cry out for God's mercy and receive the truth that there is help for you in God? For "...the mercy of the LORD *is* from everlasting to everlasting upon them that fear him, and his righteousness unto children's children" (Psalm 103:17). Will you, like David, turn to God alone in your need; though your family, friends, teachers or even fellow churchgoers declare that there is no real or practical personal help for you in God?

Will you stand on the line of Scripture and declare that Christ dwells in you, and you in Him (John 17:26). And from this shielded position, release your life to God and receive Jesus Himself to be your only authority (Lord), your only help (Savior), and the Holy Spirit your only teacher (Guide) in both spiritual and practical matters?

Prayer of Response: Set Apart

Please pray aloud with us...

Heavenly Father, thank You for Your everlasting mercy. Please release me from any attraction to self-direction or to walking according to the world's teachings, methods and ways. Like David, I repent from my sin and seek Your heart alone. I cry out for deliverance from the words of the enemy that compass me about.

According to scriptures, I believe that You are my Help, my Shield, my Glory and the One who lifts my chin in the midst

of my present situation and the practical matters of this world. Please counsel me by the Holy Spirit to hold the scriptural line as Jesus did in the face of the noisy foe. Please open the eyes and ears of my spirit to receive the counsel of Your Spirit alone, by Your Word alone, through Christ alone, to Your Glory alone. Please lead me into Your will. Thank you, Father. In Jesus' Name, Amen.

Week One, Day Four – The Work

"Knowing therefore the terror of the Lord, we persuade men; but we are made manifest unto God; and I trust also are made manifest in your consciences."

"For whether we be beside ourselves, it is to God: or whether we be sober, it is for your cause."
2 Corinthians 5:11, 13

Are you beside yourself when it comes to matters of God? Do you go about the work of your day aware of God's presence manifest in you? As others encounter you – do they see something of Jesus?

Walking in the Spirit is nothing less than crossing over from "living, moving and having your being" on the ground of man's wisdom; to being wholly beside yourself and standing upon the immovable Rock of the testimony of Jesus Christ in the power of the Holy Spirit (Acts 17:28; 1:8). Jesus taught us saying, "Woe unto you, when all men shall speak well of you! For so did their fathers to the false prophets" (Luke 6:26).

Though you may wake up in the same bed, greet the same people and circumstances, pour the same hot cup of coffee and set into the day just about the same way as yesterday; are you willing to allow the things of the world and the praises of men to fade to the background? As you take up this journey of walking unto the Spirit, God draws nearer to you (2 Chronicles 15:2-4; James 4:8).

Will you welcome Him into your foreground? (John 3:30; 2 Corinthians 8:8)

For it is written, "He that hath my commandments, and keepeth them, he it is that loveth me: and he that loveth me shall be loved of my Father, and I will love him, and will manifest myself to him" (John 14:21). Let your spirit rejoice! For even as who you are is made manifest to God; God manifests who He is – and makes Himself known to you. And through you, to others.

Perhaps, you are shaken and do not yet understand what this all means. Perhaps you imagine that having the courage to relate to friends and family that you are walking in the Holy Spirit into experiencing the manifestation of God's power in your life; leaves you feeling a bit like an over-zealous fanatic. You are in good company, for so Paul wrote: *"Knowing therefore the terror of the Lord, we persuade men."* Will you hold the line of scripture?

Some people might outright deny that practically experiencing a spiritual God is impossible. Some believe that this ability ended with the days of the apostles; yet Jesus Christ is your Rock, Fortress and Strong Habitation. From the vantage point of the gospel, you are held fast and will not be overwhelmed or ashamed (Psalm 71:1-4).

Though some will discount walking in *"the terror of the Lord;"* though others will cast a line of teaching out to save you from heavenly delusion and warn you that hearing the Holy Spirit directly is "not of the Lord;" though your family and friends may nervously avoid your eye and walk around you; though in more and more places, confessing the Name of Jesus increasingly brings a charge of "hate;" stand firm in the testimony of scripture.

Retreat to your Rock *"Knowing therefore the terror of the Lord"* and *"persuade men."* For where your physical footfalls land, there the Spirit of God is present "for ye are the temple of the living God" (2 Corinthians 6:16). It can be no wonder that some seek to put a bushel basket atop your witness!

Or perhaps you yourself are four days into this devotional still waiting to personally experience the *"terror of the Lord."* Perhaps you are crying out to know the life of Jesus Christ manifest within you and are longing to be shaken just a little; that you might actually perceive God. Perhaps the ever-present frustrating nitty-gritty of life overwhelms any sense of Christ being present and active on earth at all; let alone deeply within you.

How agonizing are the days of man, "The days of our years are threescore years and ten; and if by reason of strength they be fourscore years, yet is their strength labour and sorrow..." (Psalm 90:10). Even the great apostle Paul says, "For in this [earthly house] we groan, earnestly desiring to be clothed upon with our house which is from heaven..." (2 Corinthians 5:2).

Whether firm in Christ, or groaning under the weight of this life, the victory of the gospel is that we are now set apart in Jesus. For the gospel of Christ "is the power of God unto salvation to every one that believeth" (Romans 1:16b). You are saved; though you may cry to know *"the terror of the Lord."* This day in your spiritual walk can be likened to waiting in the Upper Room as a true disciple of Jesus, not yet knowing how Christ might come up from the grave. Yet take heart, the miracle has already happened!

Remember brother or sister that the disciples did not burst from the Upper Room into a full experience of walking in the Spirit. The ones upon the Emmaus Road walked with Jesus Himself; yet did not know it. Could this be you today? The Lord appeared to His followers many times. After *seeing* Him, hundreds of witnesses began to testify to the infallible visible proof that Jesus died, was buried and raised (1 Corinthians 15:3-8)! For them seeing was believing; but for us – believing is seeing. Some call this a spiritual inversion.

In this inversion Jesus Himself, as the sure Word of God, declares those who believe without seeing; are blessed. "Jesus saith unto him, Thomas, because thou hast seen me, thou hast believed: blessed *are* they that have not seen, and *yet* have believed" (John 20:29). Are you wondering what blessing Jesus is speaking of? Can you perceive the blessing from the Lord Himself which comes to the Believer who-has-not-seen?

When the disciples saw the Lord ascend, Jesus said, "You shall receive power, after that the Holy Ghost is come upon you; and ye shall be witnesses to me both in Jerusalem, and in all Judea, and in Samaria, and unto the uttermost part of the earth" (Acts 1:8). Upon seeing this, they returned to an upper room, "...continued with one accord in prayer and supplication," and made ready for the mission of witnessing to Jesus' resurrection (Acts 1:13-26). THEN they saw the Holy Spirit manifest in their lives and

31

descending upon them as flaming tongues of fire! At this point, they *"knew the terror of the Lord"* and took up the witness-mantle to *"persuade men."* These believed Jesus, acted upon their belief, and then knew the power of God! Believing and doing preceded seeing.

God loves you. The Lord will not leave or forsake you (Deuteronomy 31:6). Take courage if He is calling you today....and pray as He leads. Believe Jesus and act upon that belief. Sometime today, enter your upper room away from any competing voice or worldly care, and pray for the resolve to commit yourself, "to witness unto Him."

For the power of the Holy Spirit breaks-through into our lives as we move past receiving Jesus into our hearts as Lord and Savior, toward asking for the power to be living witnesses unto the resurrection of Christ the King (Acts 1:8). Will you take up the work and power of the witness-mantle and acknowledge that you believe Jesus is who He says He is?

Will you pray aloud and confirm Jesus is Savior, Lord and God (Luke 2:11; John 1:1-4); the Way, the Truth and the Life (John 14:6); the One who died, was buried, rose, ascended and is now seated at the Right of God (1 Corinthians 15:4; Mark 16:19); the One in Whom you live and move and have your being (Acts 17:28); the Immanuel (Matthew 1:23; John 14:18-21); the God whose Holy Spirit indwells you now (John 14:20)?

Will you also pray out loud and acknowledge that you believe what God says about who you are and receive the blessing for those who Believe without-having-seen? That you are born again of water and Spirit (John 3:5); that you are an adopted son or daughter of the Most High God (1 John 3:1); that you have been redeemed by the precious Blood of Jesus (1 Peter 1:19); that you are made righteous in Him (2 Corinthians 5:21); and that you are no longer your own, but are to "...glorify God in your body, and in your spirit, which are God's" (1 Corinthians 6:19-20).

Since the work of the Great Commission is for all disciples, so must the presence of Jesus, in the power of the Spirit be for all, "even unto the end of the world" (Matthew 28:19-20). As you stand in the Faith of Christ in your upper room and ask to "*know the terror of the Lord, and persuade men;*" so in His time, "Ye shall receive power, after that the Holy Ghost is come upon you: and ye shall be witnesses...unto the uttermost part of the earth" (Acts 1:8).

Will you step out in the blessing of God and take up the work of being a living witness unto the resurrection of Jesus Christ the King? *"For whether we be beside ourselves, it is to God: or whether we be sober, it is for your cause."*

Prayer of Response: The Work
Please pray aloud with us...

Heavenly Father, thank You for sending Jesus to be my Savior and Lord; to be the Way, the Truth and the Life! I believe, according to scripture that Jesus died, buried, rose, ascended and is now seated at Your Right Hand. I believe that Jesus bought

me with a price and I am Your son/daughter now. I believe that by new birth, I am now a temple of the Holy Spirit. Please empower me to hold the scriptural line, as Jesus did, in the face of the noisy foe.

I commit my life to Your cause. I humble myself before You and ask to be Your witness; that according to Your Word, I might receive power from on high, to the end that my life might be a living testimony of You. I praise and bless You right now! Thank You for sending Jesus. Thank You for sending the Holy Spirit. I release myself that I may "know the terror of the Lord" and "persuade men." Please open my lips to declare Your praise! I love you Jesus and ask all of this according to Scripture alone, by Your Holy Spirit alone. In Jesus' Name, Amen.

Week One, Day Five – Christ Awareness

"Knowing therefore the terror of the Lord, we persuade men; but we are made manifest unto God; and I trust also are made manifest in your consciences."
2 Corinthians 5:11

"For who hath known the mind of the Lord, that he may instruct him? But we have the mind of Christ."
1 Corinthians 2:16

To step out in blessing and take up the witness-mantle is to take up an ever-deepening journey into apprehending God. Therefore, we come a second time to 2 Corinthians 5:11 that we may press into an even fuller awareness of what is meant by *"knowing...the terror of the Lord."* The King James translates the Greek word behind the English as "fear" in many places, but here uses "terror." Apprehending the spiritual logic for this distinction is critical for the son or daughter of the High King who is being drawn forward into a deepening walk in the Spirit (Proverbs 3:7).

Moving from fear to terror before the Lord is a matter of moving into a fuller understanding of God's Eternal Presence. It is a matter of believing that Jesus has sat down upon heaven's throne; yet is also present with you now (Mark 16:19; Matthew 28:20). Are you aware of God's imminent presence? Do you acknowledge that the Divine Person of the Holy Spirit has filled the temple – and you are the temple (1 Corinthians 6:19)?

In Christ, you abide in the presence of God Himself (John 14:20; 17:20-23). The disciples on the Transfiguration mount fell to their face before a God-apart-from-them. Will you fall down on your spiritual face before the Holy Spirit who dwells-within-you? Will you move from fear of God apart-from-you; to an awareness of the Christ presence-within-you? If so, then you will also know "*the terror of the Lord*" and be clear before God.

For as you belong to Jesus, you have given your life to Christ. You took up the Cross and have died there. With Paul you may also proclaim:

> I am crucified with Christ: nevertheless I live; yet not I, but Christ liveth in me: and the life which I now live in the flesh I live by the faith of the Son of God, who loved me, and gave himself for me.
>
> Galatians 2:20

To take up the witness-mantle is to no longer be led by self-awareness; but by Christ alone, according to Scripture alone in the leading counsel of the Holy Spirit alone! For just as a dead man is dead to thinking and moving; in like manner, you've really died in Christ. Your new spirit is not half-alive; but you are fully alive to, by, for, in, and with the life of Jesus Christ (Galatians 2:20)!

The hard heart of your natural man, once captained by thoughts, feelings and the pursuit of the world is as gone and dead and lifeless as a body embalmed. The life you now live, "is by the faith of the Son of God, who loved" (Galatians 2:20)! This is the life of "*knowing the terror of the Lord;*" of walking in Christ-awareness instead of self-awareness!

Is such a life possible? Yes, *"by the faith of the Son of God"* (Galatians 2:20). Just as in Christ your life is no longer your own; so also your faith is not your own. Where then is your faith? In Christ where your life also is (Romans 3:22; Hebrews 12:2)!

Whose faith then do you live by? Not your own, but "by the faith of the Son" (ibid). Faith is of Jesus Christ so there is never a question of you having enough! For you are already risen and living in Him; having passed through the waters of the new birth into new life (Colossians 2:12). You have been brought from the far-country of the world, to the house of God, and are a living temple of the Holy Spirit (1 Peter 2:5).

Before the new birth, you could only know about the Lord as one knows about a famous man or woman because of reading an autobiography or seeing a documentary or encountering a historical record tracing their legacy. These heroes are known from afar with limited natural senses. Who are your heroes? If they now entered your room would you turn your eyes to them? What questions would you ask? What hospitality would you offer? Would you pause your life to entertain these? If so, how much more shall you regard the Lord who has come to tabernacle within you and in whom you now live!?

Our heroes can only be known with our natural senses; *"but we have the mind of Christ!"* The Lord has entered your temple-room! What questions are you asking? What hospitality are you offering? With awesome fear do you entertain His thoughts? Will you take up 2 Corinthians 5:16 and declare, "...yea, though we

37

have known Christ after the flesh, yet now henceforth know we him no more." If so, then you now know the *"terror of the Lord!"*

Is the watchman-of-your-mind rising up? Are you asking how this can be? Or why you have known Jesus so long and have been long asking *"who hath the mind of the Lord?"* Here is the change, Jesus is not known by your outward sense of seeing or hearing; nor is Jesus known by the inward faculties of your emotions or the logic of the mind. Man cannot comprehend the mind of God with natural awe or study, for it is written, "'Eye hath not seen, nor ear heard, neither have entered into the heart of man, the things which God hath prepared for them that love him'" (1 Corinthians 2:9).

"Having the mind of Christ" then, is coming to the very end of self-awareness and the beginning of Christ-awareness and walking in the Spirit. For Christ-followers, there is a spiritual inversion. God is no longer a subject of awe-filled study. Jesus is the source of your life and you follow His very person; which is more than a principal, or a doctrine, or a creed, or a word written upon the page, or a theology, or a philosophy, or a denomination, or an anointed teacher, or even a feeling flowing from your own heart!

You, dear brother or sister, are now an open-book on the subject of God. This is a sense of what Paul means when he says that he is laid open or bare before God and before man as he testifies that in Christ *"we are made manifest unto God"* and *"manifest in your consciences"* (2 Corinthians 5:11b).

Being laid open before God and man can be likened to being an emptied clay vessel filled with the very presence of the glory of God. For in Christ "dwelleth all the fulness of the Godhead" (Colossians 2:9), and the Holy Spirit in earnest in you (2 Corinthians 1:22, 5:5). Since you have given over your life to Christ, all you think and do occurs before the very Throne of Grace!

Hear Jesus through Paul today, "I beseech you therefore, brethren, by the mercies of God, that ye present your bodies a living sacrifice, holy, acceptable unto God, which is your reasonable service" (Romans 12:1). In Christ you have died to the body of sin and now live under Grace. Become a living sacrifice and declare, "I am crucified with Christ!" (Galatians 2:20).

Proclaim out-loud YOUR sacrifice of praise; that you are dead to self-awareness and alive in Christ-awareness! That your mind with the pride of natural thought, your emotions with their passions, and your flesh with its desires; hang dead upon the cross. Agree with Jesus that the *"terror of the Lord"* is not outside of you, but has come upon you at your invitation and you are laid bare that the King of Glory may occupy your manger.

Prayer of Response: Christ Awareness

Please pray aloud with us…

Heavenly Father, Your word says that You will not turn away a humble and contrite heart (Psalm 51:17). That You are "…faithful and just to forgive us our sins and to cleanse us from all unrighteousness" (Psalm 51:17; 1 John 1:9). Forgive me.

Receive my humbled and breaking heart. Wash me clean in Jesus' Blood, that I may live. (Confess any sin which the Holy Spirit brings to mind).

Father, please transform me from the spirit of self-awareness into Christ-awareness; that I may no longer serve my mind, or be led by thoughts about You, but that I may follow Jesus alone and be led of the mind of Christ Himself, via the Holy Spirit (John 14:26). Lay me open like a book, that who I am may be laid bare before You and before others. This so all You have taught and said may be made manifest through me. I ask this by the Faith of the Son of God; in Christ alone, according to your Word alone, to your Glory alone, through the Holy Spirit alone. In Jesus' Name, Amen.

Week One, Day Six – Out of Your Mind

"For the love of Christ constraineth us; because we thus judge,
that if one died for all, then were all dead: And that he died for all,
that they which live should not henceforth live unto themselves, but
unto him which died for them, and rose again."
2 Corinthians 5:14-15

What *"terror of the Lord constraineth"* Paul? What bound
his understanding in Christ-awareness? One thing only – *the love
of Christ.*

The love of Christ is more than an internal feeling of
dedication toward another person. It is more than putting on rose-
colored glasses named "Jesus" as lenses for deciding what to do or
be. It is more than taking off the lenses of self-awareness in an
attempt to see Christ through natural sense and experience.

Paul is not filtering what he does or what he sees through
anything other than Jesus Christ crucified. In taking up Christ, the
apostle died to himself and took up the mind of Christ (1
Corinthians 2:10, 16; John 15:15). In a manner of speaking, Paul
sought to be completely out of his mind and completely over
himself. One-thing-only held him and compelled him, One-thing-
alone directed how he lived: *the love of Christ.* Paul believed God
and received into his soul, mind and body the definitive word of
God: *"...that if one died for all, then were all dead."*

What? Dead? Is Paul here speaking of the spiritual death
that occurred in Adam and the spiritual death Jesus Christ redeems
us from? Yes. For those who are in Christ come to being in Him

by apprehending the saving work of Jesus, "...the Lamb of God who taketh away the sin of the world" (John 1:29).

You personally know Jesus if you accept that Jesus as God's Son died for your sins (1 John 4:1-3). Paul *is indeed* confessing the crucifixion of Jesus Christ and the death of Christ for the redemption of *all*. But Paul goes beyond the blessing of this elementary and fundamental word.

Paul confesses the effect of redemption in Christ, *"that if one died for all, then were all dead."* The apostle declares his own death-to-self and confirms that old-man-passed away. Paul takes up Jesus' cross as the dividing line between Saul, the winsome rabbinic prodigy rising up under Gamaliel, and Paul; "a servant of Jesus Christ, called to be an apostle, separated unto the gospel of God" (Romans 1:1). In the original Greek, the word behind "servant" is slave. Paul is separated as a slave of Jesus Christ. By what yoke is this brother held-fast? He writes, that "t*he love of Christ constraineth us."*

Most Christ-followers agree that we should preach the gospel as Jesus commanded (Matthew 28:19). But would you agree with Paul that you are dead and now separated as a slave to the gospel of Love? Have you **really** believed God and received into your soul, mind and body the definitive word of God: *"...that if one died for all, then were all dead that they which live should not henceforth live unto themselves"?*

Before going on, take a moment to pray for the Holy Spirit to guide you into all Truth and give a deeper revelation as to how it can be, *"that they which live should not henceforth live unto themselves, but unto him which died for them, and rose again."* Or said another way, "that the life you now live you live to God" (Galatians 2:20). Or yet another way, that it is "I not I who live, but Christ who lives in me." *(Please pray if led to receive this truth deep in your spirit)*.

Paul spent three days in darkness with scales over his eyes after first encountering Jesus (Acts 9:17). Perhaps you have spent what seems like three long days, though they be weeks or years – with scales over your own spiritual eyes. Let today be the day of seeing, let today be the day of the Holy Spirit! King Jesus has emptied Himself and fulfilled His word that you may now empty yourself and be filled (Acts 9:17-18).

Paul does not go about telling people the good news of what Jesus has done for him as if Jesus were apart-from-him. Paul declares himself to be dead and set-apart in Christ. Having laid down his life, he takes up living for Jesus Christ. He is not restored in the Holy Spirit unto life as he knew it; but rises up out of his mind for the Lord. Paul takes up life in Christ, constrained in and by love.

Like the apostle, you need not be bound by your own mind's limits, by the declarations of culture, or the professions, governments or any powers or principalities of this present age (Romans 8:38-39). As you take up the mantle of walking in the Holy Spirit, you are constrained by the Love of Christ. You are no longer merely a witness *to* Jesus Christ as if He were apart-from-you, but you are a witness *of Jesus Christ;* whose power filled Holy Spirit actually indwells you (Acts 1:8). "What? know ye not that your body is the temple of the Holy Ghost *which is* in you, which ye have of God, and ye are not your own?" (1 Corinthians 6:19)

Will you allow who you are this day to be decreed by Christ the Risen King, through the Holy Spirit calling into your remembrance Jesus' teaching? Consider His prayer for you. Hear Him afresh this day, not with your natural soul, mind or flesh – but deep in your spirit where the Holy Spirit is now dwelling and speaking to you. Let your old man go, release all of your expectations, withhold any judgment, receive only God's Word to your spirit and be filled with the Living Word Himself (John 1:1):

> For I [Jesus] have given them the words which thou gavest me; And they have received them, and have known surely that I came out from thee...
>
> And they have believed that thou didst send me....I have given them thy word: and the world hath hated them, because they are not of the world, even as I am not of the world....Sanctify them through thy truth, thy word is truth.
>
> And for their sakes I sanctify myself, that they also might be sanctified through the truth. Neither pray I for these alone, but for them also which shall believe on me through their word; That they all may be one; as thou, Father, art in me, and I in thee, that they also may be one in us; that the world may believe that thou hast sent me.
>
> And the glory which thou gavest me I have given them; that they may be one, even as we are one: I in them, and

thou in me, that they may be made perfect in one; and that the world may know that thou hast sent me, and hast loved them, as thou hast loved me.

And I have declared unto them thy name, and will declare it: that the love wherewith thou hast loved me may be in them, and I in them.

John 17:8, 14, 17, 19-23, 26

Having moved past an elementary understanding, will you give yourself over as Jesus' living witness? As one set-apart to the gospel and constrained as a bond-servant of Love? As a bearer of the presence of Jesus through the Holy Spirit? As one dead to self now living *"unto him which died...and rose again"*?

Since the Spirit of God is in you, the fullness of the Love of God is also in you (John 17:26). And since "God is Love" (1 John 4:16b), you are the living child of God's Love (John 1:13). You are not your own, but are a bond-servant bought with the blood of Jesus and secured by the Holy Spirit (2 Corinthians 1:22). Jesus prayed for you and gave His life that this may be so.

Perhaps you have already given Jesus permission to have all of you. Perhaps you have given Him all of your soul, all of your mind, all of your body and all of your spirit (Luke 10:27). Then your witness will move past sharing the joy of what Jesus has done for you into proclaiming His "greater works" (Matthew 11:11b; John 14:12). You will grow beyond an elementary witness, into being the living, speaking, moving word of Love in this present darkness. And by the power of the Holy Spirit you will be what you already are: Jesus' arms, hands, legs, feet, voice and eyes

45

-- the very love of God made manifest in a breaking and dying world (John 17).

Prayer of Response: Out of Your Mind

Please pray aloud with us...

Heavenly Father, thank You for loving the world so much that You sent Jesus to die. Thank You for leaving Your Spirit in me until the work on earth is done. Thank You for receiving me in love, as Your child. Please forgive me for withholding any part of my soul, mind, heart or body from You. I confess that Your word is true and I am released through the death of Christ, into living life in Him!

Father, please make this truth manifest in my clay vessel. Let the love of Christ constrain me! As I confess Jesus died for me; therefore have I died. Let the love of Christ constrain me! As I believe I live unto Jesus alone as a living vessel of His Love.

Lord Jesus, I release my life to You as a living sacrifice. Make me a bond-servant of love; take my mind, take my heart, take my hands, take my feet, take my eyes, take my ears, take my lips...for they were mine, but I give them to You now. Manifest Your Love through me, for I am Yours by Grace alone, through Faith alone in Christ alone, through the Holy Spirit alone. According to Scripture and for Your glory alone; I pray in Jesus Name, Amen.

Looking Ahead: Please ask God today to allow an extra ten minutes for next week's devotions.

Week Two, Day One – Standing Before

"'Woman, where are those thine accusers? Hath no man condemned thee?' She said, 'No man, Lord.' And Jesus said unto her, 'Neither do I condemn thee: go and sin no more.'"

"Then Jesus spake again unto them saying, 'I am the light of the world: he that followeth me shall not walk in darkness, but shall have the light of life.'"
John 8:10b-12

Are you surrounded by accusations? Are you standing before condemning thoughts which press your mind with clinging darkness? Are you wrestling with guilt or feelings of unworthiness? Do you feel stripped and exposed?

The woman standing before Jesus was "taken in adultery, in the very act" (John 8:4). She was a sinner and that personal sin was made very public. The woman stood exposed before the One who saw straight through to her heart, yet would still forgive her sin *and* go to the cross to redeem her life with His own.

The Pharisees, esteemed in knowing God's law, stood before Jesus too. In presenting the woman, they said: "Now Moses in the law commanded us, that such should be stoned: but what sayest thou? This they said, tempting him, that they might have to accuse him" (John 8:5-6).

The accused woman was not their primary target. With stones in hand, they sought to entrap and bind up Jesus through God's Word. Two purposes of their hearts were exposed. They intended to "tempt" Jesus through the law, that they might "accuse him" (John 8:6b).

Despite these intentions, Jesus did not engage these religious leaders in a conversational dispute; nor did He question the woman to test their claims. Jesus did not throw a scripture verse at the religious leaders or the sinful woman. "But Jesus stooped down, and with his finger wrote on the ground, as though he heard them not" (John 8:7).

Have you ever wondered why Jesus behaved "as though he heard them not"? With our Lord, the very thoughts of the heart are opened and exposed. There simply is no need for piercing verbal inquiry:

> For the word of God *is* quick, and powerful, and sharper than any two edged sword, piercing even to the dividing asunder of soul and spirit, and of the joints and marrow, and *is* a discerner of the thoughts and intents of the heart. Neither is there any creature that is not manifest in his sight: but all things *are* naked and opened unto the eyes of him with whom we have to do.
>
> Hebrews 4:12-13

Standing before the Lord, is there a difference between the religious leaders of Israel and the woman caught in the act? The Judge of heaven and earth exposes the heart of the matter as He commands: "He that is without sin among you, let him first cast a stone at her" (John 8:7b).

As before, so today. We all stand before Jesus. There is nothing made manifest by human hearts or hands that is out of reach of the Holy King's sight (Hebrews 4:12b-13a). As you stand before the Light of the World, you are not condemned in the darkness of either hidden or open sin (John 8:12). For King Jesus did not come to condemn you, but to save you (John 3:17). Therefore as you follow Him, all of the accusing voices are silenced and you may be quieted by your King's pardoning word: *"'Neither do I condemn thee: go and sin no more.'"*

For King Jesus promises, *"'He that followeth me shall not walk in darkness, but shall have the light of life.'"* And it is written, "But all things that are reproved are made manifest by the light: for whatsoever doth make manifest is light" (Ephesians 5:13). Jesus is the Light of the World who manifests in the darkness of your heart so that you may freely follow in the Spirit. As His Light shines, so you are transformed by receiving His word. As you *"have the light of life,"* "Ye are the light of the world" (Matthew 5:14)! And others see Him through you.

As you stand before the condemning voices, even those who seek to entrap and snare with scriptural sounding words, will you still take up stones? Will you accuse and judge those who stand to accuse and judge you? Or will you manifest *"the light of the world,"* point to the Light alone and thereby drop every judgment and accusation?

Remember that Jesus did not come to condemn the world, but to save (John 3:17). When your own heart takes up a judgmental stance to disqualify yourself or others from walking in the Spirit; or when a religious leader or theological doctrine takes

50

up a position against the plain teaching of God's Word; or when tempting voices come to tell you that you are unfit to walk in the Lord: Put down all of those spiritual stones and take up the saving sword of the Spirit of God (Hebrews 4:12; Ephesians 6:17).

Whether you have carried the hidden sins of a modern-day Pharisee, or been exposed naked in open sin as the adulterous woman, or been surrounded like Jesus by openly sinful people; will you stand before the Cross and take up the King's pardon? As you submit your sin, your broken heart and your public shame to Jesus Christ; He takes up the darkness of your grief, sorrow, sin and shame upon His cross (Isaiah 53:4; 1 Peter 2:24)! The instrument of His death is the instrument of your life. "And you...hath he quickened together with him, having forgiven you all trespasses...nailing it to his cross" (Colossians 2:13-15).

The question before you today, is not about your sin or about someone's sin against you. "All trespasses" are nailed to the cross; therefore, you are no longer bound by accusation, but are free to stand and walk in the Light of the liberty of Jesus Christ (Galatians 5:1). Will you stand before the pervading and accusing darkness of this present age as a redeemed Child of Light?

Jesus' pardon is the antidote for the stony heart of sin. As you take up the cross, the sword of the Word of God frees your spirit. You are cut loose from being conducted by soulish interpretation, accusation or zeal. You are quickened by the Spirit and separated from the darkness of man, unto the light which is of God.

Stand before Jesus even now. Pray as the psalmist, "Search me, O God, and know my heart: try me, and know my thoughts: And see if *there be any* wicked way in me, and lead me in the way everlasting" (Psalm 139:23-24)! He will lead you from darkness into Light and remove every darkening speck! For "If we confess our sins, he is faithful and just to forgive us *our* sins, and to cleanse us from all unrighteousness" (1 John 1:9).

Will you invite the Sword of the Spirit to His quickening work? Speak the Word of God in tenderness and love, both to yourself and to others. Let Christ-your-Light shine through the lamp-stand of your life. Jesus came to save, so as you stand before Him, He exchanges your darkness for His Light. For Jesus meets you "...in righteousness, and in judgment, and in loving-kindness, and in mercies" (Hosea 2:19b).

In the midst of all accusation, as before so again; Jesus stoops down. As you stand before Him covered in sin, He writes on the ground as "though he heard them not" (John 8:8c). Christ-your-Light rescues you from sin's overcoming darkness. As it is written:

> ...I will put my law in their inward parts, and write it in their hearts; and will be their God, and they shall be my people.... And they shall teach no more every man his neighbour, and every man his brother saying Know the LORD: for they shall all know me, from the least of them unto the greatest of them, saith the LORD; for I will forgive their iniquity, and I will remember their sin no more.
> Jeremiah 31:33, 32:35; see also Hebrews 8:10, 10:16

What is finished upon the cross is applied to the one standing before Him as Jesus says: "*Neither do I condemn thee: go and sin no more!*" And as you stand before Jesus in faith, you are delivered from the darkness of accusing condemnation unto the light of life declared by Jesus Christ. The Sword of the Spirit has forever divided the darkness.

And Jesus' words are fulfilled today. As you follow Him you "*shall not walk in darkness, but shall have the light of life.*" The Light of the Word of God is written upon your heart as surely as the Holy Spirit indwells your clay lamp-stand. God has written upon your hearts, the Light illumines, and the darkness cannot overcome (John 1:5).

Prayer of Response: Standing Before

Please pray aloud with us...

Heavenly Father, Holy, Holy, Holy is Your Name! Your judgments are true and right and stand from age to age. Thank You for inviting me to stand before You by sending Your Son to save me. Thank You Jesus, for dealing with all of my hidden and open sin at the cross.

I confess and turn away from every sin that You bring to mind today (as He leads, confess to Him). I cry out to You as my Lord to search me and try me continually, that from this moment forward every sin and stony stronghold that I have buried within me may be removed by the Sword of the Spirit and cleansed by Jesus' Blood.

53

I know King Jesus, that You came to save, so You shall set me free today from the darkening fear of sin into Your Light! Thank You, Father! I hold the line of scripture which declares, "They shall all know me, from the least of them unto the greatest of them...for I will forgive their iniquity, and I will remember their sin no more" (Hebrews 8:11-12)! Please stoop down Jesus. Trace these words upon my heart...that I may "go and sin no more" (John 8:11).

Please close my ears and guard my spiritual eyes from any condemning, judgmental, belittling or anxious spirit. I receive by faith the Light of Jesus and stand again upon Your Word; that "He that followeth me shall not walk in darkness, but shall have the light of life." May I "go and sin no more," walking in the Light of God's Spirit alone, to the glory of Your Name alone, to the praise of Your glorious grace. Thank you, Father. I pray in Jesus' Name, Amen.

Week Two, Day Two – Treasure Hunt

"My son, if thou wilt receive my words, and hide my
commandments with thee; So that thou incline thine ear unto
wisdom, and apply thine heart to understanding; Yea, if thou criest
after knowledge, and liftest up thy voice for understanding; If
though seekest her as silver, and searchest for her as for hid
treasures; Then shalt thou understand the fear of the LORD, and
find the knowledge of God."
Proverbs 2:1-5

"Search the scriptures; for in them ye think ye have eternal life:
and they are they which testify of me. And ye will not come to me,
that ye might have life.... But I know you, that ye have not the love
of God in you."
John 5:39-40, 42

Beloved of God, are you searching *"as for hid treasures"*?
The joy before you is that you already have both map and treasure!
The map is the Bible.   The treasure is within you: the Holy Spirit
(2 Corinthians 4:7). The hunt is the pursuit of the fathomless
depths of knowing and being known by the God you love.

"Getting saved" or "making a confession of faith" is often
understood by many Christ-followers as the utmost expression of
relationship with God; and understandably so!   For in the instant
of New Birth, fellowship with God and with the Body of Christ are
fully realized (Romans 8:9). The Holy Spirit now indwells you;
not in part, but in whole (2 Corinthians 6:16)!

"Now ye are the body of Christ, and members in particular"
(1 Corinthians 12:27). With the Spirit comes full participation in
Christ as a dedicated hand, foot, elbow, knee, finger or toe. As a

living member of the Body, you are securely in full fellowship with Christian brothers and sisters. The joy of your salvation is open to you; that is, an eternal, personal, intimate and expanding relationship with God and the Church (1 Corinthians 12:26, 13:12)!

Many brothers and sisters enjoy the wonder of participating in Christ's Living Body. These know and experience the joy of worship on the Lord's Day as well as the savor of being a family held together by Christ's Blood. Others weep and mourn as their fellowship seems riddled with bland preoccupations.

The search for hidden treasure isn't knowingly abandoned, but like a path or a maze that ever circles around itself, some go blandly through the Christian exercises. Sunday school, bible study, fellowship, prayer meeting, choir practice, committee meeting, business meeting, building meeting, mission efforts, service-projects, life-cycle groups, small groups, youth groups, accountability groups, home schools, retreats, summer camps, weekend conferences and then back again to Lord's Day worship. Yet even of Bible-study Jesus says, *"Search the scriptures; for in them ye think ye have eternal life: and they are they which testify of me. And ye will not come to me, that ye might have life..."*.

While there are different points of view as to how the biblical search for Wisdom as a persona relates to Jesus and the Holy Spirit; scripture defines "relationship" as the fundamental basis for knowing and understanding God. *"If though seekest her as silver, and searchest for her as for hid treasures; Then shalt thou understand the fear of the LORD, and find the knowledge of*

God." The Book of Proverbs even pictures wisdom as an attractive "her" to come into relationship with! Knowing God is more than studying the facts and principles or daily going through the exercises.

The purpose of the Book of Proverbs is straight-forward: "The proverbs of Solomon the son of David, king of Israel; To **know** wisdom and instruction..." (Proverbs 1:1, emphasis ours). In the linguistic world of scripture, the Hebrew word *yada* includes "knowing wisdom" and "knowing a woman." "And Adam **knew** Eve his wife; and she conceived..." (Genesis 4:1a, emphasis ours). Scripturally speaking, knowing anyone or anything at all, is profoundly relational, physical and intimate.

Most modern people believe we "know something" if we can pass a test, speak, or write eloquently. Yet a modern person does not claim to "know someone" unless they have been introduced and carried on a level of personal interaction. So there is a difference, even in modern terms, between "searching the scriptures" to "know something;" and coming to know Jesus to have life (John 5:39-40).

What begins as a journey into the heart of God and intimate relationship with the Body, sometimes veers awry into godly matters. Surely godly activities of the Body of Christ are not to be critiqued in and of themselves! Yet for the sons and daughters of King Jesus, they are not meant to be ends. For Jesus says, "I am the way, the truth, and the life: no man cometh unto the Father, but by me" (John 14:6). The hunt for hidden treasure may include the activities listed above; but apart from being compelled by the leading hand of Jesus' love and impelled by the Holy Spirit – they will not bring life.

This matter is particularly critical as you take up scripture to explore the depths of the wisdom and knowledge of God. Jesus Himself gives grave warning that it is possible to devote your life to spiritual pursuit, only to find you have missed knowing Him altogether. Will you open your spirit and receive the priceless diamond-sharp edge of Jesus' teaching?

> Not every one that saith unto me, Lord, Lord, shall enter into the kingdom of heaven; but he that doeth the will of my Father which is in heaven. Many will say to me in that day, Lord, Lord, have we not prophesied in thy name? and in thy name have cast out devils? and in thy name done many wonderful works? And then will I profess unto them, I never knew you: depart from me, ye that work iniquity.
>
> Matthew 7:21-23

If Adam had not known his wife; there would not have been the fruit of a son or daughter. In a related way, only by intimately knowing the person of Jesus Christ will there be the fruit of life in His Name. Apart from abiding in Christ, you can do nothing that sparkles in the eye of the King (John 5:5). And if prophesying, casting out devils and doing many wonderful works "in thy name" are but iniquity; what of the Christian exercises of today? Are they fruit borne of knowing Christ?

Jesus says, *"Search the scriptures; for in them ye think ye have eternal life: and they are they which testify of me. And ye will not come to me, that ye might have life...But I know you, that ye have not the love of God in you"* (John 5:39-40, 42). Have you come to Jesus? Or have you veered aside in your treasure hunt to find godly things, godly service, churchly activities, missional outreach, bible study, the worship experience, spiritual power or even the quest for a holy life – as ends in themselves?

Though the map is the Bible and the treasure is within you; loving Jesus is a never-ending, moment-by-moment decision. Jesus is calling, *"...come to me, that ye might have life."* As your spirit trembles to know Him intimately and personally; He is calling, *"come to me...have life."* And to those upon the path that leads to sin; Jesus calls, *"come to me...have life."* And as anyone truly comes to Him, they will never be turned away (John 6:37).

Praise be to God, for you are not left alone to find your way into the life of God. You are not left to depend on other men and women to find the biblical road; nor must you interpret your own way. Praise be to God, that you *"have the love of God in you."* Jesus has already given the abiding treasure (2 Corinthians 4:7); and from your clay-jar temple the Holy Spirit intercedes for you and leads you deeper and deeper into knowing the fathomless Truth of Jesus Christ (John 14:26; Romans 8:26-27).

Prayer of Response: Treasure Hunt

Please pray aloud with us...

Heavenly Father, in the Name of Jesus I cry out for the Holy Spirit to be my Guide. Thank You for placing such treasure

in my clay-jar; thank You that my search for wisdom is a never-ending journey into knowing Your Son, Jesus Christ. Thank You that I am not left to find my own way, but that Jesus Himself is the known Way of Life!

Almighty Father, please forgive and release me from a spirit of Christian effort. In the Name of Jesus, I hold the line of scripture and affirm that the Holy Spirit alone will lead me into all Truth! I am running to Jesus alone; not to Bible-study, or mission-work, or fellowship-activities or worship experience or spiritual-disciplines or any other thing which rises up. Please forgive me for those times when I confused doing things in Your Name, for being with and knowing You.

Father, please teach me by Your Spirit. I want to know Jesus. Please help me to see where You are leading change in my life-walk; that I may let go of anything which is not of Your Spirit. Please fill me with the Grace and Truth of Eternal Life in Jesus Christ unto Your Glory. In the Name of Jesus alone, Amen.

Week Two, Day Three – Natural Man

"But the natural man receiveth not the things of the Spirit of God: for they are foolishness unto him: neither can he know them, because they are spiritually discerned. But he that is spiritual judgeth all things, yet he himself is judged of no man."
1 Corinthians 2:14-15

The natural man or woman is anyone who has not entered into the new birth. This one has not confessed Jesus as Lord, or been given a new spirit, or received the Holy Spirit within. This person, though yearning and seeking — is spiritually dead.

The natural person can think about God; even attend the most prestigious universities or seminaries in the world. They may attain esteemed academic credentials and awards, publish best-selling books and speak from platform or pulpit *about* God; yet all from the far country of the human mind. It is possible to spend a life sounding very spiritual, without ever knowing Jesus as Lord (Matthew 7:23).

Knowing Jesus Christ crucified is not dependent upon the power of the mind, the expansiveness of scriptural knowledge, the sufficiency of good works, or the intensity of zeal – but upon the revelation of His Spirit to your spirit (Romans 1:17; 8:16). All of the training in the world does not improve the capability of knowing or receiving God. For the *"things of God....are spiritually discerned."*

When a natural person accepts Jesus as Lord and Savior, what is dead is made alive in Christ through water and the Spirit;

(John 3:5) and this by grace, through faith (Ephesians 2:8-9). It is written, "The Spirit...beareth witness with our spirit, that we are the children of God" (Romans 8:16). This is the present reality for those who have accepted Jesus as Lord and Savior. The Holy Spirit now testifies and teaches deep in your spirit, not only about who God is as your Father; but also about who you are as God's child and what is of God (1 Corinthians 2:9-10; 1 John 2:20, 27).

Though you may not know how to enter the spiritual dialogue deep within; the Holy Spirit Himself, "maketh intercessions for the saints according to the will of God" (Romans 8:26-27b). The Holy Spirit makes known to your spirit, a personal and direct knowledge of God.

The express proof of this knowledge is your own new birth! The manifest-evidence of scripture is your testimony that Jesus Christ crucified, raised and ascended is your personal Lord and Savior. As you gave your life to Jesus, He gave you New Life in the Spirit. In that moment of faith, you were filled with the Holy Spirit's indwelling personal presence (John 14:16, 26; 15:26). As you are now in Christ and led of the Holy Spirit, you have the spiritual discernment to "*judgeth all things*," as you yourself are "*judged of no man*."

You who are led of the Spirit, judge this matter: Does scripture testify that your Good Shepherd abandons you to the voice of the howling thief or hired hand? Where is it written that the Holy Spirit has withdrawn in silence, leaving you with only an open Bible? Does scripture report that Jesus stooped down to be

Immanuel, the "God with us," only to withhold His voice? Is the Father in Heaven denying the child who longs to hear Him?

Consider what is written according to the revelation of the Holy Spirit pouring forth within you: Jesus "calleth his own sheep by name, and leadeth them out" and "goeth before them, and the sheep follow him: for they know his voice" (John 10:3-5). Jesus testifies of the called, "It is written in the Prophets: And they will all be taught by God. Everyone who has listened to and learned from the Father comes to me" (John 6:45). And the Father, "Hath in these last days spoken unto us by *his* Son" who upholds "all things by the word of his power" (Hebrews 1:2a, 3b). And as the Holy Spirit, "...the Spirit of truth, is come, he will guide you into all truth: for he shall not speak of himself; but whatsoever he shall hear, *that* shall he speak..." (John 16:13).

The charge that God is aloof, silent, and twice-removed cannot stand. For "...your faith should not stand in the wisdom of men, but in the power of God" (1 Corinthians 2:5). It is the natural man who does not know or discern God; but the spiritual man knows the voice of the Lord (John 10:3-5).

Indeed, your faith has already come by receiving the word of God. The fact of your salvation demonstrates that you are no longer natural, but have been fitted with the supernatural. While the natural man can neither *receive* or *know* God; you are no longer a natural man or woman after the world.

Jesus is clear, "...ye are not of the world, but I have chosen you out of the world, therefore the world hateth you" (John 15:19).

63

And this is no small matter dear brother or sister, "...for know ye not that the friendship of the world is enmity with God? whosoever therefore will be a friend of the world is the enemy of God" (James 4:4). Can you perceive deep in your spirit, that the world is set to convince you that you are very natural and it is impossible to hear the Spirit's supernatural voice?

Remember that Jesus says, "I am the good shepherd: the good shepherd giveth his life for the sheep" (John 10:11) and "My sheep hear my voice, and I know them, and they follow me" (John 10:27). If the watchman-of-the-mind rises up to judge this scripture as a mere word-picture and not indicative of reality; then let the evidence stand. Jesus has died on the cross for your salvation. This is history. So then is your hearing of the Shepherd's voice; as you heard Jesus calling when you received Him! So it is written:

> To him [Jesus] the porter openeth; and the sheep hear his [Jesus'] voice: and he calleth his own sheep by name, and leadeth them out. And when he putteth forth his own sheep, he goeth before them, and the sheep follow him: for they know his voice. And a stranger will they not follow, but will flee from him: for they know not the voice of strangers.
> John 10:4-5

How then do we explain "hearing" the supernatural voice of our Good Shepherd? By way of being *"spiritually discerned; as he that is spiritual judgeth all things."* Paul explains spiritual hearing this way; "...God hath revealed...unto us by his Spirit; for the Spirit searcheth all things, yea, the deep things of God" (1

Corinthians 3:10). And "Now we have received, not the spirit of the world, but the spirit which is of God; that we might know the things that are freely given to us of God" (1 Corinthians 3:12).

The English word describing what Paul calls spiritual discernment is "intuition." Webster's Dictionary defines "intuition" as "the power or faculty of attaining to direct knowledge or cognition without evident rational thought and inference" (http://www.merriam-webster.com/dictionary/intuition, accessed 05/11/2018). If we follow the impulse of this devotional and look at an older definition of the word, it follows that "intuition" is defined as the ability of the mind to perceive "the truth of things, immediately, or the moment they are presented, without the intervention of other ideas, or without reasoning or deduction" (http://webstersdictionary1828.com/Dictionary/intuition, accessed 05/11/2018).

Intuition then, does not arise from the five natural senses, or from the mind's intellect, or from an emotional experience. "Intuition" by definition, does not even take shape based upon the transferred ideas, reasonings or deductions of other people. Intuition arises solely from within. It is in your intuition that "you know, that you know, that you know." So it is that the Christian who knows Jesus Christ is Lord and Savior "intuits" the witness of the Holy Spirit from deep within, and this invisible inspiration finds both its proof and mooring in its harmony in accord with God's Written Word (1 Thessalonians 5:19-21; 1 John 1:4:1).

Scripture is clear, *"But the natural man receiveth not the things of the Spirit of God: for they are foolishness unto him: neither can he know them, because they are spiritually discerned."* So for the natural person, natural knowledge is not rooted in God because he cannot receive *"the things of the Spirit of God."* It can then be no surprise when the wisdom of man runs contrary to God's direction.

Are you longing to perceive the deep things of God? Are you longing to hear Jesus speaking personally to you deep in your spirit? Are you longing to judge between the voices you hear in your head and the pure testimony of God? Are you longing to hear Jesus say your name and quiet you with His love (Zephaniah 3:17)?

Then Jesus is calling you. Believe what is written. Your Good Shepherd's supernatural voice shall become ever more discernible via intuition; *"as the things of the Spirit of God...are spiritually discerned."* As it is written, so it must be.

Prayer of Response: Natural Man

Please pray aloud with us...

Heavenly Father, it is written that the Holy Spirit will personally guide me into all Truth. It is written that the Good Shepherd calls Your sheep by name. I believe that Your Word stands forever! I believe Jesus is my Savior and Lord. Therefore, I believe I am no longer a natural man/woman; but am born again.

66

And my heart's desire is to hear You! According to Your Word, I believe and have received, "not the spirit of the world, but the spirit which is of God," that I "might know the things that are freely given...of God" and thereby "judgeth all things." Please teach me to discern and train me to know Your voice.

Release my spiritual ears from any spirit of worldly wisdom and knowledge. Free me from the deafening voices of the thief and stranger. In the Name of Jesus and under the authority of His Word, I receive spiritual ears for Jesus' voice alone, in the revelation of the Holy Spirit alone. May it now be that I "know His voice" and "and a stranger" I "will not follow!"

Father, please stir up a "spirit of wisdom and revelation in the knowledge of Jesus," that my intuition be awakened and strengthened; and my mind's "understanding enlightened, that I may know the hope of my calling, and the riches of the glory of Jesus' inheritance in the saints" (Based in Ephesians 1:17).

Thank you for opening my spirit so I hear You alone, through Your Grace alone, by Faith alone in Jesus Christ alone. I am listening for Your guidance, Holy Spirit! I know You are calling and leading me! In the Name of Jesus, Amen.

Author's Note: Please pray for God to provide a double-portion of time for tomorrow...or to lead you by spiritual discernment to go part way and reserve the rest for the next day according to whatever design He has prepared especially for you.

Week Two, Day Four – To the Glory of God

"The glory of this latter house shall be greater than that of the former, saith the LORD of hosts: and in this place will I give peace, saith the LORD of hosts."
Haggai 2:9

"And I will pray the Father, and he shall give you another Comforter, that he may abide with you forever.... If a man love me, he will keep my words: and my Father will love him, and we will come unto him and make our abode with him."
John 14:16, 23b

"Verily, verily I say unto you, He that believeth on me, the works that I do shall he do also; and greater works than these shall he do; because I go unto the Father."
John 14:12

"If a man love me, He will keep my words." Do you love Jesus? Are you crying out day after day to know His will that somehow you might glorify Him with your life, even in the specifics? Then your prayer is answered this day for Jesus is revealing His will for you, and from the moment you receive it, you will move forward with clarity in your spirit and soul!

Perhaps your spiritual eyes are already opened to the immutability of the Word of the Lord. Perhaps you see in scripture that God is the same yesterday, today and tomorrow and that there is no shadow of turning in Him (James 1:17b; Hebrews 13:8). Perhaps you know that the Word of God stands forever and shall never pass away (Isaiah 40:8b; 1 Peter 1:25). Perhaps you have come to confess that Jesus is the Word made flesh (John 1:14; Luke 2:11). If you are in complete harmony in your spirit with the unchanging nature of God's Word and the unchanging nature of Christ, then you are already well grounded in the basis of God's will for your life (Malachi 3:6; Psalm 33:11).

Since God does not change, God's will for His children does not change, but stands from generation to generation (Psalm 33:11). And what is the greatest commandment in both the Old and New Testament? "And he [Jesus] answering said, 'Thou shalt love the Lord thy God with all thy heart, and with all thy soul, and with all thy strength, and with all thy mind'" (Luke 10:27; Deuteronomy 6:5).

And how does Jesus define love? *"If a man love me, he will keep my words."* In His love, your Lord does not charge you with the burdensome task of receiving His word by logic and reason to achieve some spiritual objective – or avoid some spiritual pitfall (1 John 5:3). Jesus gives you His words to *keep*, by way of spiritually discerning – or knowing by intuition – the things of God (1 Corinthians 2:14-15).

Praise be to God that, *"The glory of this latter house shall be greater than that of the former"*! As there once was a time when loving God by keeping the word, was accomplished in large part through human determination and strength. In those days, God did not tabernacle *in* a human temple of clay, but in a tent or temple set *in the midst* of His people. Throughout these former times, God manifested His Presence through direct but external

69

encounter with His people by means of covenant, pillar, cloud, burning bush, tablets of stone, ark, and temple. The Lord intermittently spoke Spirit to spirit through the prophets, judges, priests and kings.

Even though the Spirit of God was external to His people, the Lord still moved in their midst. God commanded their full love in the laying up of His words in their heart and soul, upon their bodies as signs and frontlets for their eyes, upon the doorposts of their homes, and in conversations whether awake or sleeping (Deuteronomy 6:4-9, 11:18). Loving the Lord was not to be occasional on their terms, or even subject to their interpretation. They were to simply dedicate their whole life and full strength to loving God through faithfully *keeping* His Word (Joshua 1:7; Deuteronomy 12:32).

Is the watchman-of-your mind wondering what walking out God's word unto His Glory looks like today? Please take a moment to pray for a spirit of wisdom and discernment before going on. Then ask yourself if you believe that the Bible is an impersonal and insufficient expression of God's will for your life; or if you believe that by the Holy Spirit and through scripture, "the man of God may be perfect, thoroughly furnished unto all good works" (2 Timothy 3:15-17). Walking in a spirit of wisdom and discernment, consider whether you have unknowingly set aside the fullness of the revelation of God's will through scripture.

Do you believe that the interpretation of scripture informing the Christian life has changed because: "We do not live under the law, but now live under grace?" Or have you accepted the claim that "the scriptures are too heavenly minded, and no practical good; because times have changed and the Bible doesn't address modern life"? Or have you decided, "It's alright to be guided by the Bible in general doctrinal matters, but the scripture does not inform the details of my particular life"?

Or have you concluded that, "I have my individual gifts and special challenges and diverse circumstances; therefore the Bible doesn't fit who God made me to be." Or that "I cannot understand the Bible because of a lack of education, so what I believe is based on what others say"? Or that "The God of the Bible had to speak the way He did to be relevant in ancient cultures; but today, through advancements in technology and scholarship, we are freed from context and can distinguish what God really meant to say"? Or that "My own experience tells me that I do not need to follow the Bible to be spiritual"? Have you come to believe that, "God tells me to do my part, therefore I must make logical decisions about my life to apply God's word"? Any of these sound familiar?

One more question: Are followers of Christ to be hearers and doers of the Word by means of human interpretation, human logic, human experience or circumstantial evidence or to "receive with meekness the engrafted word, which is able to save your souls" (James 1:21-22)? There is a collision of kingdoms wherever human wisdom and logic qualify the leadership of God's revelation in scripture. Even the most ambitious scholarly study or spiritual

71

experience, if undertaken apart from the Holy Spirit, cannot uncover God's will.

For God alone leads His children: "I will instruct thee and teach thee in the way which thou shalt go" (Psalm 32a); "And thine ears shall hear a word behind thee, saying, This *is* the way, walk ye in it, when ye turn to the right hand, and when ye turn to the left" (Isaiah 30:21). "And when he [Jesus] putteth forth his own sheep, he goeth before them, and the sheep follow him: for they know his voice" (John 10:4).

The glory of the Lord has moved from the temple-mount to your own clay tent! Jesus prayed and the Comforter was sent to abide forever (John 14:6). *"The glory of this latter house shall be greater than that of the former."* For the Spirit of God is eternal and present in you (John 14:23b). And the mark of such a Spirit-indwelled Believer is defined by Jesus: *"If a man love me, he will keep my words: and my Father will love him, and we will come unto him and make our abode with him."*

Since you love Jesus, will you open your spirit to the leadership of the Holy Spirit? Jesus does not leave you alone to find your way or even to think your way through life. For the Holy Spirit, your Comforter and Counselor has been given to you, and the Word of God personally and directly leads (John 17:21). So the beginning and end of keeping God's will is caught up in the manifest presence of the Helper abiding within you.

Let's read John 14:21 again and notice the progression of love. Jesus says, *"He that hath my commandments, and keepeth them, he it is that loveth me: and he that loveth me shall be loved of my Father, and I will love him, and will manifest myself to him."* Notice that keeping God's word demonstrates your love, and the Father's love through you. For as you love Jesus and keep God's commands – Jesus manifests Himself to you! This is the gift of God, who is love (1 John 4:8b) and in whom there is no variability or shadow of turning (James 1:17).

Since you love Jesus, will you more deeply enter into this progression of love? Will you completely open the details of your life to the leadership of God unto His Glory alone? Jesus does not leave you as an orphan to find your way to your Father or to think your way through "how" to love Him. For the Holy Spirit, your Comforter and Counselor has been given to you, and the Word of God personally and directly leads you by the Spirit (John 17:21)! So the beginning and end of God's loving will for you is caught up in the manifest presence of God within you.

Walking in the Spirit is being led of the Word of God. Begin afresh on this journey today. Jesus says, *"Verily, verily I say unto you, He that believeth on me, the works that I do shall he do also; and greater works than these shall he do; because I go unto the Father."* Here is the progression again!

Believe and you will see the work of Jesus throughout your life! Since God knows the good works that are prepared for you; God knows His perfect will for your life (Ephesians 2:10). By the Holy Spirit of God, you receive both accurate and personal Counsel and direct liberating Comfort.

Ask Jesus today to lead you in every decision. If you do not know where to begin, just begin. Take Jesus at His Word and God's perfect design and plan will unfold in your life as you release yourself to your Savior. The will of God unfolds in the details of your life as you stand upon His word alone and cry out for leadership by His Spirit in all things.

"Verily, verily I say unto you, He that believeth on me, the works that I do shall he do also; and greater works than these shall he do; because I go unto the Father." Right here is where we invite you into our story as we give a brief testimony of how these words were actually fulfilled in our lives by the manifest power of God...

We were struggling with ordering our home and career life. We were being buffeted by chaotic schedules, chaotic rooms, and chaotic feelings. One day, we dug in our heels and asked God to demonstrate His Word in the minutia of our muddy lives.

We declared that since it is written that the Holy Spirit will "teach you all things;" we would open our spirits and listen for Him, follow Him and look for miracles in our calendar, home and heart. And deep within us, we began to perceive a leading voice, a still small voice arising from our intuition, that led with detail; from which sweater to pull from the closet, to which chore to accomplish, to which phone call to make, to which route to take to work...truly minutia.

There was a difference. Miracles happened and the chaos was pressed back. Fulfilled scripture actively wove together the doings of our hands and the moments of our day. At first, the Holy Spirit would bring a leading line of scripture to our memory, and we acted upon it. Then we began to know His voice and could finally discern what is meant by the imperative, "Therefore take no thought, saying, What shall we eat? or, What shall we drink? or, Wherewithal shall we be clothed?" (Matthew 12:31). As we sought the Kingdom, even the answers to these things were given unto us (Matthew 6:33). In these moments, we learned that believing is seeing.

As we trusted the Holy Spirit to "teach us all things" – we learned to submit, follow and walk in the Spirit. One of our most powerful prayers was that the Lord would make scripture our only thought; and before the powers of this age would teach us to "...take ye no thought how or what thing ye shall answer, or what ye shall say" (Luke 12:11); that we might walk in Christ alone.

"If a man love me, He will keep my words." As we kept Jesus' words, God manifested His loving guidance. We learned to practically refuse our own ways. We learned that the "still small voice" does still say "this is the way, walk, in it" as we insist with our whole being-enveloped-in-Faith that His Word is True (1 Kings 19:12; Isaiah 30:21b).

We learned that the will of God for our lives is always clear as light (Psalm 119:105; Proverbs 6:23). If we cannot hear God, it is because we have fallen away from His Word and are listening to another. At these times our spiritual ears or eyes are tuned to our own desires, or the world's words and/or the follow-on patterns of sin or false religion that conform us to serve them – instead of God (Romans 12:1-2). In these times, we were double-minded and did not know what we wanted (Galatians 5:17).

But as we walked unto the Spirit, we began to witness the least of the "greater works" prepared for those who follow Jesus (John 5:20). As we learned to hear God and be faithful in the details of life; He released us into more (Luke 16:10). By the Holy Spirit's guidance and in the Name of Jesus alone, we prayed and watched – fevers be driven out, bones and joints be healed; demons manifest and depart from people and homes; people be freed from addictions by the word alone; death be driven back, and we saw victory after victory over the onslaught of the enemy against the power of God and the people of God.

Underpinning all of this, was one decision – to simply stand upon Scripture alone; by Faith alone; in Christ alone, through His Grace alone, by the leading of the Holy Spirit alone – for the Glory of God alone! We stepped into the obedience of love and *"kept"* the Word. And as we *kept* the word, the Word of God *kept* us and the love of God was made manifest.

This is not surprising, as it is written: *"He that hath my commandments, and keepeth them, he it is that loveth me: and he that loveth me shall be loved of my Father, and I will love him, and will manifest myself to him."* The Word is indeed Eternal and powerfully Present (Isaiah 57:15).

Let all doubt be sent away now in the Name of Jesus Christ. For the Lord purposed to lead us, and through this devotional has

76

purposed to lead you as you invite Him to do so. The Lord will begin in the minutia of your life, and if you will receive Him – lead you into greater works unto His Glory.

Jesus is not leading you by this devotional, but by His Spirit alone. All we have to give is our obedience in love as we testify to Him. And our prayers are with you now, for Jesus has assured our hearts that those who come this far have open ears to hear Him (Matthew 11:15) and will "choose this day whom" they "will serve" (Joshua 24:15a).

In the Name of Jesus, and by the mercies of God, will you ask the Counselor to lead you into Truth even unto the nitty-gritty of life? Will you hold the line of scripture and keep the word of God alone as your only thought? Will you ask Jesus Christ to lead you through the fields of this world, by the voice of the Holy Spirit alone, to the Father's Glory alone?

If you so do, "Faithful *is* he that calleth you, who also will do it" (1 Thessalonians 5:24). We are so confident, because these are the promises of God to the people of God. And even now, we hear Him leading what is to be written on this page and in every effort and event of our lives.

It is written that the saints overcome, "by the blood of the Lamb, and by the word of their testimony" as "they loved not their lives unto the death" (Revelation 12:11). Will you take up the word as your testimony? Will you die to what you know unto the glory of God?

77

Will you give away the details of your life to Jesus? Do you love that much? If so, there is now only one move to be made, and it is the mightiest move of all. Take this matter to prayer and ask God to release the faculties of your mind, heart and soul unto the directing voice of the Spirit of God alone, unto His Glory alone.

Once again we come back around to where we left off: Will you ask Jesus today to lead you in every decision? If you do not know where to begin, just begin. Take Jesus at His Word and God's perfect design and plan will unfold in your life as you release yourself to your Savior.

Prayer of Response: To the Glory of God

Please pray aloud with us...

Heavenly Father, please forgive me for believing that I needed to walk according to my own guidance, even though Your Holy Spirit indwells me! Abba, Father! I turn around. Instead of my word, I take up Yours. I love You! Help me to keep Your Word!

In the Name of Jesus, I press back all doubt. Your Son Jesus says that those who believe in Him shall do the very works that He does. I confess the Faith of Jesus Christ now. He is the Lord and King of my life; even of the very details.

In the Name of Jesus, I ask the Counselor to lead me into all Truth for my life. Come, Holy Spirit! I ask not only to do the very works of Jesus as scripture declares, but even the greater works, because Jesus has gone to the Father. I reject every stronghold in my mind that stands against the Truth of scripture for there is no variation in You or Your Word.

Therefore, I listen for direct and personal Counsel, Guidance and Comfort now – for You are the Glory of my House. I stand on Scripture alone; and ask Jesus Christ alone to lead me by Your Holy Spirit alone, into a life lived to Your Glory alone! God help me to believe and see you manifest! In the Name of Jesus, Amen.

Week Two, Day Five – In Disguise

"LORD, who shall abide in thy tabernacle? Who shall dwell in thy holy hill? He that walketh uprightly, and worketh righteousness, and speaketh the truth in his heart."
Psalm 15:1-2

"Many will say to me in that day, Lord, Lord, have we not prophesied in thy name? And in thy name have cast out devils? And in thy name done many wonderful works? And then will I profess unto them, I never knew you: depart from me, ye that work iniquity."
Matthew 7:22-23

All who confess Jesus as Lord receive a new spirit; yet not all Believers take up the spiritual walk, as they are held-fast by firm habits of walking in other paths. Even now, break stride for this moment with what has been taught or what you have been told to do as a Christian, and for a time sit at Jesus' feet as Mary sat (Luke 10:39). Then rise up *"walketh uprightly, and worketh righteousness, and speaketh the truth"* in the power of His Name by the leading of the Spirit (Philippians 3:10).

Many spiritual-sounding church-leaders, writers and teachers claim to be Christ-followers who rightly divide God's word for life. Still others produce convincing miracles and wonderful works. Yet Jesus says to the outwardly holy who take up His Name apart from knowing Him, *"depart from me, ye that work iniquity."* Surely some of these *"walketh uprightly, and worketh righteousness, and speaketh the truth."* Can you discern the difference between what is of God and what is in disguise?

There is much at stake with this question. Mary is pictured sitting in the physical presence of Jesus. You have the same capability.

In your yearning for Jesus, to whom do you turn? As you are guided by the desire of your heart to know and come closer to God, do you choose to *"abide in thy tabernacle* and *dwell in thy holy hill?"* Turn to the right and turn to the left and you may find many church-communities who declare they are the tabernacle or spiritual "city on a hill" (Matthew 5:14). Are they? How do you know?

Let's be honest with ourselves. Most Christians look to the visible body of the church with her pastors, elders, teachers, doctrines and ministries as the spiritual focus and pathway for knowing and following God. Most Believers agree that following the world cannot lead to knowing Jesus (James 4:4) so they rightly turn aside from its teaching and influence. These brothers and sisters wisely transfer authority away from the world; yet at whose feet do they then choose to sit? Can you hear in your spirit the beginnings of spiritual dilemma?

Transferring authority over you heart from the world to the church is not the same thing as transferring authority over your heart to Jesus. Please be careful here, as we are not speaking against the Church or of being part of the Body of Christ. What is of concern is the posture of the heart before God and within a people to whom many covenant to be members. Why such a concern? Because this is the critical issue addressed by Jesus

Himself as He looks at the heart of each one as they stand before Him in heaven (Matthew 7:22-23).

Jesus is clear that it is possible to live in disguise. These are those who are outwardly righteous, yet inwardly filled with unrighteousness:

> Woe unto you, scribes and Pharisees, hypocrites! for ye are like unto whited sepulchres, which indeed appear beautiful outward, but are within full of dead *men's* bones, and of all uncleanness. Even so ye also outwardly appear righteous unto men, but within ye are full of hypocrisy and iniquity.
> Matthew 23:27-28

Though someone studies the Bible to know the things of God, or walks with the appearance of uprightness and righteousness; though their footfalls seem habituated to scriptural principle or church doctrine; though they confess they follow Jesus with a purposed desire in pursuing truth; though spiritual gifts manifest, and there be holy things, holy water and evidence of helps to the surrounding community – these all may or may not be of God.

Who then are they who rise up *"walketh uprightly, and worketh righteousness, and speaketh the truth"* in the power of His Name? Those who have inwardly climbed the Holy Hill of Golgotha, bent their knees in their clay-jar temple before their King and confessed that there is only One authority in Heaven and Earth (Matthew 28:18). These are the sheep who will not follow the voice of another; not even the voice of logic, or of sound doctrine, or of right churchly practice, or of liturgy, or of a

82

charismatic teacher, or by the experience of spiritual power or of blessing – but are led by the Holy Spirit through their new spirit into being a "doer of the Word" of God alone (James 1:22).

Those who follow Jesus, refuse to follow any voice other than His own (John 10:4-5). Since this be our Lord's testimony, there must be "other" voices to be wary of. And for good reason, because Jesus says that not a few, but:

> Many will say to me in that day, Lord, Lord, have we not prophesied in thy name? And in thy name have cast out devils? And in thy name done many wonderful works? And then will I profess unto them, I never knew you: depart from me, ye that work iniquity.
>
> Matthew 7:22-23

Perhaps your spirit trembles with our own at Jesus' warning that not a "few" will be deceived but that "many" will have followed after spiritual voices which do not lead to, but away from fellowship with Jesus Christ. And this leadership results in outwardly wonderful and apparently righteous works which only disguise iniquity.

Could it be that a son or daughter of a church lifting up the Name of Jesus Christ can drift into a spiritual walk devoted to outwardly wonderful and apparently righteous works apart from Him? Could "memorizing scripture" or "doing church" or "saying the liturgy" or "being discipled" or "manifesting spiritual power" or flourishing in this "new Christianity" or that "new spiritual practice," become ends apart from knowing Jesus?

83

Might followers become so attached to the blessings of being in a church family, or in learning the facts-of-scripture, or receiving breakthroughs of spiritual power in tongues or healing or spiritual words – that their church becomes their Jesus and spiritual power becomes their Lord? It is possible, the Bible says that "...in the last days perilous times shall come. For men shall be lovers of themselves..." and along with several other dangerous attributes, they shall be "Ever learning, and never able to come to the knowledge of the truth" (2 Timothy 3:1a, 7).

Oh dear brother and sister, walk in the counsel of the Lord! It is written that the Holy Spirit "...will guide you into all truth: for he shall not speak of himself; but whatsoever he shall hear, *that* shall he speak" (John 16:13). The Holy Spirit shall, "...teach you all things, and bring all things to your remembrance, whatsoever I [Jesus] have said unto you" (John 14:26).

The Holy Spirit guides, speaks, teaches and brings to remembrance Jesus' words; and those who keep Jesus' words are beloved of God (John 14:23). So anything that is done apart from God's leading Spirit cannot be of God. Even the most miraculous acts, beautiful liturgies, or sacrificial works of social mercy are not of God – if they are not led of the Holy Spirit.

Perhaps you are beginning to see that it is possible to lead an outwardly Christian life, independent of walking in the Spirit. Perhaps you, or others you know, have ascended what appeared to be God's holy hill and now find yourself standing atop a hill of knowledge; thinking that abiding and dwelling in God is primarily a work of the mind. Or do you find yourself atop a hill of experience; feeling that dwelling in God is primarily demonstrated by manifestations of spiritual expression? Or perhaps you are simply thanking God that you are hidden in Christ alone, already compelled and quieted by His Spirit alone.

Wherever you find yourself, rejoice in the Lord! For the Holy Spirit leads into all truth (John 16:13)! It is possible today, to give complete authority over to a pure devotion to Jesus Christ, by taking every thought captive in simple obedience to the Lord to whom all authority in heaven and earth has been given (2 Corinthians 10:5; Matthew 28:18). Let the Lord alone lead your intuition as if by the right hand (Psalm 73:23).

As you respond to the Holy Spirit, any religious or worldly habit simply falls away! As you take up the spiritual walk according to the leading of God's Spirit, you bear true power-filled spiritual fruit. And wherever you are; Christ Himself is proclaimed through you in the midst of the world or His Name-professing people. For the Church is the radiant bride of Christ and Jesus is perfecting Her that she might appear without spot or blemish before Him (Ephesians 5:27)!

Will you tune your ears to Jesus, the Author and Finisher of Faith (Hebrews 12:1-2)? Are you ready to depart from any guise of externally-focused holiness or knowledge-based pursuit of God? Will you open your spirit that you may know Jesus by the internal revelation of God via the Holy Spirit? Will you depart from pursuing the things of God, or the family of God, or the work of God, or teaching about God; to pursuing Christ alone?

Only God can deliver what He promises. No anointed leader, or mindful movement, or holy practice, or discipleship method, or purpose-driven passion can deliver the end of knowing Jesus Christ and living a life in resurrection power. *"LORD, who shall abide in thy tabernacle? Who shall dwell in thy holy hill? He that walketh uprightly, and worketh righteousness, and speaketh the truth in his heart."* Wherever you find yourself today, walk in the authority of the Holy Spirit from the hill of your mind to your new spirit, where the Holy Spirit dwells within.

Prayer of Response: In Disguise

Please pray aloud with us...

"Our Father which art in heaven, Hallowed be Thy name. Thy kingdom come. Thy will be done, as in heaven, so in earth" (Luke 11:2) Holy is Your Name! And I pray Your will be done on earth through my clay-vessel. That I may walk uprightly, do the works of righteousness, and speak truth in my heart; this out of love for You and to the glory of Your Name!

Please forgive me for any time when I substituted the teachings of a man or woman, or the fellowship or ministries of a church, or spiritual works, or religious habits, or even seeking biblical knowledge; for seeking You. Abba, help me to see and remove any disguise!

Please purify my heart by restoring a pure devotion to Jesus. Thank You for showing me where I have been tangled in worldly or churchly ways. Thank you, Jesus, for Your cleansing cross and life-giving resurrection. Thank You Holy Spirit, for leading me into all truth and for teaching my spirit only what Jesus is saying. Please open my spirit, show me where I am caught in any disguise. As You bring to mind, I confess... (take time to lay anything He brings to mind at His feet).*

God, I repent from these disguises and renounce them. Please restore me to walk by Your Spirit, in the Faith of Jesus, captained by Your Word brought to my mind by Your Holy Spirit. May I know Jesus and be known by Him as His own – forevermore. Abba, thank You for leading me by the hand into Your tabernacle! In Jesus' Name, Amen.

Week Two, Day Six – Looking for Servants

"And the Lord said, Who then is that faithful and wise steward, whom his lord shall make ruler over his household, to give them their portion of meat in due season?"
Matthew 24:45

"Blessed is that servant, whom his lord when he cometh shall find so doing."
Matthew 24:46

Who then is that faithful and wise steward? Jesus Christ who came to serve is both Faithful and True (Matthew 20:28; Revelation 19:11). And what place did He take in the Household of God? That of the Foot-Washer and of the One who died doing the will of His Father.

Jesus also taught those who follow after Him to deny themselves (Matthew 16:24) and take up the will of the Father (John 6:38) – even unto losing their lives (Luke 9:24). He charges His disciples:

> Ye call me Master and Lord: and ye say well; for *so* I am. If I then, *your* Lord and Master, have washed your feet; ye also ought to wash one another's feet. For I have given you an example, that ye should do as I have done to you. Verily, verily, I say unto you, The servant is not greater than his lord; neither he that is sent greater than he that sent him.
> John 13:13-16

Though the work of the servant be of foot-washing and self-denial, Jesus promises that those who lose their lives, find life;

88

and are blessed and honored by the Father (Matthew 10:39; John 12:26, 13:17). How happy is the one to whom God says, *"Blessed is that servant, whom his lord when he cometh shall find so doing."*

As the manifest Word of God, Jesus was not a rule unto Himself, nor did He declare a dominion apart from His Father's authority. Quite the opposite. Jesus only did what God the Father told Him to do. Jesus, as the perfect servant and Son of God says, "I do nothing of myself; but as my Father hath taught me, I speak these things" (John 8:28) and again, "The Son can do nothing of himself, but what he seeth the Father do: for what things soever he doeth, these also doeth the Son likewise" (John 5:19).

In the beginning, there were no natural or spiritual barriers between God speaking and man hearing. The sons and daughters were made in the image of God and walked with Him in full communion and obedience (Genesis 1:26, 2:15). In those days, God's children talked directly with Him in the earthly reality of time and space (Genesis 3:8). Then Eve took up conversation with the Serpent and both she and Adam ate from the garden on their own terms (Genesis 3:1-6).

By the mercies of God, Jesus Christ came into the world on His Father's terms, in a full manifestation of perfect obedience and service as the incarnate Word of God (John 1:14). As the New Adam, Jesus exemplified obedience to the will of the Father in the garden of this world (Mark 10:45; Romans 5:18; 1 Corinthians 15:22). The Son of God, "...made himself of no reputation, and took upon him the form of a servant, and was made in the likeness of men" (Philippians 2:7).

Jesus physically suffered the rejection and condemnation of His own people (John 1:11, 19:6, 14-15). He gave His life upon the cross to fulfill His Father's will (Luke 22:42). Then Jesus actually rose from the dead, appearing physically to His followers before ascending in His resurrection body to heaven (Acts 1:3, 9)! These are historic events; they are not merely spiritual acts of service, but are physical realities of the Foot-washer who died doing the will of His Father.

And so by the Grace of God, it is written of those who are in Christ, "We therefore were buried with Him through baptism into death, in order that, just as Christ was raised from the dead through the glory of the Father, we too may walk in newness of life" (Colossians 2:12). And the walk undertaken is not merely a spiritual one, but is completed in the physical gestures of a life lived in Christly obedience.

Though there is still a spirit of self-determination in the world which whispers, "Yea, hath God said....," the commission of Christ to His followers is pure and cannot be overwhelmed. Though there are many who interpret the word according to the world's perspective, it is written that the child of God overcomes "...them because greater is he that is in you, than he that is in the world" (1 John 4:4).

The Lord has actually died, risen and ascended. Your new life in Christ is the very real basis for your capability to walk unto the Holy Spirit in the obedience of Jesus. Those who follow Jesus have as a matter-of-fact, died to self in baptism, been raised to new life in Christ; and are living in Him (Romans 6:4; Galatians 2:20; Colossians 3:1-4).

Just as Jesus' death and resurrection are actual historic events, so God now considers you dead in Christ, raised and ascended to new life in Him. The disciple of Christ walks by faith, in the power of this durable, spiritual, eternal reality:

> But God, who is rich in mercy, for his great love wherewith he loved us, Even when we were dead in sins, hath quickened us together with Christ, (by grace ye are saved;) raised *us* up together, and made *us* sit together in heavenly *places* in Christ Jesus.
>
> Ephesians 2:5-6

Therefore, it pleases God when His children run to Jesus; for "it is your Father's good pleasure to give you the kingdom" (Luke 12:32).

In the garden of this world, there are many voices. Some call you to be a master of your own destiny by pursuing education, career, calling, finances, relationships and other resources as top-priorities. Some even take-up the interpretation of and application of God's Word as the paradigm for doing so. Where in these are the echoes of the foot-washing, self-denying, life-encompassing ascended life in Christ – of saying and doing only what His Father said or did?

There is a very definite scriptural precedent for self-determination and control. Though God had commanded, "Ye shall not eat" of the Tree of Knowledge (Genesis 3:3); Adam and Eve exercised their authority to choose to walk as servants *or* to be masters of their own destiny. "And when the woman saw that the tree *was* good for food...to be desired to make *one* wise, she...did eat, and gave also unto her husband with her; and he did eat" (Genesis 3:6). And herein lies the first manifestation of the mastery that this realm cries out for and imparts as the standard for being a responsible citizen in the garden-of-the-world.

However, God's *"faithful and wise steward"* walks under the authority of the counsel of God, and as a servant of the Lord Jesus alone. Every decision you make that aligns under the leading of God's Word will be a choice that arises from fidelity to the command of God. Every decision you make that arises solely out of the world's advice or training, no matter how "religious" or "wise" in appearance or "noble" in intention or goal; will be a choice that arises from fidelity to the command of the world. God has called men and women to Himself and not to be mastered or led by any word save His own (Psalm 48:14; John 6:68).

Remember Eve's deception. She chose to disobey God in full belief that she was seeking to be like Him. She acted upon the Serpent's interpretation of God's Word: "For God doth know that in the day ye eat thereof, then your eyes shall be opened, and ye shall be as gods, knowing good and evil" (Genesis 3:5). It is clear by her doings that Eve thought it was a good idea to be like God according to her own perception and mastery of the meaning of God's command. She chose disobedience unto her own end.

"Who then is that faithful and wise steward whom his lord shall make ruler over his household?" A Christian is as a matter-of-spiritual-fact ascended to heaven in Christ and set now on earth as a heavenly man or woman charged as a foot-washer sent by the Lord. The servant of the Lord takes up the things of Christ and does not turn aside (Philippians 2:21).

Will you take up the ascended life in Christ? You have already died by faith. You are set apart and sealed by the Blood of Jesus Christ and fully reconciled and restored to communion with God (1 Corinthians 1:2, 6:11; 2 Corinthians 5:17-19; 1 Peter 1:2). You have the gift of being a hearer and doer of the Word of God alone (James 1:22). *"Blessed is that servant, whom his lord when he cometh shall find so doing."*

Prayer of Response: Looking for Servants

Please pray aloud with us...

Heavenly Father, my heart's desire is to take up the service that You have appointed me to in Your house. Help me to lay aside everything that rises up in me that opposes this service to You; any spirit of self-determination, self-direction, independence, pride, worldly wisdom or any other stronghold of my mind which stands in opposition to You. In the name of Jesus, I break allegiance from these now.

Please forgive me for the times when I have chosen to take up the things of the world, and set down the things of Christ. I repent from any thought that I am the master of my own

93

destiny and take up my place as a servant of Jesus Christ. Holy Spirit, lead me ever-deeper into the will of the Father according to scriptures. Let me walk as a spiritual man/woman in obedience to Your Word. Show me the way. (Take time to pray through the changes the Holy Spirit brings to mind).

Thank You Father, for blessing me. Thank You Jesus for restoring me to fellowship by Your self-emptying obedience to the Father. I rejoice in receiving You as my Lord and Savior; please help me to live my new life in You. I entrust myself to You and pray in Your Name Jesus. Amen.

Week Three, Day One – In This Moment

"I have set the LORD always before me, because he is at my right hand, I shall not be moved. Therefore my heart is glad, and my glory rejoiceth, my flesh also shall rest in hope. Thou wilt show me the path of life; in thy presence is fullness of joy, at thy right hand are pleasures forevermore."
Psalm 16:8-9, 11

"And when he [Jesus] was demanded of the Pharisees, when the kingdom of God should come, he answered them, and said: 'The kingdom of God cometh not with observation, Neither shall they say, "Lo here! Or, Lo there!" For, behold, the kingdom of God is within you."
Luke 17:20-21

The Kingdom of God is not only demonstrated in the coming reign of Jesus or in the perfection and fullness of the New Jerusalem; it is made manifest in you in this very moment! Rejoice for your God and King is near, present and eternally close! Rejoice also for you are near, present and eternally close to your God – therefore your life, your very glory, your whole-being shall not be moved (Romans 8:38-39).

In these past weeks, the Lord has called you to an awareness of the leading of His Spirit from within the temple of your body. He has drawn your spirit, through revelation in scripture, toward a fuller understanding of the communion you have with God through the presence of His Holy Spirit. *"Behold, the kingdom of God **is** within **you.**"*

Yesterday, the Lord began drawing you from the turbulence of self-direction into the deeper calm of a life dedicated unto walking in the Spirit. Today, there is reassurance that as you get out of the old boats of thought and walk on the water of the Spirit, He shall not allow you to sink and drown in what may feel like an approaching storm of confusion or anxiety (Matthew 14:22).

Granted, habits as boats and the spirit as the surrounding water, are only word-pictures. Yet they describe what it means to step into a reality of thinking and walking in a way that is incomprehensible to the world and possible only with Christ (Matthew 14:29). Walking on water in the Spirit is a walk captained by faith.

Your spiritual walk began the moment you received the Gospel of Jesus and believed God's Word. In receiving Jesus, God received you through the saving work of His Son imparted to you through Grace – and this not of your own doing, but as God's gift (Galatians 2:8). So the contours of walking in the Spirit unfold as they began, through the Faith of Jesus, by Grace and not by works – even of the mind.

In this moment, will you by faith, entrust your mind, soul, heart and body to Jesus? It is written that the spiritual walk is "by faith and not by sight" (2 Corinthians 5:7). Will you believe Jesus when He says, *'The kingdom of God cometh not with observation, Neither shall they say, "Lo here! Or, Lo there!"'?* Walking in the presence of the Holy Spirit is accomplished only by the faith of Jesus Christ (Romans 13:14).

A deepening walk in the Spirit opens before you as you release more of yourself and more of your life to God (John 6:63). As the Spirit of God leads you into all truth, and you walk truly in faith, your heart takes up the song of speaking the truth revealed in your spirit by God (1 Corinthians 2:9-10). You move away from the habit of walking in self-confidence to walking spirit to Spirit with your God who in essence, leads you by the hand (Hebrews 10:38). As you keep step with what the Spirit is doing; like Peter before Christ, you are out of the boat in a moment and walking on water (Galatians 5:25; Matthew 14:28-31).

The Old Testament psalmist gives an accurate biblical picture of the faith-walk with God: *"I have set the LORD always before me."* This is not metaphor or wishful thinking, nor is it based on a natural observation wherefore the singer says, *"Lo here! Or Lo there!"* is God. Instead, the singer confirms the reality of the leading of the Lord in his life.

The psalmist also sings of his place in God's presence. *"Thou wilt show me the path of life...at thy right hand are pleasures forevermore."* Again, this is no mere metaphor of his nearness to God. The singer testifies that the actual attitude of his heart, his glory, and his flesh – are all affected. Though he does not apprehend God by natural observation and say *"Lo here! Or Lo there!"* – the singer experiences the "therefore" of the leading Presence of God within his personal faculties of mind, soul and body. *"Therefore my heart is glad, and my glory rejoiceth, my flesh also shall rest in hope."*

In the presence of God the singer's *"heart is glad;"* therefore it is not shaken with confusing or competing emotions. His *glory* also rejoices in God; and the soul is not striving in knowledge and wisdom apart from God. Even his *"flesh also shall rest in hope"* and is not lured away into its own desires. At the right hand of God, there *"are pleasures forevermore;"* for this is the paradise of the gladness and joy of being in the presence of Heaven's High King. This is the water-walking life.

Notice that the psalmist grabs hold of God's hand as an *external* presence; just as a child sets herself next to a parent or trusted friend by taking hold of their hand. If you would follow and *"set the LORD always before"* you. Let go of the leadership of the world and devotion to the things of the world. To follow Jesus is to be set into a new direction by the operation of your belief in Him and loving commitment to follow.

With spiritual eyes and ears purely on Christ, you are led by the *internal* presence of God. What is needed in this moment is not your understanding, or faith or love; but your radical, simple obedience in getting out of your boat and stepping out on the water. The Lord does not reach down and forcibly throw you into a spiritual walk by grabbing the shoulders of your mind, or by reining in your soul, or forcing your heart and body into obedience to Him.

The water-walking Peter isn't the only disciple who steps into the unknown with Jesus. Consider Levi for a moment. The Bible does not report that the man had even encountered Jesus prior to their meeting at the customs booth. There is no record of a lengthy inquiry by the tax-collector as to what sort of man was asking him to leave everything he had known and achieved behind. Levi got up and walked on water!

It seems Jesus showed up at Levi's job-site and spoke two words to him: "Follow me" (Mark 2:14b). Levi acted immediately, "And he arose and followed Him" (Mark 2:14c). Levi gets up and goes in response to Jesus, whose invitation and presence are very *external* for the disciple. Talk about being led of God by the right hand!

In the presence of God, Peter left the boat and Levi left the tax-booth. The psalmist takes hold of God's Word and sets it before Him. Each one demonstrates child-like obedience in rising up and following God. And each one experiences God's blessing breaking through into their lives.

The psalmist's *"heart is glad, and* his *glory rejoiceth."* Peter water-walks while his faith holds. Levi directly receives the blessing of the gladness and joy of fellowship in his own house with the Son of God! (Mark 2:25) And when you confessed Jesus as Lord, the blessing of God broke through into your life by water and the Spirit: *"Behold, the kingdom of God is within you"* (emphasis ours).

Is Jesus calling to you by the Holy Spirit to leave your boat or booth? There is no need to know your destination or your plan of action. There is no need for your heart, soul, mind or spirit to be overwhelmed or shaken with the weight of decision, the uncertainty of the world, or the press of the storm.

As Jesus calls you in a moment, so He answers you moment-by-moment with His Presence. The psalmist was unmovable in proclaiming:

I have set the LORD always before me, because he is at my right hand, I shall not be moved. Therefore my heart is glad, and my glory rejoiceth, my flesh also shall rest in hope. Thou wilt show me the path of life; in thy presence is fullness of joy, at thy right hand are pleasures forevermore.

At Levi's table Jesus said, "They that are whole have no need of the physician, but they that are sick: I came not to call the righteous, but sinners to repentance" (Luke 2:17). Then the Physician Himself became the cure, "...in that, while we were yet sinners, Christ died for us" (Romans 5:8). Jesus has offered His Life upon the cross as full satisfaction for all the sin that barred your way to restored communion; and in the moment you repented and believed, you received the Holy Spirit (Acts 2:38).

Yet you are still given a choice as to whether you will rise up in Christ, forever leave life as you know it, and step out moment-by-moment as one "born of water and of the Spirit" (John 3:5). Will you *"set the LORD always before* yourself?*"* Will you take up a life devoted to the reality that the *"kingdom of God is within **you?**"* Will you embrace the wonder that this heavenly life is not somewhere out there for you to find in some practice or work? The path of life is revealed in Jesus Christ (John 14:6) and the presence of the Holy Spirit is within you (1 Corinthians 3:16).

"Thou wilt show me the path of life; in thy presence is fullness of joy, at thy right hand are pleasures forevermore."

Prayer of Response: In This Moment

Please pray aloud with us...

Heavenly Father, Thank You that Your Kingdom is within me. Thank You for releasing me from looking at the "here's" and "there's" of my circumstances to find Your will for me. Thank You for the indwelling and leading presence of Your Holy Spirit.

Lord Jesus, I rise up in radical and simple obedience. Though my future is unknown to me, I step out in faith and set You "always before me," confident that "I shall not be moved." I take up the life You died to give me and receive gladness of heart, joy of mind, peace and stillness of soul, and hope for my frame. Please lead me by the right hand that I might leave behind any devotion to the world, either by choice or by habit.

Moment-by-moment, lead me in the "paths of life," "fullness of joy" and "pleasures forevermore" of Your Presence. Thank you for new life in the Spirit wherein I am released from the striving of my mind, the pride of life and the luring desires of the flesh. Come what may, let the Kingdom come and Your will be done. Let my thinking and doing align to Your will, according to Scripture, by the leading of the Holy Spirit unto Your Glory; in the Name of Jesus, Amen.

Week Three, Day Two – By Faith

"There is none that understandeth, there is none that seeketh after God."
Romans 3:11

"John answered and said, 'A man can receive nothing, except it be given him from heaven.'"
John 3:27

The holiest person on earth cannot by means of religion, come to God. The most zealous person on earth cannot by means of passion, draw near to God. The most knowledgeable man on earth cannot, by means of wisdom, find God. The only path to God is by way of a gift from heaven. It is written, *"A man can receive nothing, except it be given him from heaven."* And Jesus says, "No man can come to me, except the Father which hath sent me draw him" (John 6:44).

And how does the Father draw each one unto Himself? Jesus answers saying, "It is written in the prophets, 'And they shall be all taught of God.' Every man therefore that hath heard, and hath learned of the Father, cometh unto me" (John 6:45).

And now, have you come to Him? If so, by what means? There is only one way, by way of being drawn and taught of the Spirit of God.

Do you know you are taught of God? It is written that "...the Comforter, which is the Holy Ghost, whom the Father will send in my name, he shall teach you all things...." (John 15:26).

What you know of God in your spirit is therefore a gift of God Himself.

And what does the Holy Spirit teach? What Jesus has declared: "I am the way, the truth, and the life: no man cometh unto the Father, but by me" (John 14:6). Therefore, communion with God does not come by an instrument, or by way of worthiness; but through Jesus Himself!

Apart from being drawn by the Father and coming by way of Jesus, *"There is none that understandeth, there is none that seeketh after God."* A relationship with God cannot merely be a work of the intellect, heart, or hand.

It is received by faith. The Lord teaches this lesson as the disciples pass a fruitless tree which Jesus had cursed. Mark 11:22 translated directly from the original language reads: "And answering, Jesus said to them [the disciples], 'Have the faith of God.'"

In fact, Romans 3:26b in the original language simply says that "the one who has faith of Jesus" is justified of God! And St. John writes of this same mountain-drowning faith in Revelation 14:12 as he describes the victorious saints as "...those who keep the commandments of God and hold fast to the faith of Jesus."

The Lord tells them that a doubt-free "faith of God" can move mountains into the sea (Mark 11:23). Is this a surprise given that Jesus is faith's Author, Source and Perfecter (Hebrews 12:2)? For through Jesus, "all things were made" (John 1:3). And this

Jesus is the way, truth and life by whom you came to both physical and spiritual life.

Indeed, *"A man can receive nothing, except it be given him from heaven."* Our Father in heaven gives, "Every good gift and every perfect gift" (James 1:17a). By way of saving faith, you are justified before God and the mountain of your sin falls under the blood of Jesus (Romans 3:26).

In all of these examples "of faith," the little English word "of" is moored in the possessive in the grammar of the original Greek language and points to a substantial truth when directly translated. Jesus says, 'Have the faith of God" (Mark 11:22). Paul says that "the one who has faith of Jesus," is justified (Romans 3:26). John says, those who conquer "hold fast to the faith of Jesus" (Revelation 14:12). Each of these references to faith are in the Greek possessive case and "the faith" that is spoken of is "of God."

What does this mean? The possessive is the grammatical case of ownership. A colloquial translation of Mark 11:22, Jesus' instruction to "Have the faith of God," can be written, "Have God's faith." In Romans 3:26, Paul's teaching can be rendered, "the one who has Jesus' faith," is justified. And John's description of the victorious saints in Revelation 14:12 can be translated, "hold fast to Jesus' faith."

When you take up Christ by faith, whose faith do you take up? Your own faith in something or someone? By no means. Though you are given faith in measures (Romans 12:3), even the smallest is mountain-moving because it is "God's faith" or "Jesus' faith." The gift, though received, does not depart from the presence of the Giver. *"A man can receive nothing, except it be given him from heaven."*

Scripture testifies that Christian faith is not founded in the belief, effort or understanding of man; but flows from God. As it is written, *"There is none that understandeth, there is none that seeketh after God."* There then cannot be anyone who knows God by their own means; for the mortal and finite cannot seek the eternal and infinite unknown. Just as an ant cannot purpose to understand a man, a human being cannot purpose to know a God infinitely greater than himself.

Yet, God in His mercy has made a way for us. Our Lord Himself confirms; "I am the way, the truth, and the life: no man cometh unto the Father, but by me" (John 14:6). There is no other gate, no other way, no other channel or road by which we may know God:

> Then said Jesus unto them again, Verily, verily, I say unto you, I am the door of the sheep. All that ever came before me are thieves and robbers: but the sheep did not hear them. I am the door: by me if any man enter in, he shall be saved, and shall go in and out, and find pasture. The thief cometh not, but for to steal, and to kill, and to destroy: I am come that they might have life, and that they might have *it* more abundantly.
>
> John 10:7-10

When Jesus called you by name and you confessed your belief, you received the first installment or "measure of faith" (Romans 12:3). For "no man can say that Jesus is the Lord, but by

105

the Holy Ghost" (1 Corinthians 12:3). Though this gift of faith be received with little understanding and be even smaller than a mustard seed, its measure secured your salvation and the mountain of stone that sat cold and hard deep within you became a "heart of flesh" (Ephesians 2:5-8; Ezekiel 36:26). A "new spirit" was placed within you and the mind began its transformation as Jesus Christ took up residence and tabernacled within by the quickening of the Holy Spirit (Acts 11:17; John 17:22-23)!

Faith then, does not come by natural knowledge or by the operation of the physical ears. Faith does not come by works or by the operation of human striving, moral behavior or holy habit. Faith does not come by a winsome word or through the expanding feeling of a warming heart.

"So then faith *cometh* by hearing, and hearing by the word of God" (Romans 10:17). Faith comes, when Jesus-the Word comes "which effectually worketh also in you that believe" (1 Thessalonians 2:13), and Jesus comes when the mind, heart and body accept a word spoken not of man, but of God – who draws through His Son all people unto Himself (John 12:32).

Is there room in your mind for Jesus or is it filled with other pursuits? Do you recall that Jesus was not born at the inn of Bethlehem because there was no room for him? Some minds are stack-piled with knowledge from Christian books or even Bible translations – yet are no longer an open manger to receive by faith what is given of Jesus through the Spirit.

106

Some hearts are no better as they are clothed with feelings of warmth, acceptance and connection in the church or are wrapped-up in highs of zealous worship, tear-filled prayer, or passionate service. These are so filled with loving the experience of faithful service that there is nothing left to swaddle Jesus with.

For if the body of the manger itself; if its hands and feet are so busy scrubbing and filling the mind by words and works while swaddling the heart with emotional wonders; if its openness to being the birthing place of heaven, the abode of the Holy Spirit, a temple through which God is known by faith is already full...how is the gift of heaven to be received?

"A man can receive nothing, except it be given him from heaven." The holiest person on earth cannot by means of religion, come to God. The most zealous person on earth cannot by means of passion, draw near to God. The most knowledgeable man on earth cannot, by means of wisdom, find God. The only path to God is by way of the Faith of Jesus Christ through the gift of the Holy Spirit.

Prayer of Response: By Faith

Please pray aloud with us...

King Jesus, I repent from believing that the more I studied about You; the more I would know You. I repent from believing that the more I did for You; the more I would please You. I repent from believing the more I took up the religious habit or spiritual disciplines, the closer I would be to You.

Thank You Jesus, for taking up the cross that I may be drawn unto You (John 12:32). Thank You for taking all of my iniquities and failings. I confess my sins before You. Please forgive me for... (share any specific things the Holy Spirit brings to mind).

Heavenly Father, I believe Your Word as recorded in the Bible is true. Thank You for every gift You give. Thank You for the gift of the Faith of Jesus Christ. Please let me receive a fuller measure of Jesus' Faith.

I know that "A man can receive nothing, except it be given him from heaven." Lord, thank You for releasing me to simply open my spirit and invite You to come in. Let my mind be as an open manger to receive You and my heart be as swaddling clothes to embrace You.

Thank You that by the Faith of Jesus Christ, I am filled in the Holy Spirit. Thank You Jesus for such a great gift! Thank You Father, for drawing me unto Your Son. Please lead me by Your Spirit alone to Your Glory alone. In Jesus Name, Amen.

Week Three, Day Three – Wake Up

"For the Son of man is as a man taking a far journey, who left his house, and gave authority to his servants, and to every man his work, and commanded the porter to watch. Watch ye, therefore: for ye know not when the master of the house cometh...Lest coming suddenly he find you sleeping."

"And what I say unto you I say unto all, Watch."
Mark 13:34-37

Remember the childhood song, "Are you sleeping, are you sleeping? Brother John, Brother John? Morning bells are ringing, morning bells are ringing, ding-ding dong, ding-ding dong." Perhaps a sibling or bunk-mate would cajole you out of bed with such a melody as the sun rose. There is a real scriptural echo in this song. Is the Holy Spirit singing a similar song to you? "Awake thou that sleepest, and arise from the dead, and Christ shall give thee light" (Ephesians 2:14)!

As the Spirit of God is quickened and moving within you (John 6:63; 1 Corinthians 3:16), you receive this light as the gift of God-in-you. Therefore, it takes no additional authority to rise up in the Spirit and take up the watch or the work the Master has prepared for you (Ephesians 2:8-9).

Just turn your spiritual eyes toward the light, and the darkness is pressed back. For "...all things that are reproved are made manifest by the light; for whatsoever doth make manifest is light" (Ephesians 5:13). For the light of spiritual watchfulness is the Spirit of the Lord who shows you the way, prepares and equips you. Alleluia! *"For the Son of man is as a man taking a far journey, who left his house, and gave authority to his servants, and to every man his work, and commanded the porter to watch."*

Those who sleep-in these days are not quietly lying in some tranquil spiritual cemetery. Quite the opposite. Those who are asleep are wide-awake to the press of each day. Their physical eyes are open-so-wide that their spiritual eyes are blinded shut. The world is so challenging, work is so demanding, family schedules are so pressing, health concerns are so debilitating and circumstances, circumstances, circumstances become so overwhelming that even the Believer may pick up a spirit of anxiety or stress and have difficulty perceiving that the Lord is with them.

If this goes on long enough, some almost completely lose sight of the Lord (Proverbs 3:7). They "do each day" out of obedience and in a sort of languid desperation that if they just keep moving – something will change. In their effort, some even conclude that God Himself has left them alone to be tossed by life's battles. The deathly doldrums press and the days come and go, and this Child of God feels marooned on a dizzying and endless merry-go-round of struggle.

Let the Word of God deal with these mind-numbing doldrums. It is written that *"...the Son of man...left his house, and gave authority to his servants."* Though the Master has left as if *"taking a far journey;"* Jesus did not ascend to heaven without preparing and equipping those left behind to manage until He

110

returns! As you believed and confessed Christ, you have taken up Jesus' faith and are established "in" the Lord's house now:

> ...ye are no more strangers and foreigners, but fellow citizens with the saints, and of the household of God, And are built upon the foundation of the apostles and prophets, Jesus Christ...being the chief cornerstone.
>
> Ephesians 2:19

The Lord prepares His people in two powerful areas. Jesus *"gave authority to his servants, and to every man his work."* The authority given is the transferred authority to stand in place of the Master and conduct the business of the day according to His will (Romans 8:14; 2 Corinthians 5:17-20). The basis for your authority on earth is none other than the finished work of Jesus' death on the cross, His resurrection and ascension (Ephesians 2:1-10).

When you took up the faith of Jesus Christ, as a matter of scriptural fact, you received the gift of the guiding Presence of the Holy Spirit (Acts 2:38). In receiving Jesus, His Word is fulfilled as your Counselor comes: "Nevertheless I tell you the truth; It is expedient for you that I go away: for if I go not away, the Comforter will not come unto you; but if I depart, I will send him unto you" (John 16:7). And just before ascending, Jesus confirms, "...ye shall receive power, after that the Holy Spirit is come upon you: and ye shall be witnesses unto me" (Acts 1:8).

By giving your life to Christ, you have accepted the authority of the Lord's Spirit and appointed your will to follow

God. You have said that you are no longer your own Lord, but have proclaimed that Jesus is your King and your God. And to those who believe in His Name, "...gave he [Jesus] power to become the sons of God" (John 1:15b).

A son or daughter of God is not marooned in this world as an orphan. For the Presence of God tabernacles within. And "...greater is he [God] that is in you than he that is in the world" (1 John 4:4). Therefore, in Christ, every Believer has authority to deal with all of the business in the house-of-this-world; even unto standing in authority over the hidden powers, principalities, powers of darkness and spiritual wickedness in high places (Ephesians 6:12) operating behind natural realities. Are you awake to the Master's call? *"And what I say unto you I say unto all, Watch."*

Scripturally speaking, there is no question of your authorization or your authority as a son or daughter in the household of God! Yet have you acknowledged this authority and received the work Jesus has prepared for you? *"For the Son of man is as a man taking a far journey, who left his house, and gave authority to his servants, and to every man his work, and commanded the porter to watch."*

Jesus has not left you to wonder at what work you are assigned in the King's house. You and your fellow servants were created "...unto good works, which God has before ordained that we should walk in them" (Ephesians 2:10). The direction of scripture is clear regardless of your natural status. Whether slave or free, salary or hourly, white collar or blue collar, professional or trade, employee or homemaker: "Whatsoever thy hand findeth to do, do *it* with thy might" (Ecclesiastes 9:10) and "With good will doing service, as to the Lord, and not to men" (Ephesians 6:7).

In whatever natural work is yours in the world, are you spiritually awake to your authorization and authority in the Lord? Two fundamental spiritual matters are of great concern upon taking your watch; seeking the Kingdom of God with a mind set on Jesus (Matthew 6:33; Colossians 3:2), and standing firm before the devil who comes to steal, kill and destroy (John 10:10). In this there is a great reversal because the world commends seeking a "living" or a career and then platforming any Kingdom service upon that (or despite it). Yet the *"Son of man...left his house...gave authority to his servants, and to every man his work."* Therefore, in the Kingdom of God, finding your work means finding Jesus first!

Will you take up the watch? Will you lift your spiritual eyes and tune your spiritual ears to apprehend the leading of the Holy Spirit? Will you awaken in the spiritual legacy bought for you by the Master's blood? Will you take up the charge of the Lord to keep His house and watch in complete vigilance for His return? *"And what I say unto you I say unto all, Watch."*

The servant who keeps watch in the Master's house attends to the matters of their Lord and is set upon the direction of God's Spirit. Taking up spiritual work does not mean a life of passivity, or empty-headed meditation, but full engagement. As is written, "...whatsoever ye do, **do *it* heartily**, as to the Lord, and not unto men" (Colossians 3:23, emphasis ours) and "Whatsoever thy hand findeth to do, **do *it* with thy might**" (Ecclesiastes 9:10, emphasis ours).

And though your authorization in every undertaking of God may be resisted, in the Spirit you will not be defeated (Isaiah 54:17; 1 John 4:4). As you take up the work of God and watchfully follow the leading of God's Spirit through the noisy battles on your work-front and home-front; you will conquer "Not by might, nor by power, but by my spirit, saith the LORD of hosts" (Zechariah 4:6). Therefore, the watchful servant mightily engages the practical work of the Master's house under the leadership of God's Spirit alone!

Whether at home or in a factory, whether working a field or building the city, whether standing firm in the marketplace or operating advanced technologies, whether defending the nation or caring for the infirm or elderly, whether teaching the young or waiting tables – whatever your post, as a Believer you may rise above human endeavor and be conducted in all things by God's Spirit (Matthew 28:19-20). Your authority and work are of divine appointment and not of this world; for *"the Son of man...gave authority to his servants, and to every man his work."*

Jesus, your Lord calls you to *"Watch."* Are you awake and ready? When Jesus shows up, everything changes. Peter gets out of the boat and walks on water. Matthew gets up and leaves the tax booth. The man who finds treasure buries it again, sells all he has, and buys the field in which it resides (Matthew 13:44). And as the Master returns, you will finally be called out of the fields of the world unto the House of our Lord (Matthew 24:30-31; John 24:2). In the meantime, Jesus is appointing you to tend to the matters here.

Brother or sister, "Are you sleeping, are you sleeping? – Morning bells are ringing, morning bells are ringing!" Ask the Lord to open your spiritual eyes to the breaking light and sounds of the Kingdom of God! Ask the Lord of Heaven and Earth to equip you to stand firm in this present darkness, that you might take up your authority and place in Him.

> For the Son of man is as a man taking a far journey, who left his house, and gave authority to his servants, and to every man his work, and commanded the porter to watch. Watch ye, therefore: for ye know not when the master of the house cometh...Lest coming suddenly he find you sleeping. And what I say unto you I say unto all, Watch.
> Mark 13:34-37

Jesus will come. Will He find you wide-awake to the things of the world, yet spiritually a-slumber? Let that not be. Take up the Master's end-time warning as it were today:

> Be watchful, and strengthen the things which remain, that are ready to die: for I have not found thy works perfect before God. Remember therefore how thou hast received and heard, and hold fast, and repent. If therefore thou shalt not watch, I will come on thee as a thief, and thou shalt not know what hour I will come upon thee.
> Revelation 3:2-3

Jesus is calling now, will you "Remember therefore how thou hast received and heard, and hold fast, and repent"? Wake up in the Spirit by rebuking any devotion to "...the cares of this world, and the deceitfulness of riches, and the lusts of other things entering in;" which "choke the word" (Mark 4:19). Actively cry out for the Word of God to cut all spiritual ties to walking in your own will, your own accomplishments, or any counsel apart from God. Be awake – as you are led of God right now (Romans 8:14)!

Prayer of Response: Wake Up

Please pray aloud with us...

My Lord and my God, I cry out for a spirit of wisdom and understanding! Please break through the voices of this world and stir up my spirit. Open my spiritual eyes and ears! Please free me from any spiritual dullness and all deceptions of the "one who seeks to steal, kill and destroy" (John 10:10).

Lead me through Your Word unto "keeping watch" per Your command. Forgive me for all of the times that I have substituted world-based thinking for following the logic of the Holy Spirit. Forgive me for all of the times I have kept my eyes and ears on worldly things or worldly ways. Please restore me now to be wide-awake in the legacy, authority and charge of your Name to the work that You have given me.

Lord Jesus, I give you charge over my spiritual and practical work. Let me hear from You in my intuition. Show me if there is anything to let go of – or anything to take up – that I may simply stand in Your Spirit. Confirm, by Your Word, the form of the watch I am to take in the practical work of life. I submit my spirit to Your own. Thank you, Lord Jesus!

Thank you for leaving Your Spirit to guide and lead me into all Truth! "Thy word is truth" (John 17:17b). Sanctify me! Let Your will, and not my own be the sum of my spiritual understanding and my practical work. Awaken me by Grace and to Your Glory, in the praise of Your Son's Name! I pray in the Name of Jesus, Amen.

Author's Note: Tomorrow's prayer is woven through the devotion. As the Holy Spirit brings things to mind for you to take up or set down, consider taking note of them in the margins to test them in the light of this week's readings.

Please ask the Holy Spirit for a double provision of time, and/or the wisdom to journey in stages through this devotion...

Week Three, Day Four – Commandant

"The first of all the commandments is, Hear, O Israel; The Lord our God is one Lord; And thou shalt love the Lord thy God with all thy heart, and with all thy soul, and with all thy mind, and with all thy strength; this is the first commandment. And the second is like, namely this, Thou shalt love thy neighbour as thyself. There is none other commandment greater than these."

"And the scribe said unto him, 'Well, Master, thou hast said the truth; for there is one God; and there is none other but he; And to love him with all the heart, and with all the understanding, and with all the soul, and with all the strength, and to love his neighbor as himself, is more than all whole burnt offerings and sacrifices."

"And when Jesus saw that he answered discreetly, he said unto him: 'Thou are not far from the kingdom of God."
Mark 12:29-34

How far are you from the kingdom of God? It is possible to know. For those who are near are firmly standing in Christ and have one indissoluble, perpetually binding tie – the stability of the commandments of God (Matthew 24:35). These commandments are more than guides for moral or godly behavior (Hebrews 4:12).

How many Bible classes or Sunday schools have you attended where a seasoned teacher or facilitator reads a word of scripture and then asks, "What do you think it means to *'love the Lord thy God with all thy heart, and with all thy soul, and with all thy mind, and with all thy strength?'* or 'What does that verse mean to you in your circumstances?'"

Perhaps the teacher means to draw out what the Lord is commanding in your individual experience – and that is a God-honoring question (Acts 17:11)! Yet how many people hear this question as a request for personal interpretation and thereby assume that walking in the Spirit is subject to their own understanding, experience and circumstances?

Giving a witness to what God is doing in your life is effective in shaking the opponents of God; for the saints conquer "by the blood of the Lamb and the word of their testimony" (Revelation 12:11)! Yet the word of our testimony must abide under God's own testimony (John 12:49, 16:13). If the two are parted by interpretation or application arising from any other source, a dangerous shift has occurred.

The enemy seeks to part the conquering Word from its Source and make the knowledge of good and evil central to the human mind (Genesis 3:5). When this is accomplished, a stronghold is built in a man's mind and God is no longer *received* as the substantial Living Word (John 1:1,14; 2 Corinthians 10:4-5). Instead, God's commandments are merely *perceived* as some ephemeral idea or wise saying that can be analyzed, understood and applied apart from God.

Then follows the belief that some people have a better understanding of God's commands based upon biblical studies in the original language, or theological education, or by their authority as a church leader, or in battling demons, or showing signs and wonders. These are not new claims, for Paul writes of

119

his fear, "...lest by any means, as the serpent beguiled Eve through his subtilty, so your minds should be corrupted from the simplicity that is in Christ" (2 Corinthians 11:3).

While God mightily uses Spirit-led men and women deeply invested in biblical studies, ecclesial leadership, missional outreach, deliverance and healing ministries; a worldly education, church ordination, mission-appointment or the demonstration of signs, wonders and miracles is not the basis for *receiving* the fullness of God's word (Proverbs 2:6). All of these are but manifestations of walking in pure devotion to the "simplicity that is in Christ" (2 Corinthians 11:3)!

The pure fullness of God's Word cannot come from the complex of human authority, churchly pedigree, theological interpretation, or apologetic argument; but only through the leading presence of the Holy Spirit (1 Corinthians 2:9-10) within the one who loves *"God with all...heart, and with all...soul, and with all...mind, and with all...strength."* There is a difference between working with all of your heart, soul, strength and mind to learn the Bible and build your own moral, successful, and upright life; and receiving God's Word with *"all thy heart, and with all thy soul, and with all thy mind, and with all thy strength."*

Please take a moment to read the opening scripture for today's devotion again. Can you perceive that the religious teachers and scribes were basically asking Jesus the same questions asked in discipleship circles and bible studies today? In essence, they were asking, "What does this verse mean to you?" or

"How do you live out God's word in your life?" Yet their questions were intended to "catch him in his words" (Mark 12:13b).

Even so, Jesus did not disqualify their questions; but answers them! Jesus did not disqualify the leaders who asked the questions, but stood in their midst and embraced them:

> And one of the scribes came, and having heard them reasoning together, and perceiving that he had answered them well, asked him, Which is the first commandment of all? And Jesus answered him...
>
> Mark 12:28-29

Yet among those religious inquirers who conversed with Jesus, there was only one man who *received* Jesus' teaching. This scribe, "having heard them [religious leaders and Jesus] reasoning together, and perceiving that he [Jesus] has answered them well, asked him, 'Which is the first commandment of all?'" (12:28). This scribe did not ask with the intent of grappling with Jesus in debate – but with sincerity. *"And when Jesus saw that he answered discreetly, he said unto him: 'Thou are not far from the kingdom of God.'"*

Long ago Jesus walked and talked in the temple, but now our conversation with God manifests by the revelation of the Holy Spirit in the temple of our spirit (Romans 8:9, 16). As Jesus really stood before and spoke with the religious leaders; so now the Holy Spirit of God really indwells and communicates...with you.

121

Is the watchman-of-your-mind pressing for a discreet answer? Is the scribe challenging you to wonder at a conversation with Jesus? Do you believe that you are in the presence of the Holy Spirit of God who indwells, teaches and leads those who receive with sincerity? Do you believe God is conversing with you? Are you the one among many who will *receive* Jesus at His word?

Or do you believe that only the scholar, or the ordained, or the sainted, or the miracle-worker, or the author, or the aged, or the virgin-pure can be vessels who hear God's Spirit? Or perhaps you have believed that God's Spirit is not active today due to some sort of cessationism; or because you yourself have not heard God-speaking and have not seen evidence of God's miraculous hand in your life?

Or perhaps you have believed that God's Word cannot be foundational and true, because God was bound by ancient cultures to be relevant and acceptable. Or perhaps you embrace the teaching that God is so expansive that there is an ever-expanding, changing and broadening interpretive horizon for scriptures based upon the new technologies and insights of man.

Reading this devotional will not clarify a "right" belief on these matters. Reading the Bible alone will not clarify a "right" understanding of God's will. Only an open conversation with the Holy Spirit of God can lead you into apprehending the perfect will of the Father:

> Howbeit when he, the Spirit of truth, is come, he will guide you into all truth: for he shall not speak of himself; but

whatsoever he shall hear, that shall he speak: and he will shew you things to come. He shall glorify me: for he shall receive of mine, and shall shew it unto you. All things that the Father hath are mine: therefore said I, that he shall take of mine, and shall shew it unto you.

John 16:13-15

~Prayer Pause~

Please pray aloud, taking a moment to ask the Lord to fulfill His word in you...

> **Heavenly Father, Your word is True (John 17:17). And Your Holy Spirit will guide me into all truth as the Holy Spirit "will not speak of himself; but whatsoever he shall hear, that shall he speak" (John 16). Father, upon the basis of scripture alone, in the Name of Jesus alone, I take up a simple devotion of Jesus Christ (2 Corinthians 11:3). I renounce any teaching which departs from Your Word as revealed in Jesus Christ by the Holy Spirit.**

> **Father, I take Your Word as Your simple command for me today. Let me "love the Lord** my **God with all** my **heart, and with all** my **soul, and with all** my **mind, and with all** my **strength; as this is the first commandment. And the second is like...to love** my **neighbour as myself"** *(pronoun and tense changes ours).* **I repent from impurely loving You and impurely loving those around me.**

> **Please write Your Word upon my heart and lead me by Your Holy Spirit, in the Name of Jesus, according to Scripture and to Your Glory!** *(Please take time to pray as the Lord leads you before continuing on.)* **In Jesus' Name, Amen.**

We pray that you may receive these words from Jesus just as they are:

> He that rejecteth me, and receiveth not my words, hath one that judgeth him: the word that I have spoken, the same shall judge him in the last day. For I have not spoken of myself; but the Father which sent me, he gave me a commandment, what I should say, and what I should speak. And I know that his commandment is life everlasting.
>
> John 12:48-50a

Dear brother or sister, the commandment of God is life everlasting. It is written that the Holy Spirit bears witness to your spirit that you are a son or daughter of the High King of Heaven (Romans 8:16; John 1:12; Galatians 3:26)! It is written that the Holy Spirit *will* lead you into all Truth (John 3:16), *will* teach you all things (John 14:26, 16:13), *will* instruct you as to what to speak and *will* cause you to remember all that Jesus says (Luke 12:12; John 14:26).

It is written that you are not left as if an orphan, but that the Lord Himself is with you until the end of the age (Matthew 28:20). It is written that the Holy Spirit is sent as the Paraclete that serves forever as your Counselor and Comforter even unto future matters (John 14:16, 26-28, 16:13). It is written that you will be taught of no man; but of God and the voice of the Father will speak through you (Matthew 10:20; John 6:45). It is written that the sheep hear the voice of their Shepherd and will not follow, but flee from the voice of another. (John 10:3-5). Judge for yourself this day as the sincere scribe judged in Jesus' day; wherein lies the division

124

between the doctrines of God and the commandments of man (Mark 7:1-14; Luke 12:47)?

There is a distinct division between the teaching of God and the wisdom of man. Those who belong to the Good Shepherd flee from and thereby refuse to follow "the voice of another" (John 10:5). The Good Shepherd's voice is clear as Jesus calls you with the greatest commandment of God; to love the Lord with all of your heart, mind, soul and strength. Are you wondering how this single-minded, single-hearted, single-souled, single-strengthed love is possible?

As you take up the confession of Jesus Christ and are quickened to life in the Holy Spirit – you are no longer of the world's flock (Ephesians 2:19). Therefore, you need no longer be conducted by competing voices in the world which say, go here or go there – believe this or believe that – do this or do that – eat this or eat that (Luke 17:21).

> But God, who is rich in mercy, for his great love wherewith he loved us, Even when we were dead in sins, hath quickened us together with Christ, (by grace ye are saved;) And hath raised us up together, and made us sit together in heavenly places in Christ Jesus.
>
> Ephesians 2:4-6

Do you believe and receive these words as true? That you are "quickened...together with Christ" and "raised...up together" and spiritually "sit together in heavenly places in Christ Jesus" (ibid)? Therefore, in the "great love wherewith he [God] loved;" you are together now by God's Holy Spirit with the Lord. As you have taken up Christ, you have been taken up into living in the love of God (Galatians 2:20)! According to scripture, you are now living in an eternal, intimate relationship together with God. This is not merely some ephemeral idea, but scriptural reality!

God even promises that as you devote yourself to Him, your inner man will be strengthened that you may comprehend, test, prove and thereby do His will (Psalm 138:3; Romans 12:1-2). For through blessing, God works "in you that which is well pleasing in his sight, through Jesus Christ" (Hebrews 13:21b). "For it is God which worketh in you both to will and to do of *his* good pleasure" (Philippians 2:13). And it is "the word of God which effectually worketh also in you that believe" (1 Thessalonians 2:13b).

The love which God commands is the same love which God supplies. "God is love" and He supplies Himself to you (1 John 4:16a). Therefore, Divine Love lives and works within you (John 15:5, 17:26). As you allow, Divine Love is life!

How exactly is it that you dwell in the love of God? Not of yourself, but "by the faith of the Son of God" (Galatians 2:20b). By faith you may proclaim, "Christ liveth in me: and the life which I now live in the flesh I live by the faith of the Son of God, who loved me, and gave himself for me" (Galatians 2:20). It is Jesus Christ who loved you and gave Himself for you.

And now in the 24/7 press of life, the Holy Spirit sheds His love in your heart that you may give yourself back to Him (John 17:26; Romans 5:5). And in Christ, by the Holy Spirit "...*love the*

Lord thy God with all thy heart, and with all thy soul, and with all thy mind, and with all thy strength" and *"love thy neighbour as thyself."*

When "...the Father sent the Son *to be* the Saviour of the world" (1 John 4:14); He really did. This side of heaven, you are living an after-death experience. Jesus died, that you may move from a self-centered life, to living a love-compelled life in Christ (2 Corinthians 5:14-15). This is scriptural fact (Romans 6:11, 7:6), and through a pure devotion to Christ and living in Him you may now, "...*love the Lord thy God with all thy heart, and with all thy soul, and with all thy mind, and with all thy strength"* and *"love thy neighbour as thyself."*

How is God's love received? By "the faith of the Son of God" (Galatians 2:20b). Who sheds the love of God abroad in our hearts? The Holy Spirit does (Romans 5:5b). Who works in you to "will and to do of his pleasure" (Philippians 2:13)? God the Father does. And how do you walk in His will? By God's Word working in you (1 Thessalonians 2:13). This is why Paul can so confidently proclaim, "I can do all things through Christ which strengtheneth me" (Philippians 4:13).

Here we come to the end and to the beginning. There is a difference between working with all of your heart, soul, strength and mind to learn the Bible and build your own moral, successful, and upright life; and **receiving** Jesus Christ with *"all thy heart, and with all thy soul, and with all thy mind, and with all thy strength."*

Jesus did not disqualify the questioning pharisees or scribes; but stood in their midst and answered them. Today, Jesus does not disqualify you, but fills you with His presence and His power. That led by the love of God, which is the Word of God, you may now, "*...love the Lord thy God with all thy heart, and with all thy soul, and with all thy mind, and with all thy strength"* and *"love thy neighbour as thyself."*

Living in the love of God in the heavenlies, really does get worked out in the earthlies (Ephesians 5:2)! Now, with the help of God, you may exhibit on earth what is true in heaven. And others will know that you are Jesus' disciple by your love (John 13:35).

Prayer of Response: Commandant

Please pray aloud with us...

Abba, Father! Thank You for hearing and receiving me along with all of my questions. Thank You for not leaving me alone in the world to find my way. Thank You for loving me so much that You sent Jesus to fulfill Your law. Thank You for sending the Holy Spirit and opening my spirit to be led into all Truth (John 3:16), and learn all things (John 14:26, 16:13), and remember all that Jesus says (Luke 12:12; John 14:26).

Believing what is written, I attest that the Holy Spirit is my God-given Teacher, Counselor and Comforter. Believing what is written, I attest to receiving Your Heavenly Counsel by way of the Faith of Jesus Christ an in accordance with scripture.

Believing what is written, I take up the confession that in Christ who strengthens me...all things are possible. Believing what is written, I lay down what I have done in the strength of my mind, heart, soul or body and ask for You to forgive me. Thank You, Father.

Abba, Father! Your Holy Spirit dwells within me! Abba, Father! Jesus Christ lives in me! Abba, Father, by Faith alone, I may now love You with all of my heart, soul, mind and strength! Abba, Father! Nothing can separate me from Your love (Romans 8:38-39)!

How near indeed am I to the Kingdom of God! Alleluia! I praise You and bless You in the Holy Name of Jesus! Amen.

Week Three, Day Five – Gasping for Air

"I had fainted, unless I had believed to see the goodness of the LORD in the land of the living."
Psalm 27:13

"And the LORD shall scatter you among the nations, and ye shall be left few in number among the heathen, whither the LORD shall lead you. And there ye shall serve gods, the work of men's hands, wood and stone, which neither see, nor hear, nor eat, nor smell. But if from thence thou shalt seek the LORD thy God, thou shalt find him, if thou seek him with all thy heart and with all thy soul."
Deuteronomy 4:27-29

"Wait on the Lord; be of good courage, and he shall strengthen thine heart; wait, I say, on the LORD."
Psalm 27:14

Are you near to losing heart? Are you compassed round about by sorrows, loss, overwhelming circumstances and heartache? Do you find yourself in the midst of those who say they are following Jesus, only to find yourself receiving the compassion and counsel of Job's companions?

Are you pressed down, gasping for the Lord to breakthrough with just a drop of grace, a sip of mercy, a swallow of freedom-from-the-world and its idols? We stand this ground with you; we come alongside today and pray that even now the wells of the Spirit would break forth with the balm of Comfort from the Comforter Himself! *"Wait on the Lord; be of good courage, and he shall strengthen thine heart; wait, I say, on the LORD."*

For we are in the world, but not of the world (John 17:16). We walk in the Spirit in the realm of the natural; for our feet still pound the pavement whereupon we are punching the clock, filling out the time cards, staying atop of the appointment calendar, staying abreast of homework, finishing degrees, investing quality time, nurturing relationships, paying rent, repairing the house, fixing the car, finding time for exercise, managing a diet, going to the doctor, implementing preventative care, getting our prescriptions filled, going out to dinner, doing a bible study, home group, Sunday worship – then saying our prayers, all within our prayer closets – only to do it over again the next day, or for the next month, or until the next year. *"Wait on the Lord; be of good courage, and he shall strengthen thine heart; wait, I say, on the LORD."*

In the world, and in many places the "church," have both become impersonal drivers. Our culture and education form and inform us to live in the name of being responsible, productive, educated, competent, professional, self-sustaining, contributing members of society. Many Sunday schools and discipleship groups ingrain us to become plugged-in, bible-studied, active church-members committed to a vision statement of growing disciples for Jesus. We have been set and have set ourselves under many authorities.

We can praise God together that though some of these authorities may be as *"gods, the work of men's hands, wood and stone, which neither see, nor hear, nor eat, nor smell"* – the Lord is

131

greater than them all. The True God does not call us out of the world, but in the midst of the twenty-four seven, promises to be manifest to those who are pursuing Him (John 17:15-23). In the midst of every challenging circumstance or commandeering system we are to: *"Wait on the Lord; be of good courage, and he shall strengthen thine heart."*

It is worth repeating that Believers are not called out of the world, but into the manifest Presence of God in the midst of the twenty-four seven (John 17:15-23). Wherever you stand in the idol-occupied world, if you seek God with all of your being, *"from thence"* – you shall find Him. This word stands yet today; *"...seek the LORD thy God, thou shalt find him, if thou seek him with all thy heart and with all thy soul."*

Experience verifies that the commandeering and conforming systems of the world have done what they have set out to do: train up minds, hearts and souls to independent action. Today, the biblical imperative to *"wait on the Lord and be of good courage"* is often spurned as ridiculous, far-fetched or even fanatical by both Christians and unbelievers alike. The well-trained watchman-of-the-mind objects, "Doesn't *real* help come from finding better answers and making changes in our own lives?" Before going farther, let the watchman-of-the-mind hear what Jesus says, "...be of good cheer; I have overcome the world" (John 16:33).

Jesus overcame the world, because there was something to overcome. Whether we like it or not, Romans 12:2a is clear that we are commanded to "...be not conformed to this world." Webster's Dictionary defines "conform" as "to give the same shape, outline, or contour to" or to "bring into harmony or accord" (https://www.merriam-webster.com/dictionary/conform, accessed 01/04/2018). In essence, the world can be likened to a pattern that forms people as a die-press stamps a pattern out onto wax.

Real helps comes to our aid in dealing with these patterns through the Word of the Lord. If we peek behind the English at the original Greek of Romans 12:2 "And be not conformed to this world: but be ye transformed by the renewing of your mind, that ye may prove what is that good, and acceptable, and perfect, will of God." The verb that is translated into English as "conformed" is in the Greek perfect tense, passive voice. *"Wait on the Lord and be of good courage"* as we wade through the depths of the grammar of scripture together..."*and He shall strengthen thine heart!"*

Grammatically speaking, the Greek perfect tense describes a completed action with continuing results way up until the present. The completed action of being "conformed to this world" has already happened to us. The die has fallen upon the wax; and we each have been impressed with its mold. The continuing results of this verbal form can be likened to the wax holding this shape even after the die-press has been lifted and removed.

The ongoing outcome of being "conformed to this world" is a life of continuing harmony and accord to the contours of the pattern of the world. This pattern shaped and continues working to shape our understanding of who we are, what we are to be, and what is acceptable and unacceptable to do. The world conforms patterns via the operations of culture, language, family-history, education, religion and technology.

Continuing even deeper into the Greek verbal form of "be not conformed;" one uncovers the passive voice. The passive voice of the Greek verb has a similar meaning to the passive voice of an English verb. The passive indicates that the action of the verb is something done unto the subject. This means that "conformation" is something happening to the natural person without their active participation.

To apply the passive voice in the example of the wax – it can be said that the wax receives the stamp of the die-cut through no doing of its own. The wax is impressed upon as a matter of it simply being where it is. In like manner, the world actively shaped and acts to shape the "wax" of the mind, heart and soul of the natural man; by virtue of citizenship in the world. Here the cry of Isaiah rises up, "Then said I, Woe *is* me! for I am undone; because I *am* a man of unclean lips, and I dwell in the midst of a people of unclean lips..." (Isaiah 6:5).

All of this affirms, dear brother or sister in Christ, that your experience of being hard-pressed by the world is real. Both your need of a sip of God's mercy and for freedom from daily oppression is confirmed in the very grammar of scripture! The world pushes and pulls at you without your consent, and even despite your faithfulness to the Lord. But in these *40 Days* you will move to firmer ground as a heavenly citizen who no longer must walk in conformance (Philippians 3:20).

God assures us in scripture that from the midst of ANY captive or captivating structure; *"...if from thence thou shalt seek the LORD thy God, thou shalt find him...."* Jesus Himself puts it this way, "For every one that asketh receiveth; and he that seeketh findeth; and to him that knocketh it shall be opened" (Matthew 7:8). And assures those gasping for air that, "All that the Father giveth me shall come to me; and him that cometh to me I will in no wise cast out" (John 6:37).

The world and all its training does not overwhelm your capability to seek God. Nor will Jesus spurn you or turn you away! You have been bought with the blood of Jesus Christ and His precious gift to you is freedom and life in Him (1 Corinthians 7:23; Romans 8:2).

But is this freedom to be found only in the "someday" of heaven? Has God, as circumstances seem to testify, set the world in motion and then as a great clock-maker departed to leave things to unwind as they will? Or did Jesus die on the cross only to save you from sins so that you may have heavenly eternal life, but live through hell on earth?

Has the hand of God and the goodness of the Lord been banished from the land of the living? Do you believe the goodness of the Lord is seen this side of heaven? Or do you gasp for air waiting for heaven? *"I had fainted, unless I had believed to see the goodness of the LORD in the land of the living."*

135

Scripture does not say, "seek the LORD with all thy flesh," with physical eyes or through the operation of the natural human senses. Scripture does not say, "seek the LORD through the proof of thy circumstances." Indeed, King David authored Psalm 27 as he was straining against worldly foes who desired to consume him (Psalm 27:2b). Can you sense that there are very real powers seeking to destroy the lives of God's anointed today?

Seeking Jesus with *"all thy heart and with all thy soul"* is a matter of turning your spiritual eyes away from the world and setting them upon your Lord; even as your physical eyes register the tangible outcomes of the spiritual war against the inhabitants of the earth (Hebrews 12:2-3). While your physical eyes see the impact of sin and of a culture who has departed from God; the substantial reality of the Kingdom of God is not subdued (John 16:33b). Accessing this realm is your gift as a Redeemed of the Lord Jesus (Luke 17:21; Philippians 3:20)!

While this may sound like a riddle to seek God with spiritual eyes, it is one that you have already solved. For those who receive Jesus as Lord, Savior, King and God have *"believed"* and *"seen the goodness of the LORD in the land of the living."* Those who follow Jesus have perceived the spiritual, even in the midst of the natural.

Upon what evidence was your decision for Christ made? A few can say they saw Jesus with their physical eyes or heard His voice with their physical ears or felt Him in their physical circumstances and in that moment knew Him! Some have met

Him in dreams and visions as the Good Shepherd who personally brings them to Himself. But most hear the Word of God and believe with their hearts, confess with their lips, then receive a new spirit and become a pavilion of the Holy Spirit without the natural touch of Jesus in this world (Romans 10:9, 17).

What greater manifestation of the *"goodness of the LORD"* than salvation in Christ might come to you *"in the land of the living"* to strengthen your fainting heart? Praise the Lord that once you believe, then you receive a new spirit and begin to see spiritually through eyes of faith. Thank God the riddle of spiritual sight is already solved!

With the gift of faith, your spiritual eyes are opened to *"see the goodness of the LORD in the land of the living."* When you believed, you received a new spirit by which to perceive. As you believe, you begin to see spiritually through eyes of faith. Now you "walk by faith, not by sight" (2 Corinthians 5:7).

"Waiting on the Lord" is not the inaction of sitting and being a do-nothing. *"Waiting on the Lord"* is more like the image of entertaining guests in your home. Do you sit by passively as you *"wait"* on your guests? More than likely, you actively extend your love to them by preparing for their presence and providing for their needs as well as you can while they are with you.

In a similar manner, *"waiting on the Lord"* is actively seeking Him in the midst of the conforming and commandeering forces of the world. Indeed, you stand as one scattered amidst the various cultures and priorities of the world's powers. Like Israel of

old, you stand in the midst of a world turning around itself...yet the Lord is found with you:

> *And the LORD shall scatter you among the nations, and ye shall be left few in number among the heathen, whither the LORD shall lead you. And there ye shall serve gods, the work of men's hands, wood and stone, which neither see, nor hear, nor eat, nor smell. But if from thence thou shalt seek the LORD thy God, thou shalt find him, if thou seek him with all thy heart and with all thy soul.*
> *Deuteronomy 4:27-29*

Will you actively *"wait on the Lord"* and be freed to receive your Lord's blessing even in the midst of the busyness and hard press of life? For as you consider Christ in the midst of the contradicting world, you will not faint or grow weary (Hebrews 12:3, 1:3)! And as you have, you will see the *"goodness of the Lord in the land of the living!"*

Prayer of Response: Gasping for Air

Please pray aloud with us...

Heavenly Father, Holy is Your Name! You are not a "work of men's hands." You are the Living God! You have shown me Your power by drawing me to Jesus. LORD of Heaven and Earth, I praise and bless You!

I acknowledge that Jesus has overcome the conforming powers of the world. Though I walk in the midst of a fractured and overwhelmed people, I ask You today to cover the lintel of my mind with the Blood of Jesus and there-under, give fresh sight to

my spiritual eyes.   This Lord so that I may continuously see through eyes of faith; that Your Word would be fulfilled in my life and the power of Your Hand made manifest in and through me.

Jesus, You died so that I may not faint, nor be held captive to idols, but be freed unto Your service alone.   By Your blood, You bought me.   By Your blood, I am no longer held-fast by worldly structures (1 Peter 1:18-19).

Holy Spirit, please fix my eyes upon Jesus and help me be as a waiter rising to the service of hospitality.   Teach me to "wait" that I may celebrate Your goodness in the "land of the living." May this be so to the Glory of Your Holy Name; through the guiding of the Holy Spirit, in the power of the Name of Jesus. Amen.

Week Three, Day Six – Integrity

"Judge me, O Lord; for I have walked in mine integrity: I have trusted also in the Lord; therefore I shall not slide."
Psalm 26:1

"My heart is fixed, O God, my heart is fixed: I will sing and give praise."
Psalm 57:7

"Evening and morning, and at noon, will I pray, and cry aloud: and he shall hear my voice."
Psalm 55:17

In Christ, personal integrity is no longer a matter of your judgment, holiness or moral character; but is a matter of Christ's completed work (Romans 8:9). Trusting in the Word of God as your fundamental, substantial reality, binds you in love – spirit, soul, mind and body – into an interwoven integral in Jesus Christ (1 John 3:24). You are wholly the Lord's (1 Corinthians 6:19-20) and conquer through God's purchase and the word of Spirit-led testimony (Revelation 12:11).

With the psalmist, you may confidently say, *"Judge me, O Lord; for I have walked in mine integrity: I have trusted also in the Lord; therefore I shall not slide."* Indeed, you *"shall not slide"* as you choose a Spirit-led walk in the integrity of full trust in the Lord. In Christ, your *"heart is fixed;"* for you dwell in Christ and Christ dwells within you (Galatians 2:20; Ephesians 3:17). With your heart literally set in Christ, you may also sing, *"My heart is fixed, O God, my heart is fixed: I will sing and give praise."*

There is an inversion in the spiritual walk. Integrity is no longer of man, but of God. "For he hath made him [Jesus] *to be* sin for us, who knew no sin; that we might be made the righteousness of God in him" (2 Corinthians 5:21). The integrity that you have is no longer your own; but is imputed by God (Romans 4:24-25). In Christ, you are made "the righteousness of God." In Christ, you are made anew (2 Corinthians 5:17).

Your new integrity is revealed of God via the conduit of trust – which is faith-applied (Romans 15:13). With all joy, peace and hope, do you act in the faith of God by entrusting Him with your life-direction and daily provision? If the answer to this is a heart-wrenching variation of "sometimes" or "no," coupled with a sense that God sometimes leaves you high and dry to be decimated by the world and its systems, please ask Father to free you through this devotional reading.

The greatest inversion in walking in faith by trusting in God, is to be led thought-by-thought and step-by-step by God's Spirit alone, through faith alone, according to scripture alone. This is not the same as being led line-by-line and application-by-application through the Bible. Why? Because Jesus directly tells us that the scriptures do not and cannot lead our lives: "for in them [scriptures] ye think ye have eternal life: and they are they which testify of me. Yet you refuse to come to Me to have life" (John 5:39-40).

Your integrity in Christ is revealed as you say in your soul, *"Evening and morning, and at noon, will I pray, and cry aloud:*

141

and he shall hear my voice." Praying and crying aloud IS acknowledging by prayer before the Throne of God that Jesus has fixed your heart as His very own. Why? Because in prayer, you run to God, and not to yourself. In this very moment, as you take up a conversation of prayer and praise unto God, you are no longer conformed to the world's patterns of self-direction, but have overcome them (1 John 4:4). In prayer, you turn aside from self-counsel, worldly counsel, and even the lingering counsel of the enemies of God.

What is apprehended in the conversation of prayer cannot be overwhelmed by the world or even by the reports of reality registered by your natural senses. The Lord indelibly fixed your heart in Him by your new birth in the Spirit (Acts 2:38; Psalm 91:1-2). His leadership and protection are not intermittent, for God's presence within you is never-changing and eternal. "And this is life eternal, that they might know thee the only true God, and Jesus Christ, whom thou hast sent" (John 17:3; James 1:15). Walking in the Spirit is the result of knowing "the only true God" and thereby being held-fast in the presence of an uncompromising God (John 14:20).

Now many of you may feel the watchman of the mind saying, "Jesus is only talking about salvation when He speaks of 'life eternal,' not about the nitty-gritty of what I do every day." Tell the watchman that eternal life begins in the moment of salvation; yet extends, even in the natural realm, from that moment on! Your natural life is covered in eternity; because your life is hidden in Christ (Colossians 3:3).

Yes, the scriptures really say that Christ lives in you (Galatians 2:20). Is your mind echoing in confusion in considering the question, "Did God really say that Christ lives in me?" Look up what is written. Write it out long-hand in the margins of this page and train the watchman in truth.

Many of God's children do not yet believe that the word of God is true (John 17:17b). They have never considered that as they question the truth of the scriptures, they are at the same time questioning the integrity of the Holy Spirit. Because they are unaware of what is at stake, like Eve, they allow their minds to depart from a pure devotion to God's Word and instead, derive their own meaning – not only of scripture, but also of their purpose in life, and what they are to do and be.

To be led of God, is to receive the word of God as true. As you take up Jesus via scripture, you hear the voice of your Shepherd and learn to walk and work in the pastures of this world. This is of course, what it practically means to be walking in the Spirit. The Spirit's leading begins and ends in the word of God – not the book alone – but in Christ (Acts 4:12-14)!

The word of God is true (John 17:17). To walk in the truth includes every single moment of our lives; for in Christ we are caught up in the Word-made-flesh. We no longer can divide between "our lives" and Christ's life, because "to live *is* Christ" (Philippians 1:21). God's word is definitive on this.

You may have already written this verse in the margins, but here it is again. Take a moment to read it aloud: "I am crucified with Christ: nevertheless I live; yet not I, but Christ liveth in me: and the life which I now live in the flesh I live by the faith of the Son of God, who loved me, and gave himself for me" (Galatians 2:20). So if your life is in Christ, your integrity must also be where your life is.

Jesus Himself promises to be with you always until the very end of the age (Matthew 28:20) and also says, "I will not leave you comfortless; I will come to you (John 14:18). So there is no dark-night for the soul who lays off every hurdle of sin and pride (which is the ultimate form of self-guidance) and runs to the arms of the Savior by the guiding hand of the Holy Spirit!

Will you take these words by the One in whom all authority is given? It is written, "Jesus came and spake...saying, All power is given unto me in heaven and in earth" (Matthew 28:18). And the Lord has and will forever fulfill what is written; that "The LORD is nigh unto them that are of a broken heart; and saveth such as be of a contrite spirit" (Psalm 34:18) and "The LORD is nigh unto all them that call upon him, to all that call upon him in truth" (Isaiah 50:8).

Does this scriptural testimony seem too impossible to be true? If so, there is a reasonable cause. The adversary of the kingdom of God, the serpent and accuser, roams around and makes "...war with the remnant which keep the commandments of God, and have the testimony of Jesus Christ" (Revelation 12:17b).

This roaring lion works continually to overwhelm the sons and daughters of God and to devour their testimony. Why? Because the children of God "...overcome him [the accuser who has been cast down] by the blood of the Lamb, and the word of their testimony" (Revelation 12:11).

If the accuser can effect your thinking and shake your life to the point that what you perceive with natural eyes or feel with the soul, is judged in your mind to overshadow the truth of God's word – by your own judgment are you stripped of the conquering testimony of God. Without the conquering testimony; that is, without believing God's word and walking in the Spirit, you are bound by doubt into the pain and agony of walking under natural circumstances.

Doubt is a powerful tactic of the adversary. Eve was firm in the counsel of God until the adversary led her to question (Genesis 3:1). So perhaps it is time to conquer all doubt. For you have an overcoming gift: "For by grace are ye saved through faith; and that not of yourselves: *it is* the gift of God" (Ephesians 2:8). Your faith did not save you. Your best decision-making does not bring you life – God's grace did and does (Mark 9:24).

God is Faithful (1 Corinthians 1:9). Ask Him now to fulfill His word in your life. Ask Jesus.... *"Judge me, O Lord; for I have walked in mine integrity: I have trusted also in the Lord therefore I shall not slide."*

The judge upon the bench sits as one who must make a decision between what is legal and illegal. Judging, in its essence, is decision-making. Every decision made entirely on the bench of the human mind without prayer and apart from the leading presence of the Holy Spirit is led of the human spirit and not of God.

Do you know that even the Holy Spirit of God does not act independently on His own authority? Jesus says of the Holy Spirit: "...he will guide you into all truth: for he shall not speak of himself; but whatsoever he shall hear, *that* shall he speak: and he will shew you things to come" (John 16:13).

Since the Holy Spirit of God does not Himself decide what guidance you are to receive – surely the son or daughter of God is to take up the same counsel. Scripture confirms, "apart from God, you can do nothing (John 15:5b) and "whatsoever *is* not of faith is sin" (Romans 14:23) and "My sheep hear my voice, and I know them, and they follow me" (John 10:27). Sheep are counted lost if they self-direct and depart from the leading-presence of the shepherd.

Even before you call out for the leading-presence of heaven for practical guidance, "Father knoweth what things ye have need of, before ye ask him" (Matthew 6:8b). Take up the conversation of prayer; that *"Evening and morning, and at noon, will I pray, and cry aloud: and he shall hear my voice."* As you seek the King, what is needed is provided day-by-day (Matthew 6:33-34). And it pleases the Father, when you ask, to rescue you from your troubles (Psalm 37:17-22, 23-26); to not bring you a stone or a serpent, but sustaining bread (Luke 11:11-12).

146

Perhaps you have asked God to lead you even as near as yesterday, and your spiritual sense is that you remain empty, crushed and weighed down. Perhaps you are extending your hand to the Lord for help out of the mind-choking quicksand of the world, but it seems He has not acted and is not acting on your behalf. Are the promises of God first perceived by spiritual or physical sight? Do you walk in the Spirit by faith or by sight (2 Corinthians 5:7)?

It may be that sunny circumstances accompany a walk in the Spirit! Yet it may also be that the brightness of the things of the world occlude the spiritual eyes and what appears to be blessing and consolation is but the trappings of prosperity, or affluence, or privilege, or success. A Christian can have all of these prizes of the world and be praising God for them; yet be walking far from the Spirit of Jesus. The Lord cautions us that a rich man enters the kingdom of heaven with great difficulty (Matthew 19:23).

Many Believers rightly look for consolation, but interpret the leading of God by means of physical, instead of spiritual eyes. So when their emotions are happy, circumstances are sunny, and their lives are filled to the brim with fulfilled desires for "healthy relationships" or "meaningful work" or "advancing success" at the home front or on the career field; they say, "Praise God, for I am walking in consolation and blessing!" Yet be warned about this, for is it not the way of the adversary, to masquerade as an angel of

147

light (2 Corinthians 11:14)? Does he not deceive the world in his shining glimmer?

Desolation is the opposite of consolation. In the Latin, it means "walking without light." Perhaps your circumstances seem dark and desolate; there is no work, debt is accumulating and overwhelming, there are not enough hours in the day for the piling on work and the break-neck pace of busyness. Perhaps life at church is dry, family is fracturing as a spouse leaves, a child takes up drugs, or worse; there may even be an erroneous judgment made against you by the court authorities of this world. It seems that no prayer, no intervention, no help stops the avalanche and ends the surrounding chaos.

In spiritual desolation, the spirit of a man believes it cannot perceive God's leading hand. There seems to be no outpouring from God, no spiritual balm, no companionship in the spirit. Add to this a piling-on of stress in a broken and dying world and the poison of doubt seeps into the mind as natural eyes take in the pain and the heart feels wrecked and fainted within.

Though this feels like spiritual darkness and natural bleakness, does the word of God declare that you are ever without consolation? Many would claim that the dark night of the soul is just that – a time when you are beyond the glimmer of the light of God. There are also the medical and psychological diagnoses of depression, anxiety and phobia. Is there not a higher power that has conquered both spiritual confusion and mental darkness?

The eternal life of Jesus does not ebb and flow inside of you because there is no condemnation upon you. Believers no longer move from consolation to desolation as a matter of position in Christ! Jesus paid it all; therefore, all that is brought to light is made light (Titus 2:14, Ephesians 5:13). Yet so many do not comprehend this blessing because they are looking to their circumstances, or their religion, or their Bible; instead of looking to Christ for life.

Does the watchman-of-your-mind stir at the thought that even studying or poring over the Bible might not be looking to Christ? Jesus warns that it is possible to read the Bible and not have "his word abiding in you" (John 5:38). He calls the Christian through Scriptures to go beyond the page and not stop short; as it is written: "Search the scriptures; for in them ye think ye have eternal life: and they are they which testify of me. And ye will not come to me, that ye might have life" (John 5:39-40). The consolation of Christ abides in coming to Him alone.

If you believe or have believed that you are "walking without the light" of God and are being sifted and shaken by the world – you are in good company. To the disciples, Jesus says: "...behold, Satan hath desired *to have* you, that he may sift *you* as wheat" (Luke 22:31b). The "you" is in the second person plural...

Most of those who are hard-pressed and sifted by the adversary are those who are nearest to making an incredible impact in the world for the kingdom of God. Satan doesn't bother with sifting friends; just enemies. And the enemy is the one who longs for the integrity of walking in the Spirit.

Walking in the Spirit, is walking in the applied-integrity of God's Word. Though the world change, though mountains fall into the sea, though the ones who say they love you sin against you, though the world calls you and all you stand for – worthless, hateful and intolerant; though you are personally labeled fanatic, lunatic, blasphemous and outrageous by loved ones – "set yourselves, stand ye *still*, and see the salvation of the LORD with you" (2 Chronicles 20:17).

Take hold of the everlasting arms of God's Word. Take hold of the words of the psalmist, fix your heart on God, that you may walk out His judgments in the integrity of your walk, and freely sing praise knowing that the Lord hears your cry and will keep you from sliding or stumbling. For "...the word of the Lord endureth for ever. And this is the word which by the gospel is preached to you" (1 Peter 1:25).

Perhaps you have asked for God to lead you, and you are receiving the spiritual sense of God laying down a breadcrumb-like path falling from the bread of His Word. Or perhaps you have asked God to lead you, and your spiritual sense is that you remain crushed and weighed down; that you are extending your hand to the Lord for help out of the quicksand of the world that chokes mind and body; or perhaps you "perceive" or "conceive" no strong leading word.

150

Whether in one place or the other, hold your integral position in God's Word. Ask yourself which is true – your judgments? Your circumstances? Or the integrity of the Word of the Testimony of Jesus Christ.

Prayer of Response: Integrity

Please pray aloud with us...

Heavenly Father, please forgive me for the occasions when I have judged my circumstances, my experience or my judgments to be above Your Word. I know Your Word is true! "My heart is fixed, O God, my heart is fixed: I will sing and give praise!"

Lord, let me walk in the truth and integrity of Your Word alone. Please judge me and all my ways, for as I trust in You, I shall not slide. I set down my own personal integrity and take up the integrity of walking in the Spirit. Thank you Jesus for being my integrity, for taking sin and defeating death, "so I shall not slide."

I call upon You Jesus! "Evening and morning, and at noon, will I pray, and cry aloud" and I know You "shall hear my voice." Sanctify me in the unswerving confidence and eternal presence of Your never-changing, enduring Word (John 17:17). Sanctify me in the unswerving confidence of Your never-changing, eternal and present Holy Spirit (Isaiah 57:15).

Release me from any spirit of doubt. Release me from any spirit of condemnation. Set me at liberty to walk in the

151

consoling light of Your Word. I set all things under Your authority; my feelings, my thoughts, and my circumstances and my prayers. "Evening and morning, and at noon, will I pray," even continually will I cry aloud: and You "shall hear my voice." "My heart is fixed, O God, my heart is fixed: I will sing and give praise!"

Guide me as if by the hand to walk in integrity led of the Holy Spirit alone, by Your Grace alone, through Your Faith alone, according to Scripture alone, through the perfect integral of the Name of Jesus alone. Alleluia! Thank you, Jesus! To God be all glory! Amen.

Week Four, Day One – Mind Idol

"It is the spirit that quickeneth; the flesh profiteth nothing: the words that I speak unto you, they are spirit, and they are life. But there are some of you that believe not. For Jesus knew from the beginning who they were that believed not, and who should betray him. And he said, Therefore said I unto you, that no man can come unto me, except it were given unto him of my Father. From that time many of his disciples went back, and walked no more with him."
John 6:63-66

The Lord has brought you to the crossroads; will you turn back? *"It is the spirit that quickeneth; the flesh profiteth nothing: the words that I speak unto you, they are spirit, and they are life."* Are you ready to set down the flesh and take up the full-inheritance of a daughter or son of the Kingdom? If you are a Believer, "God hath sent forth the Spirit of his Son into your hearts, crying, Abba, Father" (Galatians 4:6).

Whether you received the Gospel of Jesus yesterday or half a life-time ago, you received the full inheritance of the saints (Colossians 1:5, 12-14). That is, you are completely covered by the blood of Jesus, the Lamb of God, who takes away the sins of the world – even yours (John 1:29). God placed in you a new spirit and the Holy Spirit dwells in you now (Ezekiel 36:26; 2 Corinthians 5:17).

There is no more eternal salvation to find or receive, nor is there any greater righteousness of God to pursue, or some greater presence of God's Spirit to attain (Proverbs 8:35; John 17:3). The fullness of God dwells in Jesus, "and you are complete in him" (Colossians 2:9-10). *"It is the spirit that quickeneth; the flesh profiteth nothing: the words that I speak unto you, they are spirit, and they are life."*

If you are uncertain that you are a Believer, turn back to the beginning of this book and begin again. For "...he that was born after the flesh persecuted him that was born after the Spirit, even so it is now" (Galatians 4:29). The Promise of God in you is opposed by the conforming powers of those who belong to the world (2 Chronicles 36:15-16; Matthew 23:34-36). If there be vagueness in your spirit, honor God by going deeper in love, into that which He has already worked in you. Please pray now...and whether you turn back to week one in obedience, or go on in obedience, God will accompany you along the way and bring you again to this same crossroads (John 14:21)! God loves you and will manifest Himself to you as you are drawn along in the Father's love (John 14:21).

The most difficult crossroads for many of Jesus' personal followers was receiving the spiritual reality that *"It is the spirit that quickeneth; the flesh profiteth nothing."* Many disciples departed from following Jesus altogether when He denied the power of their mind, soul, body and might to contribute to their own holiness before heaven or in the earth. Consider that Jesus preached this stunning and mind-shattering message in the midst of a religious culture where fulfilling the law of God was *the* highest work-of-man.

The scribes and teachers were the esteemed intelligentsia of Jesus' day. Those people who followed along after the Lord were shaped and formed under these schoolmasters (Galatians 4:3). So they wondered how Jesus could say that all the hours devoted to studying Torah, and all the works of ritual cleansing and sacrifice, and all of their festival pilgrimages, and all of their carefully constructed personal prayers and piously executed daily rituals were of-no-profit before God?

Jesus was shaking their world. Jesus was asking them to put away everything they had done. Jesus led them to the same crossroads where He now stands with you.

To be clear, the practice of the Jewish faith in Jesus' day had departed from the revelation of the law of God. Despite its pure foundation and God's clear warning, Israel heaped on additions to God's revelation (Deuteronomy 4:2, 12:32; Acts 15:10; Matthew 23:4-6). Even those with truly circumcised hearts were brought up and hard-pressed under the schoolmaster of the law and could not meet its expectations (Galatians 3:24). If you are led, read Matthew 23:1-39 for a succinct picture of the cultural and religious landscape during Jesus' ministry.

Though you may arrive wearily; do you see the crossroads before you now? Will you receive Jesus' teaching? Will you lovingly set all of your study, interpretation and application of God's word at the feet of Jesus and invite Him to reveal Himself to you Spirit-to-spirit?

God in His mercy, meets you where you are at (Matthew 11:28). Though some schoolmasters say that knowing God is taking up the Bible and going verse-by-verse with mindful dedication, proper interpretation, and finally – godly application; there is another way. *"It is the spirit that quickeneth; the flesh profiteth nothing."*

Perhaps you are feeling a little bit of what Jesus' disciples felt. Most modern cultures disciple their students to believe in and walk under a paradigm of "mind over matter." Under this paradigm, knowing anything comes as a result of the dedication of the physical and natural mind to study, comprehension, problem-solving and implementation. Ideas and thoughts captain the body and therefore, the schoolmaster of this age subtly teaches that "thinking" defines both "being" and "doing."

The mind is the modern idol, as ideas and thoughts are exalted above the body. The mind is the modern idol, as by it many followers of Jesus believe they both receive and interpret the word of God. By this, so many are led to esteem human thoughts or ideas about the word of God, above the quickening Spirit of God.

There is a plethora of such teaching available; yet does the word of God move forth in power? Is the church in the United States or Western world expanding? Jesus says that a tree is known by its fruit (Matthew 12:33). *"It is the spirit that quickeneth; the flesh profiteth nothing: the words that I speak unto you, they are spirit, and they are life."*

156

Scripture addresses the pairing of the work of the mind and the work of the flesh; as this is not a new cultural invention. The next several paragraphs will unravel the difference between walking quickened in the Spirit and walking under the idol of the mind. St. Paul's letter to the Ephesians reads:

> **And you hath he [Jesus] quickened**, who were dead in trespasses and sins; Wherein in time past ye walked according to the course of this world, according to the prince of the power of the air, the spirit that now worketh in the children of disobedience: Among whom also we all had our conversation in times past in the lusts of our flesh, **fulfilling the desires of the flesh and of the mind**; and were by nature the children of wrath, even as others.
>
> Ephesians 2:1-3 (emphasis added)

In his second letter to the Corinthians, St. Paul writes:

> For though we walk in the flesh, we do not war after the flesh: (For the weapons of our warfare **are not carnal, but mighty through God to the pulling down of strong holds**;) **Casting down imaginations**, and every high thing that exalteth itself against the knowledge of God, and **bringing into captivity every thought to the obedience of Christ**.
>
> 2 Corinthians 10:3-5 (emphasis added)

St. John explicitly warns of the idols of mind and flesh as he exhorts Believers to:

> Love not the world, neither the things *that are* in the world. If any man love the world, the love of the Father is not in him. For all that *is* in the world, the **lust of the flesh, and the lust of the eyes, and the pride of life, is not of the Father,** but is of the world. And the world passeth away,

and the lust thereof: but he that doeth the will of God abideth for ever.

> 1 John 2:15-17 (emphasis added)

Yet the penultimate warning of scripture is the command of the Father:

> And the LORD God commanded the man, saying, "Of every tree of the garden thou mayest freely eat: But of the tree of the knowledge of good and evil, thou shalt not eat of it: for in the day that thou eatest thereof thou shalt surely die."
>
> Genesis 2:16-17

Having walked through this brief testimony of scripture, let us re-approach Jesus' appointed words for today – John 6:63-66. Please consider praying Jesus' words aloud as the pure testimony of your mind, heart, soul and spirit...

> It is the spirit that quickeneth; the flesh profiteth nothing: the words that I speak unto you, they are spirit, and they are life. But there are some of you that believe not. For Jesus knew from the beginning who they were that believed not, and who should betray him. And he said, Therefore said I unto you, that no man can come unto me, except it were given unto him of my Father.
>
> John 6:63-65

Jesus tells us explicitly that *"the words that I speak unto you, they are spirit, and they are life"* and that *"no man can come unto me, except it were given unto him of my Father."* Jesus did not say that the human intellect or ritual acts were means to the Father, or are the means of life. Indeed, it is the opposite, as Jesus says, *"the flesh profiteth nothing."*

158

There is yet one more manifestation of the *"works of the flesh"* to be addressed. Under this paradigm, knowing God comes by way of passionate experience. The problem in this approach centers in being led of human emotions in the interpretation of spiritual experience.

These would-be Christ-followers passionately seek Jesus in the experience of the spiritual gifts, or even the thrilling beauty of worship, or ministries of social impact or justice. Once again, a tree is known by its fruit (Luke 6:44). There is a plethora of such experiences available; yet does the word of God move forth in power? Is the church in the United States or western world expanding? *"It is the spirit that quickeneth; the flesh profiteth nothing: the words that I speak unto you, they are spirit, and they are life."*

Just as scripture points to knowing the word of God by way of knowing Jesus Christ, so scripture points to interpreting spiritual experiences by the revelation of the Holy Spirit (John 16:13). Acts 1:8 at once encourages Believers to rest in the authentic power of God's Spirit; yet prayerfully interpret spiritual experience by way of Jesus Christ alone – and not by human passions or perceptions of spiritual power. Just ascending, the Lord says:

> But **ye shall receive power, after that the Holy Ghost is come upon you: and ye shall be witnesses unto me** both in Jerusalem, and in all Judaea, and in Samaria, and unto the uttermost part of the earth.
>
> Acts 1:8 (emphasis added)

The Holy Spirit of God witnesses to Jesus Christ alone. The work of the Spirit witnesses to Jesus Christ alone. Believers who witness the presence of God through spiritual gifts, signs, wonders or miracles can be assured these manifestations of power *will* **witness to Jesus Christ alone** and manifest in an expanding movement of the gospel from a local community to the surrounding world.

The manifestation of the gifts of the Spirit will never be an end in and of themselves, or be the purview of a man or woman to draw people unto themselves, or be sought-ought for the sake of a power-filled experience. The true servant of the Holy Spirit of God can only point to Jesus Christ, Son of Man, Son of God (1 John 4:2). And through the true-witness, the Holy Spirit of God witnesses in the earth to Jesus Christ alone unto the healing of the nations.

Though you may arrive wearily; do you see the crossroads now? Perhaps now you perceive in your spirit why so *"many of his disciples went back, and walked no more with him"* when Jesus said, *"no man can come unto me, except it were given unto him of my Father"* and *"It is the spirit that quickeneth; the flesh profiteth nothing."*

What about you? Will you set the mind idols of knowledge and experience at Jesus' feet and receive His teaching? Rest assured, for as you do, Jesus will not deny you (Matthew 11:28).

Prayer of Response: Mind Idol

Please pray aloud with us...

Heavenly Father, You sent Jesus to be the Savior of the world (1 John 4:14); therefore, I am not my own savior. The Holy Spirit came to Teach and to Guide (John 14:26, 16:13); therefore, I am not my own teacher or my own guide. Father, You draw me unto Yourself (John 6:44). So it cannot be that by my thinking, my understanding of the Bible, my passionate engagement, or by the depth of my spiritual experiences – that I come to You.

So I repent from working out-of-my-flesh to find and follow You. "It is the spirit that quickeneth; the flesh profiteth nothing" (John 6:63). Thank You Father, for drawing me to Yourself! Jesus, thank You for revealing the Father! Holy Spirit, thank You for quickening me!

Heavenly Father, Jesus died to save me that I may give my whole self to You (Matthew 22:37). I pray that You cover my mind, soul and body with the Blood of the Lamb as a living witness of Your Glory and Kingdom! I have come to the cross-roads and walk forward by the Holy Spirit alone. In Christ I take up my inheritance as Your son/daughter and lay down my mind idols.

May Your Will be done in the earth, by and through me. I set my mind, my intellectual work, my spiritual gifts, and all of my passions down and take up Jesus Christ crucified and

161

ascended. I rebuke a spirit of self-direction and declare with your Word that my life is hidden in Jesus Christ (Colossians 3:3).

Lord Jesus, please deliver me from all fear as I am quiet and emptied before You (Psalm 46:10). I am relying on You to quiet my soul that I may know You. Thank you for being at hand (Philippians 4:5). Take all of me, Father. In the Name of Jesus, Amen.

Week Four, Day Two – Abiding Rest

"Abide in me, and I in you. As the branch cannot bear fruit of itself, except it abide in the vine; no more can ye, except ye abide in me. I am the vine, ye are the branches: He that abideth in me, and I in him, the same bringeth forth much fruit: for without me ye can do nothing."
John 15:4-5

Are there days when the fingers of exhaustion grab hold of your heart? Perhaps these days are wrapped up in the garlands of responsibility and duty; but deep down, you know there is little-to-nothing left to give. These days have the potential to become miracle-filled in Christ! It takes coming to the end of abiding in oneself to find Jesus (Zechariah 4:6; Psalm 20:6-8). There is nothing more real, more visceral, more rubber-meets-the-road practical, than abiding in the secret place of the most High God (Psalm 37, 91; 1 Corinthians 12:15).

To abide in Christ is to choose to dwell and remain in Him even as you open your spirit so He may abide in you (Revelation 3:20; John 14:20-21). God in His love, does not bind an unwilling branch to the vine. He does not pump its frame full of sap, swell its leaves and hang fruit upon it without the branches' fullest confession (Acts 2:38). Indeed, some of us have been willing enough branches, but our twigs are almost leafless and we are wondering for our life where God's fruit is to be. We are hanging around thinking we need God to fill us; certain that He will if we just get the "abiding" right.

163

Yet God is Spirit, the Holy Ghost is Spirit and your new spirit is prepared by God as His pavilion – and is an actual tent-of-meeting (John 4:23-24). By your confession of faith and the accompanying new birth, "...your body is the temple of the Holy Ghost *which is* in you, which ye have of God, and ye are not your own" (1 Corinthians 6:19). Therein lies the filling and the abiding in the secret place of the Most High God. The Holy Spirit is in your temple now, wherein you are in communion with God.

As we read yesterday, the Word of the Lord is *spirit* and *life* (John 6:63). Knowing God is therefore a matter of growing in spiritual wisdom and a power-filled life through the quickening power of the Holy Spirit. As you abide in Christ, you are taught, led and equipped by the Holy Spirit of God (John 6:45, 63).

Does abiding in Christ by the power of the Holy Spirit mean staying "plugged in" to the sap of the local congregation? Or to a daily Bible study or prayer regimen? Or to rehearsing His Word over and over again during the day? Or spending quality time in meditation? Or practicing the Presence of God? Or listening to Christian radio? Or writing a journal or blog? Or reading this devotional? Definitely....when and only when these are arising from loving obedience to the leading of the Holy Spirit in the secret place of your own heart (John 5:19). As God leads, He fills and uses these practices as blossom-bases for growing fruit through you.

The parable of the vine and the branches is a living picture of receiving the life of Christ. In Christ the Father is glorified as you bear fruit; however, your fruitfulness is not your own as Jesus says that apart from Him, *"you can do nothing."* A branch that does nothing falls to the ground and is cast into the fire (John 15:6). There is no life coursing through it; there is no Kingdom abiding, nor harvest, nor produce, nor fruit (Psalm 37:1-7, 9).

Why? There is finally no life-giving sap in that branch. It has dried up for lack of communication with Jesus. The Bible is explicit: "In him [Jesus] was life" (John 1:4a). In Jesus is life, therefore a branch apart from Christ is dead. So it is that, "...*the branch cannot bear fruit of itself, except it abide in the vine."*

The vitality of the branch is set and maintained in Jesus Christ alone from its new birth unto eternal life in God (Romans 6:1-11). You are united in Christ by the presence of the Holy Spirit forever; and your destiny unfolds with Jesus Christ (John 14:6). Indeed "...the salvation of the righteous *is* of the LORD:" [justification] *"he is* their strength in the time of trouble" [sanctification] and "transgressors shall be destroyed together: the end of the wicked shall be cut off" (Psalm 37:38-39). "But those that wait upon the LORD, they shall inherit the earth" [glorification] (Psalm 37:9).

Does the watchman-of-your-mind yet cry out; "What does it mean that I must abide? Am I simply a do-nothing?" The Master Gardener speaks through scripture today, "... yield yourselves unto God, as those that are alive from the dead, and your members *as* instruments of righteousness unto God" (Romans 6:13). The branch who wishes to bear fruit is not passive, but actively "yields"

165

to the Hand of God. For the branch cannot at once yield to the flesh and live in the Spirit (Romans 8:5).

"For when we lived according to the flesh, the sinful passions aroused by the Law were at work in our bodies, bearing fruit for death" (Romans 7:5). And the sinful passions, as we learned yesterday, arise from man thinking and acting in his own mind according to human interpretations of God's word and human interpretations of experiencing God's Spirit. The fruit of mindful thinking and acting are the "imaginations, and every high thing that exalteth itself against the knowledge of God" (2 Corinthians 10:5). This is the fruit of death (Romans 7:5); "for whatsoever *is* not of faith is sin" (Romans 14:23b).

Remember when St. Paul and his disciples were on the mission trail, they once tried to go the direction they planned "but the Spirit suffered them not" (Acts 16:7). Though they were on the very mission of the Gospel; they were not permitted to choose where they would go, or what they would do, apart from God's leading. In so far as they were in Christ, they would not transgress His will. For to transgress is to pass a boundary, and in pursuing our own plans we depart from abiding in God, forego the Spirit's sap and take up the world's ways.

Too often, the Branches of God wither on the vine because they undertake "kingdom work" in the name of a Bible verse, ministry organization, for the cause of social justice, or even out of their own personal compassion and love for the hurting and broken. Lest the flow of sap that comes from the High King's command leads these ministries, there may be results in the natural, but devastating effects in the spiritual. As the branch grafted into the vine prefers and performs its own ministry apart from the Lord's direct Holy Spirit bidding, it will fall from its heavenly vine to the ground of the earth that it loves.

Yet there is something worse than withering. The dry branch is finally cut off, thrown to the ground and burned. Those who at the same time confess Christ, but choke and constrict the flowing life of the Spirit's sap, actually refuse Christ in the now and present – which is also the eternal. These branches who once confessed His Name, continuously refuse to abide and fruit. Are these to be "cut off" and burned (Palm 37:1-2, 7, 9-10)?

Yet the Branch who abides in Christ receives His life-giving word and manifests the power of that word! Jesus is clear on this point, "He that believeth on me, the works that I do shall he do also" (John 14:12). In His love and mercy, we are grafted into Christ through His death and resurrection and His love binds us to Himself and to each other (Colossians 3:14). Christian service impelled by the Holy Spirit embodies the testimony of scripture (so will never move contrary to God's word), manifests Christ (John 14:21) and never leads to death.

Jesus Himself says, *"He that abideth in me, and I in him, the same bringeth forth much fruit."* What is the fruit of such a vine? In Matthew 7, Jesus teaches His disciples to discern the difference between natural results and spiritual fruit. He teaches them:

Enter through the narrow gate. For wide is the gate and broad is the road that leads to destruction, and many enter through it. But small is the gate and narrow the road that leads to life, and only a few find it. Matthew 7:13

You may be wondering what Jesus' discussion of entering the narrow gate has to do with bearing fruit. Everything: because Jesus is the vine and its grounding life. The fruit-filled life of the Christ-follower is the life of the narrow way of abiding in Christ (John 15:8). Walking the narrow way has everything to do with the Branches of God bearing fruit. For our Lord Jesus continues:

Beware of false prophets...Ye shall know them by their fruits. Do men gather grapes of thorns, or figs of thistles? Even so every good tree bringeth forth good fruit; but a corrupt tree bringeth forth evil fruit. A good tree cannot bring forth evil fruit, neither can a corrupt tree bring forth good fruit. Every tree that bringeth not forth good fruit is hewn down and cast into the fire. Wherefore by their fruits ye shall know them. Matthew 7:15-20

And here is the mystery: you are both branch and fruit of Heaven's Vine! For it is written that "Of his [the Father's] own will begat he us with the word of truth, that we should be a kind of firstfruits of his creatures" (James 1:18). "For it became him, for whom *are* all things, and by whom *are* all things, in bringing many sons unto glory" (Hebrews 2:10).

The fruit and branches of The Vine are the children of God; the healed broken-hearted, the delivered captive, the seeing blind-man, and the liberated bruised (Luke 4:18). As a Believer, you are now engrafted into the Family of God (Ephesians 2:19). You are not rescued out of the world, but are spiritually rooted and grounded in Jesus Christ. And from your position in Christ, impelled of the Holy Spirit, you branch out and witness to the abundance of eternal life in Christ! By your testimony, others receive the word of God in power (Acts 1:8); these are spiritual sons and daughters and the fruit of your communion in Christ.

> Wherefore, my brethren, ye also are become dead to the law by the body of Christ; that ye should be married to another, *even* to him who is raised from the dead, that we should bring forth fruit unto God.
> Romans 7:4

Since you are "married to another, even to him who is raised from the dead," is your witness accompanied by the fruitfulness of the greater works of Christ Himself? Are you impelled by a never-ending cry for the leading of God's Spirit to "bring forth fruit unto God" through you (Romans 7:4; John 14:12)? No matter what has gone before, will you as a living branch, cry now to the Living God, "What must I do to work the works of God?" (John 6:28)

Dear brother or sister, it became Jesus, "for whom *are* all things, and by whom *are* all things" – to bring you unto glory (Hebrews 2:10)! The Dove of the Holy Spirit alighted upon Jesus as He was baptized and began this public mission to the world (John 1:32). The Holy Spirit has come upon you in your baptism and engrafted you into the Father's glorious mission of drawing all people unto Himself through Jesus (Matthew 28:19-20).

You already know that apart from God's leading, you can do nothing. But now in Christ, you know the Father's will (John 5:19)! Just as the sayings and doings of Christ were compelled of God as He walked on earth in full communion with God; so now, the sayings and doings of Christ are compelled of God as you – His Branch – empty yourself and are filled with the life-sap of the Holy Spirit (Galatians 5:1).

Do you believe that you are a Branch bound in the love of God in the Life of the Vine? Are you longing to see the power of God break forth through your Branch and through the Branches of God who are your brothers and sisters in Christ? Or does a nagging doubt keep you from emptying yourself and receiving what Jesus is calling forth in your spirit?

Will you go into your spiritual tent-of-meeting today? While outwardly this may be a prayer-closet, corner-room or favorite chair, inwardly, it can only be the secret place of the New Spirit within you. Jesus gives you the authority to open your spirit to receive Him. He says, "Behold, I stand at the door, and knock: if any man hear my voice, and open the door, I will come in to him, and will sup with him, and he with me" (Revelation 3:20). Do you hear in these words the truth of the matter of abiding in Christ?

The more you open the door to the secret place within, the more you abide, and allow the revelation and instruction of God's Spirit to flow through your spirit; the more you empty yourself and decrease, the more He will increase and become manifest to you (John 14:21; John 3:30). The more you die to self, the more you will green in leaf and bear fruit unto God (Psalm 1:3).

Have you asked for and received the instruction of the Holy Spirit in your secret place? By way of intuition, do you receive and then practically demonstrate the loving testimony of the Living Word with all of your faculties? As you do, the greater works that the Lord has prepared for you from the beginning of time will begin to manifest (John 14:12). Through you the Lord will "bring forth fruit unto God" (Romans 7:4) unto the Glory of the Holy Name of Jesus! For this you are made a Living Branch in the Kingdom of God: *"I am the vine, ye are the branches: He that abideth in me, and I in him, the same bringeth forth much fruit."*

Prayer of Response: Abiding Rest

Please pray aloud with us...

Heavenly Father, I know that Your Love has taken hold of me, set me in Jesus Christ the Vine and filled me. Thank you for grafting me into Jesus and quickening me in the Spirit! I repent now from all efforts of seeking to fill up my own life.

I know that apart from You, I can do nothing (John 5:30, 15:5). Please forgive me for every occasion I have preferred abiding in myself over abiding in Jesus. Holy Spirit, I repent from self-determination and take up the Promise of Abiding in the Vine. I open the door to fully receive Your gift of Abiding Life with You as my Guide, my Comfort and the One who

Quickens the life of God in me. Thank you for making me Your temple (1 Corinthians 6:19). I honor You.

Holy Spirit, in faith I ask that just as Christ received the will of the Father and did and said only what was revealed – that You would show me the will of the Father that I may also say and do only what He asks and shows. I pray Your power would pour down over my mind and my broken, fissured heart that I may receive Your Counsel in my spirit.

I take hold of the Word of God and pray this scripture: Jesus said, "I am the vine, you are the branches." So I agree and declare now that "I abide in the Vine as Christ's Branch!" Father, let Your Word be fulfilled in me, that I may be a witness of Jesus Christ, demonstrate Your power and bring forth much fruit to Your Glory! According to Your Word alone, in Your Faith alone, by Your Spirit and in the Name of Jesus – Amen.

Week Four, Day Three – God's Word v. Natural Facts

"And being not weak in faith, he [Abraham] considered not his own body now dead, when he was about an hundred years old, neither yet the deadness of Sarah's womb: He staggered not at the promise of God through unbelief; but was strong in faith, giving glory to God; And being fully persuaded that, what he had promised, he was able to perform."
Romans 4:19-21

Abraham did not stagger before the promise of God. Can you imagine being him today? What mockery would medicine make of his testimony of faith? Or what allegorizing would religion apply to bring into harmony the revelation of God and the natural facts of Abraham and Sarah's age?

Medicine would declare the birth of a child impossible – and suggest adoption. Religion might receive the Promise but point to the New Testament Paul who was the spiritual father of many children – and suggest Abraham would be a spiritual father to many heirs. As you wonder at the Promises of God, notice that this second interpretation is partly true. Abraham is a spiritual father, but only by receiving the Promise of being a natural father!

"Being not weak in faith," Abraham did not look at the natural facts of his situation. When he was nearly 75 years old, he left Haran to go where God was leading (Genesis 12:4). At 99 years old, Abraham was circumcised according to the covenant God had made with him; *then* the son of the Promise was

conceived and Isaac was born (Genesis 17:1,19,23). God gave Abraham a physical son "of his bowels" (Genesis 15:4). Through that son, Abraham became the earthly father of the nation of Israel and the spiritual father of all who walk in faith (Romans 4:16). God perfectly completed his pure and accurate Word!

Abraham took hold of the Promise of God and appropriated that promise into his life. Abraham did more than spiritually or intellectually wait upon God; he acted in faith upon the calling of God (Genesis 12:1). And as the years unfolded, God demonstrated his word to Abraham when he moved according to God's leading.

Throughout those itinerant years, God provided a covering of protection over Abraham's family (Genesis 15:1), gave victory over peoples who declared war against him (Genesis 14:15-17, 20) and filled his tent with abundant riches, even though Abraham gave Lot first choice of the verdant valley (Genesis 13:2, 10-11). God even manifested angels at Abraham's table and deliberated directly with him over the destruction of Sodom and Gomorrah (Genesis 18:1-14, 16-33). The many details of Abraham's faith journey are recorded in the Book of Genesis, chapters 12-22. God will draw you into these chapters if it is His plan for you.

As a spiritual son or daughter of Abraham, have you wondered at your own legacy? Abraham, by faith embraced the Promises of God as though they were (Hebrews 11:13). What about you? Have you, by faith embraced the Promises of God as though they were? Consider reading this question a couple times over; especially if the watchman-of-your-mind is demanding attention or your spirit is quivering.

Here is the simple, direct answer: Abraham believed and appropriated what God said. He moved beyond allowing the world to tell him what was possible. He moved beyond allowing his mind to tell him what was possible. He even moved beyond what his family told him was possible (Genesis 18:10-11).

Your father in the faith accepted the word from God in its direct and simple meaning. Abraham acted in faith and along came Isaac (Genesis 21:5). Now, several thousand years later...you are born a spiritual son or daughter of Abraham (Romans 4:16).

Will you walk as Abraham walked? Will you take hold of the simple, direct and pure meaning of what God is saying to you today? Will you believe God in every matter of your spiritual and natural life? For what is taken hold of in the spiritual breaks forth in the natural (Zechariah 3:7; 1 Peter 2:9; Matthew 6:10).

Abraham trusted God and accepted what God said without interpreting that word through the lenses of the world. When God told him that he would be the father of nations, Abraham believed this would be so (Abraham 15:6). He did not, nor could he run to scripture and find confirmation of his name being the name of a nation, or many nations. He could not run to a local pastor or teacher and be counseled in the word. Abraham heard God, believed and acted upon what God said!

This is very critical dear brother and sister.

Abraham received God's word expecting a manifestation of God's power in his life. He believed that the power of God and the Presence of God would be experienced in the land of the living (Genesis 15:1-7). Even though God had promised his descendants the Land of Canaan and many future blessings, Abraham walked in the reality of those blessings the day that God revealed them. He grabbed hold of the word of God with his spirit and soul for his here and now.

Your father in the faith took hold and would not let go. Scripture reports that there were days when Abraham decided he was going to naturally help God along with fulfilling the Promise; but the chord of his faith held firm. The New Testament declares that the substance of his belief did not change (Hebrews 11:8-12). Abraham only got into trouble when he turned aside from walking in a pure confidence that the Lord had the power to complete what He had promised to perform (Psalm 138:8; 1 Corinthians 1:8).

Abraham took up natural solutions to God's supernatural promise under the influence and advice of his dear wife who hoped to "obtain children" by Hagar (Genesis 16:2). Oh beware of your counselors, dear brothers and sisters. There is only one Counselor for you and His Name is the Holy Spirit of God (John 14:26)! And in these days, you have the Scripture as a foreground for the Spirit's leadership!

In his day, your father in faith took matters into his own hands. Abraham embraced Hagar without the command of God to do so. He followed his wife's advice and veered from a pure

176

reliance upon God. Abraham departed from the Promise and took up a human interpretation and culturally sanctioned application of God's word.

Did Abraham falter in his faith? No. Romans 4:20-21 testifies that Abraham, "...did not waver through unbelief regarding the promise of God...being fully persuaded that God had power to do what he had promised."

So what happened? Abraham held fast to the supernatural Promise of God, yet worked out his own natural solution. He sought to secure the Promise of God by interpreting it through his natural circumstances.

"Interpretation" is a controversial word. The scholars and the doctors argue that every word must be interpreted for meaning to be made. We grant them their point; but not the ground of their argument.

We must be direct. Scripture interprets scripture; according to the leading of God's Holy Spirit. Man's wisdom and knowledge, no matter how theological or traditional or logical, can never be brought to bear to sit as an authority over God's Holy Word. Will you take hold of these scriptures and God's word for you today?

> Who hath directed the Spirit of the LORD, or *being* his counseller hath taught him? With whom took he counsel, and *who* instructed him, and taught him in the path of judgment, and taught him knowledge, and shewed to him the way of understanding? Have ye not known? have ye not heard? hath it not been told you from the beginning? have ye not understood from the foundations of the earth? *It is* he that sitteth upon the circle of the earth, and the

inhabitants thereof *are* as grasshoppers; that stretcheth out the heavens as a curtain, and spreadeth them out as a tent to dwell in: That bringeth the princes to nothing; he maketh the judges of the earth as vanity.

Isaiah 40:13, 21-23

O the depth of the riches both of the wisdom and knowledge of God! how unsearchable *are* his judgments, and his ways past finding out! For who hath known the mind of the Lord? or who hath been his counseller? Or who hath first given to him, and it shall be recompensed unto him again? For of him, and through him, and to him, *are* all things: to whom *be* glory for ever. Amen.

Romans 11:33-36

But the natural man receiveth not the things of the Spirit of God: for they are foolishness unto him: neither can he know *them*, because they are spiritually discerned. But he that is spiritual judgeth all things, yet he himself is judged of no man. For who hath known the mind of the Lord, that he may instruct him? But we have the mind of Christ.

1 Corinthians 2:14-16

Then answered Jesus and said unto them, Verily, verily, I say unto you, The Son can do nothing of himself, but what he seeth the Father do: for what things soever he doeth, these also doeth the Son likewise.

John 5:19

For I have not spoken of myself; but the Father which sent me, he gave me a commandment, what I should say, and what I should speak.

John 12:49

Howbeit when he, the Spirit of truth, is come, he will guide you into all truth: for he shall not speak of himself; but whatsoever he shall hear, *that* shall he speak: and he will shew you things to come.

John 16:13

According as his divine power hath given unto us all things that *pertain* unto life and godliness, through the knowledge of him that hath called us to glory and virtue.

2 Peter 1:3

We have prayed and asked the Holy Spirit of God to bring to mind the incredible meaning of the simple phrase "scripture interprets scripture." Simply put, scripture reveals that: 1) God has given us all things pertaining to "life and godliness" (2 Peter 1:3 – see above), 2) These things are received, not by the natural mind – but by the spiritual man (1 Corinthians 2:14 – see above), and 3) Jesus and the Holy Spirit reveal the perfect Truth of God's Word as they speak and do all things in perfect accordance with the Words of the Father (John 5:19, 12:49, 16:13 – see above), 4) therefore, scriptural interpretation is not a matter of natural facts or natural information, but comes only by the supernatural revelation of the Word of God (1 Corinthians 2:10 – see below)! As it is written:

'For my thoughts *are* not your thoughts, neither *are* your ways my ways,' saith the LORD. 'For *as* the heavens are higher than the earth, so are my ways higher than your ways, and my thoughts than your thoughts.'

Isaiah 55:8-9

But as it is written, Eye hath not seen, nor ear heard, neither have entered into the heart of man, the things which God hath prepared for them that love him. But God hath revealed *them* unto us by his Spirit: for the Spirit searcheth all things, yea, the deep things of God. For what man knoweth the things of a man, save the spirit of man which is in him? even so the things of God knoweth no man, but the Spirit of God. Now we have received, not the spirit of the world, but the spirit which is of God; that we might know the things that are freely given to us of God. Which things also we speak, not in the words which man's wisdom teacheth, but which the Holy Ghost teacheth; comparing spiritual things with spiritual.

1 Corinthians 2:9-13

Now some interpreters will say that based on the nearby context, or advances in modern exegetical methods, or by way of an expanding hermeneutic of grace, or through improved anthropological and cultural understanding, or by the application of the most sophisticated computer analysis of scripture – that the true meaning of God's word must be decoded and explained by way of a present and relevant interpretation.

Other interpreters will admit that "scripture interprets scripture" yet excerpt verses from scripture and explain them by way of the world. These believe that by a logical and methodical study of God's word, even in the original languages – God may be known. Unfortunately, God's word does not testify that this academic or apologetic process has power in and of itself to reveal anything about Him at all.

The word of God is clear: "Howbeit when he, the Spirit of truth, is come, he will guide you into all truth" (John 16:13).

Thereby it is only by the leading of God's Spirit that we may ever know anything about God at all.

Scripture does indeed interpret scripture – when and only when – the interpreter is led by the Spirit of God through God's Word. The Holy Spirit Himself is the Interpreter of God's Word as He brings it across from the supernatural realm into the Believer's spirit that the Believer may know the things of God.

> Now we have received, not the spirit of the world, but the spirit which is of God; that we might know the things that are freely given to us of God. Which things also we speak, not in the words which man's wisdom teacheth, but which the Holy Ghost teacheth; comparing spiritual things with spiritual.
>
> 1 Corinthians 2:12-13

So the Believing scholar, preacher, expositor or disciple who begins in and remains in the Holy Spirit; ends in the revealed Word of God. But anyone who walks apart from the Holy Spirit's leading, ends up following the same path as Abraham as he embraces Hagar. A son is born, but not the son of the Promise (Genesis 16:1-5, 15).

When Abraham and Sarah "helped" God by way of Hagar, did the Promise of God come to fruition? Quite the opposite. As these two applied God's word into the reasonable and culturally accepted interpretative paradigm of their day, strife entered into their natural family and into the entire spiritual family of God (Genesis 16:4-6, 11-12).

Ishmael was born; conflict grew between Sarah and Hagar; Ishmael scoffed at Isaac; Sarah demanded that the very child she had asked for through Hagar be sent away; and the family was divided (Genesis 21:8-17). Today we still experience deadly division and conflict between the sons of Ishmael (Islam) and the sons of the Promise (Israel) and the sons of Faith (Christian Gentiles).

Can you see the danger in adding "our best interpretation and application" to the Promise of God? What of our families today? Do Christian families or churches suffer from division and conflict?

Herein lies the faith of Abraham: not in interpreting God's word into his life, but interpreting his life into God's word. Isaiah puts it this way, "And thine ears shall hear a word behind thee, saying, This *is* the way, walk ye in it, when ye turn to the right hand, and when ye turn to the left" (Isaiah 30:21). And Jeremiah, "Thus saith the LORD; Behold, I set before you the way of life, and the way of death" (Jeremiah 21:8).

Jesus makes the spiritual faith-walk pure and clear: "I am the way, the truth, and the life" (John 14:6) and the Holy Spirit has come to lead you into all truth (John 16:13). *"He staggered not at the promise of God through unbelief; but was strong in faith, giving glory to God; And being fully persuaded that, what he had promised, he was able to perform."*

Though Abraham once veered, as he climbed Mount Moriah, built an altar, laid his son upon it and raised the knife –

182

Abraham applied his mind, soul and body to living God's direct command (Genesis 22:6-8). And as Abraham climbed the mountain, the Lamb of the sacrifice was racing down the mountain from heaven to the site where the altar would be built and faith would be exercised. At the altar, both Abraham and Isaac would see the supernatural Faith of God as the Lord provided the Ram who would be the bound and slain of God (Genesis 22:9-14).

Abraham did not climb the mountain with eyes set on the natural facts. As it is written that when Isaac asked about the sacrifice, Abraham answered: "My son, God will provide himself a lamb for a burnt offering: so they went both of them together" (Genesis 22:8). As Abraham walked with Isaac; he walked with a living demonstration of God's supernatural life. The facts would argue that Isaac could not exist...but Abraham and Isaac knew the power of God. Both the Father of Faith and the Son of the Promise willingly climbed the mountain together.

How do we know Isaac was willing? Sons and daughters, Abraham was over 100 years old. Scripture testifies that Isaac was strong enough to carry the wood needed to consume an offering – for three days (Genesis 22:3-4). And Isaac's mountain was a little higher to climb. He carried wood for the altar, then allowed himself to be bound upon the mount of altar-stones (Genesis 22:9).

Isaac's willingness to lay on the altar-mount waiting for "a lamb for the burnt offering" and Abraham's willingness to offer Isaac to God in full faith that "God will provide himself a lamb," bring to life what God is asking of Believers today (Genesis 22:8).

183

Your spiritual fathers have shown you what it means to walk out the simple meaning of the word of God. Abraham and Isaac "went both of them together" and climbed the mountain in total faith that God would provide. Will you join them?

Will you receive the word of God and walk in it? Will you allow your natural mind and the issues that flow from it, to be bound and laid upon the altar as an offering to God (Romans 12:1-2)? Will you go beyond the natural facts and every interpretation or application of scripture made apart from God, and be led by the Holy Spirit into a life where the power of God's word manifests in the presence of Jesus Himself?

Jesus, the Lamb of God Promises:

> He that **hath my commandments, and keepeth them, he it is that loveth me:** and he that loveth me shall be loved of my Father, and I will love him, and **will manifest myself to him.**
>
> John 14:21 (emphasis ours)

May what is said of Abraham, be said of you:

"He staggered not at the promise of God through unbelief; but was strong in faith, giving glory to God; And being fully persuaded that, what he had promised, he was able to perform."

Prayer of Response: God's Word v. Natural Facts

Please pray aloud with us...

Heavenly Father, I cry out to You to free me from the conforming powers of a world that taught me to be self-directed

and self-sustained. By Your Grace and in Your Mercy, please release me from the bondage of the natural.

Abba! I repent for every time I have asked for Your Hand upon my life, only believing it was up to me to receive Your blessing through the interpretive effort of my mind, applied through the diligence of my soul and by the strength of my hand. Take away this spirit of self-direction and striving.

Thank You Father for taking my matters into Your own Hand. Thank You for sending Jesus, the Lamb of God. Thank You for forgiving me.

Dear Holy Spirit, insofar as I have grieved You by asking for revelation only to turn aside to my own ways; I repent. Knowing I stand forgiven in Christ, I take up the faith of Abraham my father who "staggered not at the promise of God through unbelief; but was strong in faith, giving glory to God; And being fully persuaded that, what he [God] had promised, he [God] was able to perform."

My Lord and my God, as Father Abraham believed, he then saw the Promise of God fulfilled in Sarah's dried up body! As Abraham and Isaac believed and walked together, they then saw the ram manifest in the thicket!

Father, I believe! In Your Mercy and Love, please let me see! Let me see Your Word fulfilled in my dried-up life. Please let me walk together with the Holy Spirit and see Jesus the Lamb of God manifest Himself in my life (John 14:21).

185

Walking by Faith alone, I open all that I am to receive the supernatural Promise of your Word. Looking to Jesus Christ alone, quickened by Your Spirit alone, I look past my natural facts and circumstances to the supernatural revelation of the Holy Spirit, and the pure guidance of my Shepherd, who is the Promised Son of God and the Lamb Who was slain– Jesus Christ my King. Amen.

Week Four, Day Four – This Little Light

*"...I am the light of the world; he that followeth me shall not walk
in darkness, but shall have the light of life."*
John 8:12

*"But ye are a chosen generation, a royal priesthood, an holy
nation, a peculiar people; that ye should shew forth the praises of
him who hath called you out of darkness into his marvellous light."*
1 Peter 2:9

"For with thee is the fountain of life; in thy light shall we see light."
Psalm 36:9

Are you straining for the light of Christ? Have you
endeavored to find a church, or a pastor, or an elder, or just plain
anyone who "...looked unto him, and were lightened: and their
faces were not ashamed" (Psalm 34:5)? Have you sang the song
about "this little light of mine" and confirmed in your heart that
your life is to be a "city on a hill" (Matthew 5:14); yet are left
yearning for the radiant faces of those who know Jesus? Does
your own face shine with the light of God?

These are not questions about pulling yourself up by the
bootstraps, or putting on a happy face, or gritting your teeth and
setting yourself toward love, or obedience, or faith, or truth. This
is not about the power of positive thinking or the practice of
uplifting "self-speak." Nor does finding this light require finding
new insightful teaching.

The light of Christ is not located in our mind; nor can our
mind break forth of its own efforts with supernatural life. The

light of Christ is not a matter of bright emotions or happy countenances or stirring expressions of joy; for our human emotions cannot convey the love of God or the joy of the Lord. The source of Christ's supernatural light is not located anywhere other than in Christ, the Three-In-One sitting upon heaven's throne! *"For with thee is the fountain of life; in thy light shall we see light."*

The supernatural light of Christ shines forth from God into our spirit and radiates into all that surrounds; the mind, the soul and the body. *"...I am the light of the world; he that followeth me shall not walk in darkness, but shall have the light of life."* Christ's Light is not some sort of reflection of the pure light of God, as Jesus is more than a mere reflection (Colossians 2:9). Jesus is penetrating light, as it is written, "This then is the message which we have heard of him, and declare unto you, that God is light, and in him is no darkness at all" (1 John 1:5).

Jesus Christ is a blazing fire (2 Thessalonians 1:8; Hebrews 12:29). And as your clay jar is the temple of the Holy Spirit, so the Light of Christ is manifest in this world through you. As the light of the sun passes through a magnifying glass – so the Light of Christ is magnified through you. For you, dear clay jar, are kept as the apple of the eye of the Most High God (Deuteronomy 32:10).

In the original language, the "apple of the eye" is the eye itself; even the cornea or lens. As the apple of God's eye, you are the lens or window for the light of heaven to break forth on the earth. And see what light breaks forth from the eyes of the Ancient of Days! Your Heavenly Father has "...eyes as lamps of fire...and the voice of his words like the voice of a multitude" (Daniel 10:6 b, c). Like His Father, Jesus' eyes shine "as a flame of fire...and his voice as the sound of many waters" (Revelation 1:14a, 15b).

When you received Jesus as your Lord, you became part of this family of Light! And as a Believer, you are God's child now (1 John 3:2; Galatians 3:26) and a spiritual child of Father Abraham (Romans 4:16). In the hard press of this world, you are led of God. As before, so again. God leads His own "...in a desert land, and in the waste howling wilderness; from there he led him about, he instructed him, he kept him as the apple of his eye" (Deuteronomy 32:10).

So whose eyes do you have? The natural remain as they were, but you are spiritually the "apple of God's eye" now. And *"in thy light shall we see light;"* but not as light before you, nor as a world lighted up with the brightness of God. You now walk as a shining star in the darkness of this generation along the narrow way lighted by the beam of the torch of God's will for your life (Philippians 2:15).

You are a walking lamp, lit and shining and illumining the path of life for you and for others! The Psalmist describes walking in the Light this way: "Thy word is a lamp unto my feet, and a light unto my path" (Psalm 119:105). But now the Word of God has come in the flesh: *"...I am the light of the world; he that followeth me shall not walk in darkness, but shall have the light of life."*

Jesus has declared that YOU *"have the light of life"* and are a living lamp shining forth and bearing witness to Him unto the world. Jesus Himself says, "Ye are the light of the world" (Matthew 5:14) therefore, "Let your light so shine before men, that they may see your good works, and glorify your Father which is in heaven" (Matthew 5:16).

Are you yet straining to see Christ's Light and receive Jesus' own Word that you walk in Light? Let us then ask, does a magnifying lens strive to receive light? Or does a clay-lamp strain to show the light set in its midst? Or do each of these simply fulfill the work for which it is purposed?

Since you have accepted the Light of the world and are now a clay-temple of the Holy Spirit; let the Sword of the Word defeat any spirit of straining that comes upon you. For it is written, *"...ye are a chosen generation, a royal priesthood, an holy nation, a peculiar people; that ye should shew forth the praises of him who hath called you out of darkness into his marvellous light."*

Tell the watchman-of-your-mind that "In Christ, the Word of God is life and light and I HAVE the Light and Life of the Lord Jesus Christ!" As it is written, "In the beginning was the Word, and the Word was with God, and the Word was God" and "In him was life; and the life was the light of men" (John 1:1, 4). If this scripture does not set easily on your soul, pray for the Holy Spirit's wisdom and read John 1:1 and 4 out loud until your spirit is settled that this REALLY is what Jesus is saying.

The Light of God is not a beam removed from Him, but burns from the Father, through the Son, by the Holy Spirit, through you – to the world! *"...I am the light of the world; he that followeth me shall not walk in darkness, but shall have the light of life."*

Walking in the Spirit then, is nothing less than walking in the gift of the light of the wisdom and knowledge of God. For it is written, "...if we walk in the light, as He is in the light, we have fellowship with one with another, and the blood of Jesus Christ his Son cleanseth us from all sin" (1 John 1:7). You have been cleansed from sin now and are "translated...into the kingdom of his dear Son" (Colossians 1:13).

When you were Born Again, you received this Light. There is no need to find it with your natural faculties. The supernatural Holy Spirit is your Teacher, Helper, Comforter and Guide; therefore, you are free to walk in the Light of God though your natural footsteps fall in the midst of this present darkness (1 John 1:5-10).

As you walk in the Light today, so you will tomorrow and forevermore. As it is written that you are now led of God; for "the Comforter, *which is* the Holy Ghost, whom the Father will send in my name, he shall teach you all things, and bring all things to your remembrance, whatsoever I have said unto you" (John 14:26). And it is Jesus who promises that the Holy Spirit shall be with you forever (John 14:16-17). And forever is now!

In these dark days, the Word does not walk outside of us. There is no need to strain to see the Light of Christ. "For God, who commanded the light to shine out of darkness, hath shined in our hearts, to *give* the light of the knowledge of the glory of God in the face of Jesus Christ" (2 Corinthians 4:6). Jesus is shining in your heart and giving you the knowledge of the glory of God!

The Lord Himself does not leave you to the work of deciding how to interpret and apply God's wisdom. Jesus has saved you from the darkness of your own thinking and your own limited strength. Jesus has delivered you unto a full life lived in the "light of the knowledge of the glory of God in the face of Jesus"!

So today these words are fulfilled in you: *"With thee is the fountain of life; in thy light shall we see light."* So you surely are the Light of the world and can declare according to the Word of God: *'With* ME *is the fountain of life; in* JESUS' *light shall* I *see light!'* [pronoun/noun changes ours].

Can you apprehend that you are released from straining for the pure light of Christ? For you are in Christ, and "in him is no darkness at all" (1 John 1:5). May you walk now into the Light, in the joy of the Lord!

Prayer of Response: This Little Light

Please pray aloud with us...

Heavenly Father, I set the eyes of my heart upon Jesus, the Light of the world! I know that with the Presence of your Holy Spirit in my heart, I now have the Light of life. Father,

Your Word is true. And it is written that those who follow Jesus "are the light of the world." So this is what I am now.

Thank You, Father God and Lord Jesus, for not leaving me stranded in an overcoming darkness. Thank You for delivering me into the Light of the knowledge of Your wisdom and glory! I am Your lamp in this dark world.

I pray for Your Light to fill me; that I would evermore be conducted by Your Holy Spirit unto the cause of Christ. I repent from any teaching that holds that I walk by the natural light of men; by earthly opportunity, human wisdom, knowledge or personal skill.

Please deliver me from all darkness and fill me up with Your Light, that I may be as a shining star led of Your Spirit alone – to the praise of Your Glory alone, according to Your Word alone, by Grace and in Faith! Alleluia! Come, into my heart Lord Jesus and let Your Spirit shine through me. Thank You, Jesus. I pray all this in Jesus' Name, Amen.

Looking Ahead: Tomorrow's devotion focuses on "How to Hear The Spirit." Please take up the Light of Christ in you and put on the Armor of Light; as the enemy's desire is to overwhelm the still, small voice of God.

Please take time to prepare for tomorrow by putting on the armor of God. You may choose to go to Ephesians 6 or be led into the prayer on the following page. We are believing that all who press through shall hear the Voice of the Shepherd as this is the Promise of the Shepherd to all Sheep (John 10).
Our prayers are with you and for you...

Prayer of Preparation: "How to Hear the Spirit"

Please pray aloud with us…

Dear Lord Jesus, as I prepare for tomorrow's devotion, I ask for the full armor of God to cover me against any attack of the enemy. I close my spirit to anything but the Pure Word of God. I set the watchman-of-my-mind under the Truth of Your Word.

Let the Helmut of salvation, the Breastplate of Righteousness, the Belt of Truth, the Shield of Faith, the Sword of the Spirit and the Shoes of Peace be completely effective. I know that my life is hidden in You; therefore I cannot be shaken.

I take up Psalm 34:7. It is written that, "The angel of the LORD encampeth round about them that fear him, and delivereth them." I appoint this word to be active in my life!

Let tomorrow be a day of complete victory as there is complete victory in Your Name! I pray the Blood of Jesus over every aspect of my life. Thank you, Jesus for dying so that I may have life in You. I pray in Your Holy Name. Amen.

Week Four, Day Five – How to Hear the Spirit

"My little children, let us not love in word, neither in tongue; but in deed and in truth. And hereby we know that we are of the truth, and shall assure our hearts before him. For if our heart condemn us, God is greater than our heart, and knoweth all things. Beloved, if our heart condemn us not, then have we confidence toward God. And whatsoever we ask, we receive of him, because we keep his commandments, and do those things that are pleasing in his sight."
1 John 3:18-22

"For our rejoicing is this, the testimony of our conscience, that in simplicity and godly sincerity, not with fleshly wisdom, but by the grace of God, we have had our conversation in the world, and more abundantly to you-ward."
2 Corinthians 1:12

Many Christians today have questions about testing the spirits, and it is written that "many false prophets are gone out into the world" (1 John 4:1). The test of the Spirit of God is direct: "Every spirit that confesseth that Jesus Christ is come in the flesh is of God" (1 John 4:2). Yet something about these simple words leaves most people working very hard to determine if what is being spoken into their lives comes from God or from the enemy. Some even wonder if what they are hearing in their inner man is just another trip of the mind.

The first step in testing the spirits is to be able to receive direction from God. As we learned in Week Two, Day Three, this communication pours forth deep within you. Such intuition does not arise from the five natural senses or from the mind's intellect, or from an emotional experience. "Intuition" by definition, does not even take shape based upon the transferred ideas, reasonings or deductions of other people. Intuition arises solely from within.

It is in your intuition where Faith was received and you came to "know, that you know, that you know" that Jesus Christ is Lord. The Holy Spirit bears witness deep within you (Romans 8:16; 1 Corinthians 2:10); this witness is brought forth to the mind through your intuition. Yet, you say, how does one know that intuition is arising from the Spirit and not an impure source? Herein we go to a deep place within; for the deeper things of God are revealed from deep to deep (Daniel 2:22; 1 Corinthians 2:6-16)!

The one who can clearly hear the Holy Spirit above the din of the enemy is the one whose heart is clear before God. The one whose heart does not condemn him is tested and tried in dialogue with the Spirit of God by way of the written word of God (Romans 12:1-2). *"For if our heart condemn us, God is greater than our heart, and knoweth all things. Beloved, if our heart condemn us not, then have we confidence toward God. And whatsoever we ask, we receive of him, because we keep his commandments, and do those things that are pleasing in his sight."*

Knowing Jesus Christ crucified and being cleansed in His blood is your eternal basis for hearing God (Hebrews 9:14). Today, in learning how to hear the Holy Spirit, your heart will be tested and purified in *"confidence toward God."* You will comprehend that if you know Christ, you know the Word – as surely as it is written "the Word was God" (John 1:1).

Even now, before going farther, let your heart be assured that you are: "...born again, not of corruptible seed, but of incorruptible, by the word of God, which liveth and abideth for ever" (1 Peter 1:23). And where does this Abiding Word live and dwell? Within you via the presence of the Holy Spirit. "Hereby know we that we dwell in him, and he in us, because he hath given us of his Spirit" (1 John 4:13).

Scripture *is* reliable – and the revelation of the logic of the Spirit is easily carried from the Holy Spirit through the spirit and into the mind of the son or daughter who is willing to receive. Scripture is the revealed word of God. As the Holy Spirit begins to bring its meaning alive in your heart, you are being led as if by God's hand toward a clear conscience before God.

With the open book of scripture, your mind and spirit are guided in tandem into godly understanding and action:

> Every Scripture *is* God-breathed and profitable for instruction, for conviction, for correction, *and* for training in righteousness, that the man of God may be perfect, thoroughly furnished unto all good works.
> 2 Timothy 3:16-17

If you believe "every Scripture is God-breathed" and believe in your heart and have confessed with your mouth that you are Christ's and He is yours; then along with this God-breathed scripture whisper…"*whatsoever we ask, we receive of him, because we keep his commandments, and do those things that are pleasing in his sight.*"

In the early days of hearing the Spirit, the Paraclete will guide you into all truth by the hand of God's Word (John 16:13; Psalm 139:10). As your spirit receives the guidance of the Comforter and you see the coordination of God's Word in the nitty gritty circumstances of your life, you begin to experience the personal Voice of God's Spirit! It is as if the Holy Spirit takes up a beautiful highlighter and draws a glowing line over the scripture you are reading and illustrates that Word in your life.

Here we must divert for a moment to understand the idea of "heart." In scripture, the heart can be likened to a seat of decision where our soul, emotions and will coincide together. Indeed, the terms "heart" and "soul" are almost interchangeable as they both speak to the conscience of the integral inner man. The Holy Spirit guides, comforts and teaches through God's word, as it is received in the supernatural gift of the new spirit and believed upon in your heart or innermost self.

The Holy Spirit brings out the highlighter and colors the page of your inner man via the sure Word of Scripture. The deep place within you where your mind and spirit touch receive the gift of the Comforter. There God's Spirit intimately and lovingly tends to every inclination and question of your soul (John 15:11; Zephaniah 3:17).

Today many people see the mind as the organ where decisions are made for Jesus. But a decision of the mind is often a false start for the Believer. As it is written, "...with the **heart** man believeth unto righteousness" (Romans 10:10a, emphasis ours).

Since we are speaking to convince the mind of the priority of the conscience or heart being led directly of God, you may want to read the following verse in your favorite translations. Romans 10:10 reads, "For with the heart man believeth unto righteousness; and with the mouth confession is made unto salvation." Ask yourself, can the decision of the mind make you right with God?

Again, let us reiterate that the watchman-of-the-mind is likely to rise up and demand proof of such things. The proof will come; but from above and not from below. Proof must come by the Holy Spirit's whisperings in your intuition as you are led through God's Word. Apart from God's revelation, there is no proof at all.

So for a time, command the watchman to stand down and be still before God (Psalm 46:10). Rest assured that in Christ the way forward is not by "mind over matter" but in receiving God's Word and perceiving the revelation of God's Spirit in the depths of conscience. Minds set on earthly proofs or fleshly arguments are set in opposition to hearts tuned to God's Spirit (Philippians 3:19; Romans 8:5). As it is written:

> *This* I say then, Walk in the Spirit, and ye shall not fulfil the lust of the flesh. For the flesh lusteth against the Spirit, and the Spirit against the flesh: and these are contrary the one to the other: so that ye cannot do the things that ye would.
> Galatians 5:16-17

Confusion and error seep into the Church through modern ideas which incorrectly picture the heart as the seat of emotion alone; and the mind as the organ of decision. Yet an untroubled heart is the biblical picture of single-minded belief in God. Remember these words of Jesus, "Let not your heart be troubled: ye believe in God, believe also in me" (John 14:1). So a decision for Christ is not a matter of the mind alone.

The man or woman who operates in and by their own thoughts – no matter how spiritual-sounding or feeling – is led of him or herself and not of a supernatural God (Isaiah 55:8-9). On the other hand, a spiritual man or woman can testify with scripture; "...*our rejoicing is this, the testimony of our conscience, that in simplicity and godly sincerity, not with fleshly wisdom, but by the grace of God, we have had our conversation in the world, and more abundantly to you-ward.*"

The mind and heart of man cannot divide itself and serve both the logic of the Spirit and the logic of man. He must love one and despise the other, because this is as God says it is. "No servant can serve two masters: for either he will hate the one, and love the other; or else he will hold to the one, and despise the other" (Luke 16:13a). A mind captained by the natural logic of man serves one master, but a mind captained by the logic of the Spirit serves another.

Indeed, the Christian who attempts to walk according to the Spirit and according to the world, "*is* unstable in all his ways" and cannot expect to receive anything from God (James 1:7-8). Jesus warns those who divide their loyalty are as:

...whited sepulchres, which indeed appear beautiful outward, but are within full of dead *men's* bones, and of all uncleanness. Even so ye also outwardly appear righteous unto men, but within ye are full of hypocrisy and iniquity.

Matthew 23:27b-28

Yet even in this darkened generation, we have not entirely lost a sense of what it means to be led of something other than the mind. Even unbelievers speak of an internal or "moral compass" which directs the internal thought-life of man. Let us take the compass point as being Christ Jesus and allow the Holy Spirit to calibrate our heart and mind to the destination of the Word of God alone. May we rise from the definitions of worldly matters to being led by faith of God's Spirit alone, with an undivided mind and heart set in the power of the gospel (1 Corinthians 2:1-5).

Such logic of the Spirit is plain in scripture: "That which is born of the flesh is flesh; and that which is born of the Spirit is spirit" (John 3:6). The mind of man itself is capable of producing nothing but natural thought. However, the Holy Spirit produces the supernatural revelation of God and delivers this through the waters of baptism in your New Birth of the spirit within (John 3). This revelation-receiving spirit is already borne in you!

As it is written, "...we have received, not the spirit of the world, but the spirit which is of God; that we might know the things that are freely given to us of God" (1 Corinthians 2:12). God has given every believer a new spirit through which He intends that you know the things of God! And the logic of revelation belongs to His Spirit as "God hath revealed them unto us by his Spirit: for the Spirit searcheth all things, yea, the deep things of God" (1 Corinthians 2:10). So it is that the knowledge of the things of the Spirit are freely given to you by way of your new God-given spirit!

Now you know what it means to be guided of God's Spirit alone, through an undivided and pure spiritual heart! Now you know what it means to be led of the Spirit with a mind calibrated through transformation by the Spirit of God (Romans 12:1-2; John 14:1-2). When led of the Spirit of God, the heart believes (Romans 10:10a); then the mind receives (Romans 12:1-2); and then the lips confess the revelation of Jesus Christ! Can you hear the subtle ordering of the spirit as captain to the mind and body? This is what Paul means when he exhorts, "But we have the mind of Christ" (1 Corinthians 2:16).

Jesus says, "Verily, verily, I say unto thee, Except a man be born of water and *of* the Spirit, he cannot enter into the kingdom of God" (John 3:5). And through what internal spiritual gate did you enter the kingdom of God? Through hearing the revelation of Jesus Christ. For it is written, "I am the way, the truth, and the life: no man cometh unto the Father, but by me" (John 14:6) and "I am the door: by me if any man enter in, he shall be saved" (John 10:9a).

Therefore, all revelation of the Holy Spirit is summed up in hearing Jesus Christ and the whole testimony of God's Word (John 16:13b). Knowing God begins in the moment of salvation; but continues in every moment that follows on as the Christian walks by way of Jesus Christ. And scripture is clear that, *"There is* therefore now no condemnation to them which are in Christ Jesus, who walk not after the flesh, but after the Spirit" (Romans 8:1).

As you walk "after the Spirit" you take hold of Jesus Christ, who is the Living Word of God abiding within you and are led by His Holy Spirit (Romans 8:9; John 14:12, 17). As you are receiving the internal Holy Spirit, you are led by the One who "is greater than you and knoweth all things" (1 Corinthians 6:17) into the "greater works" of Jesus Christ (John 14:12). Your life becomes activated in the Spirit, and your mind is freed to step in the service of God as you are taught of Him (1 John 2:21, 27; John 6:45).

Surely God disciplines the ones He loves and chastens the one accepted as daughter or son (Hebrews 12:6). Yet in Christ your conscience is covered by the Blood that you might be freed from walking in the natural works of your mind, unto serving the Living God (Hebrews 9:14).

Do you yet feel stuck in your own head and lost when it comes to hearing God? Give no cause to worry. St. John writes, *"...if our heart condemn us not, then have we confidence toward God."* Sin or the deception of the worldly life, is already conquered by our confession before God and has already fallen under the power of the Blood of the Lamb and the word of the Testimony (Revelation 12:11). Therefore, in Christ your spirit is no longer burdened and you may approach and receive the conversation of God unimpeded.   This is a matter for prayer and a matter we will take up at the end of today's devotion.

But now, let us take one more spiritual step.   Though it is by your spirit that you are taught of God, the natural organ of the mind is not useless.   The mind transformed by Christ actively yields its own thoughts and desires to become an instrument of God (Romans 12:1-3).   St. Paul describes such a spiritual offering of the mind this way:

> Neither yield ye your members *as* instruments of unrighteousness unto sin: but yield yourselves unto God, as those that are alive from the dead, and your members *as* instruments of righteousness unto God.
> Romans 6:13

To have the "mind of Christ" is not to receive a new natural mind; but to actively submit all thinking and doing to the instruction of God (Romans 12:1-3; Acts 17:28).   The mind is the bridge between the new spirit, your internal thought world, and the working out of faith in the external activities of your body.

Walking in the Spirit is a moment by moment yielding of yourself to God; soul, mind and then body (Romans 10:9-10). Ultimately, your choice is to take God at His Word and walk accordingly; or to take God's word, interpret it with mindful logic and walk in the instruction of the world (Ephesians 2:2).

God does not command your mind – you do.   If this were not so, you would not be given the option to "present your bodies a living sacrifice, holy, acceptable unto God" (Romans 12:1).   Jesus did not give His life upon the cross, only to take the minds, hearts and bodies of His people. He gave Himself freely; that we may freely give ourselves to Him (John 1:12; Galatians 5:1).

Walking in the Spirit is freely submitting your mind to Christ in the moment by moment, step by step living-in-Christ life. There is therefore no middle-ground for Christ-followers to walk in their own counsel and to walk in the Spirit's Counsel. Jesus commends the Believing saying: "If ye continue in my word, *then* are ye my disciples indeed" (John 8:31).

Dear brother or sister, "Fear not, believe only!" (Luke 8:50). Jesus Himself has refined and purified you by His death and resurrection; thereby making you the righteousness of God (2 Corinthians 5:21). "For he will be like a refiner's fire or a launderer's soap. He will sit as a refiner and purifier of silver" (Malachi 3:2-3).

And what does a refiner and purifier of silver do? Smelt it until He can see His own face as if in a mirror. May you be led out from the thick din of the enemy with a pure conscience by His counsel alone by His Holy Spirit Alone (Psalm 73:22-24).

Are you ready to quiet your mind? Ask the Lord now to show you where any obstacle of sin restrains and condemns your heart from having confidence toward God. Then offer your bodies – mind first – then soul, heart – and body as a living sacrifice.

Ask to hear the Holy Spirit and receive what has already been given in your new birth. Turn and return again in prayer whenever the conversation with the Holy Spirit seems absent or to be but flickering or fading. And remember....to be led of the Spirit of God, your heart must firmly believe...then your mind, transformed by Christ, must actively yield its own thoughts and desires to become an instrument of God.

Beloved, if our heart condemn us not, then have we confidence toward God. And whatsoever we ask, we receive of him, because we keep his commandments, and do those things that are pleasing in his sight.

For our rejoicing is this, the testimony of our conscience, that in simplicity and godly sincerity, not with fleshly wisdom, but by the grace of God, we have had our conversation in the world, and more abundantly to you-ward.

Prayer of Response: How to Hear the Spirit

Please pray aloud with us...

Our Father, who art in Heaven, Holy is Your Name! Your Kingdom come! Your will be done in my life on earth as it is in Heaven! (Matthew 6:9-13). Thank You for sending Jesus and making a way for me to be reconciled to You.

I believe Jesus is Your Son and has taken my sin unto Himself. Thank You Jesus for giving Your life that I may live. Thank You for making a way for me to come into the Father's Presence. Alleluia! The veil has been torn! (Matthew 27:51)

Forgiven and covered in the Blood of Jesus, I rise up before You in great need. Holy Spirit, please reveal any hidden sin in me that I may confess my sin now. *(Confess as led until your conscience is clear before God).*

206

Since Jesus has saved me, I know that there is no condemnation for me. Thank You, Jesus. Father, I pray that You would perfect me through Your Word for:

> *Every Scripture is God-breathed and profitable for instruction, for conviction, for correction, and for training in righteousness, that the man of God may be perfect, thoroughly furnished unto all good works.*

> *2 Timothy 3:16*

I know that only Your Spirit can reveal You and train me in righteousness. I invite Your Holy Spirit to be my Teacher, Counselor, Comforter and Guide.

I believe according to Scripture, that the Holy Spirit <u>shall guide</u> me into all Truth (John 16:13, emphasis ours). I believe the Holy Spirit "will not speak of himself; but whatsoever he shall hear, that <u>he shall speak</u>" (ibid). I believe according to Scripture, that the Holy Spirit <u>shall speak</u> to me and show me "things to come" (ibid). I stand in Your Word, open my spirit and receive the personal Counsel, Teaching, Comfort and Guidance of Your Holy Spirit, in the Name of Jesus. So now, let my spiritual ears be healed and any stronghold of my mind to be demolished; that I may evermore clearly hear and be led in knowing You.

Father in Heaven, my desire is to walk out Your will on earth. Please come, Holy Spirit. Please open the scriptures to me with all godly wisdom.

I take the authority that the Father has given me. I choose this day to set down the crown of my will and take up the cry of heaven; "Thy will be done on earth as it is in heaven!" Abba, Father!

Thank You Jesus for manifesting Yourself to me (John 14:21). I stand waiting with open belief that Your Word is true. I will not follow the voice of another and will wait to hear You in my spirit. I pray this according to scripture alone, by Your grace alone, in the Name of my Lord Jesus Christ, by the Holy Spirit. May Your Name be Glorified! Hold me fast in the Peace of Christ. Amen.

Week Four, Day Six – Rising Love!

*"And we have known and believed the love that God hath to us.
God is love; and he that dwelleth in love dwelleth in God, and God
in him."*
1 John 4:16

*"For God hath not given us the spirit of fear; but of power, and of
love, and of a sound mind."*
2 Timothy 1:7

Where the Father is, the fullness of His love dwells. Where
Jesus is, the fullness of God is present. Where the Holy Spirit is,
there is the light of the power of God. For can God be manifest
without the fullness of grace, love, majesty, victory, peace, power
and all of His Attributes?

"Hear, O Israel: the Lord our God is one Lord"
(Deuteronomy 6:4a) and with Him "there is no variableness,
neither shadow of turning" (James 1:17). God does not present
Himself in one way today only to change and be another way
tomorrow; for then God would not be an integral or "one." Indeed
that constant fullness is testified even unto Christ who is "...the
same yesterday, and to day, and for ever" (Hebrews 13:8). When
we encounter God, we encounter His unchanging and unwavering
grace, power and love.

Though God does not change, the meeting-place for
encountering the fullness of God began as a garden, then became
wilderness, then moved into the camp tent and glorious temple.
But now, according to God's master-design, Love is now manifest

in a mere earthen vessel or clay jar. In this progression from the Old Testament to the New Testament, we see a movement from a pillar of fire and smoke, to the glory of the Lord filling the temple, to Jesus walking the Jerusalem road, to God tabernacling within His sons and daughters as the blazing light of the Holy Spirit of God!

The movement of God's fire from "outside" of His people into the tabernacle of the secret place of their spirit is the movement of God's Love into the center of the camp. The deepest place of your New Spirit now radiantly dances with the bright light of the Spirit; for *"he that dwelleth in love dwelleth in God, and God in him."*

And this radiant indwelling Spirit spills over into your spirit, and then into an illumined life-walk that proclaims the Love of God to the world! *"For God hath not given us the spirit of fear; but of power, and of love, and of a sound mind."* Such is the joy-filled dance of walking unto the Holy Spirit! All praises and blessings to Our God and Father, through the Name of Jesus, by the quickening Light of the Holy Spirit! Alleluia!

As you are in Christ, your clay jar is quickened with the life of the Spirit of God and filled with the blazing love of God!

> ...if the Spirit of Him that raised up Jesus from the dead dwell in you, he that raised up Christ from the dead shall also quicken your mortal bodies by his Spirit that dwelleth in you.
>
> Romans 8:11

This is why Jesus says, "Ye are the light of the world" (Matthew 5:14a)!

And who are those who are quickened? Those who confess Jesus as Lord; those who do not love the world or the things in the world; those who love their brothers; those who hate the darkness of sin; and those who obey God and "doeth righteousness" (1 John 2-3). Indeed, when you love the Lord your God with all your heart, mind, soul and strength; you are witnessing to the fullness of the love of God deep within! *And we have known and believed the love that God hath to us. God is love; and he that dwelleth in love dwelleth in God, and God in him.*

And the fullness of this love is not your own; but is the very same love of Jesus Christ made manifest within your body now (1 John 4:12). So it is that the love of God does not come apart, or depart from the presence of, all of the rest of His Attributes! "Hear, O Israel: The LORD our God is one LORD" (Deuteronomy 6:4).

And Jesus has promised to be with you until the very end of the age – so He is (Matthew 28:20). The Lord does not "come and go." Jesus Himself declares His eternal and personal presence to you: "And lo, I am with you alway, even unto the end of the world. Amen" (Matthew 28:20). How great is the "Amen" of Jesus Christ!

You may feel cold and dark right now. Perhaps you are still waiting for the clearing voice of the Holy Spirit. Hear the "Amen" of Jesus again in Matthew 28:20! The eternal presence of Jesus

211

Christ has already been given to you. We pray that even now, you will perceive in increasing measure that the Lord **is** kindling the warmth of His Love within you.

And as a cold, cast-iron wood-stove is kindled to full flame by even one ember; so shall the Love of God come to the fullness of its light in you (Philippians 2:15-16). For it is written, "the path of the just is as the shining light, that shineth more and more unto the perfect day" (Proverbs 4:18). As it is written, so it must be...and so shall you see!

Rejoice for "...ye are a chosen generation, a royal priesthood, an holy nation, a peculiar people; that ye should shew forth the praises of him who hath called you out of darkness into his marvellous light!" (1 Peter 2:9) Delight in your God, as "...the LORD hath taken you, and brought you forth out of the iron furnace, even out of Egypt, to be unto him a people of inheritance, as ye are this day!" (Deuteronomy 4:20) "For the LORD'S portion is his people!" (Deuteronomy 32:9) And as your spirit is stirred to rejoice and praise the Lord, His inhabiting Presence dispels the darkening gloom (Psalm 22:3). *"For God hath not given us the spirit of fear; but of power, and of love, and of a sound mind."*

O Glorious Day! (Isaiah 9:5-7) God's Love tabernacles in you **now**, and you have been gathered under the wings of your Lord as a brooding hen gathers her chicks under her wings (Matthew 23:37). Your hiding place is **now** in His secret place. For the Lord, "He shall cover thee with his feathers, and under his wings shalt thou trust: his truth shall be thy shield and buckler"

(Psalm 91:4). And the love with which the Father has loved the Son is **now** yours (John 17:23).

God loves you in the same manner as He loved His own Son; as you are His child! (1 John 3:2) Does the birth of a second or third or even fourth child diminish or change the love of the father toward each? By no means!

So, dear child of your Father in Heaven, He loves you with the same love that He loves Jesus! You are "rooted and grounded in love" (Ephesians 3:17b). Your life is hidden in Him (Colossians 3:3). How great and unceasing is the steadfast love of God toward you (Lamentations 3:22-24; Nehemiah 9:17)!

Hear these words as recorded in the perfect record of scripture. Jesus said, "As the Father hath loved me, so have I loved you: continue ye in my love" (John 15:9). There is no doubt about the nature and breadth of this love. Even as the Father loves His Son; the Son loves the Father. And the very love of the Son for the Father is the very same love sheltering you. *"For God hath not given us the spirit of fear; but of power, and of love, and of a sound mind."*

You have likely sung the song "Jesus Loves Me....because the Bible tells me so." Here is what the Bible says: you are more than the object of God's love. You are the abiding place of God's love. For Jesus prayed, "...I have declared unto them thy name, and will declare it: **that the love wherewith thou hast loved me may be in them**, and I in them" (John 17:26, emphasis ours). Do you see now why the darkening thoughts and fears must be dispelled?

"God is love; and he that dwelleth in love dwelleth in God, and God in him." And what kind of dwelling is this? Just as stones are not piled at random by a mason; so the master-builder lovingly chooses, cuts and places every stone according to His plan and expertise. Indeed, Christ came as "a chief cornerstone, elect, precious: and he that believeth on him shall not be confounded" (1 Peter 2:6b).

Jesus your Cornerstone, is the sure basis or foundation for God's Love. So you are established upon Christ and appointed to be a "lively stone" built together with others into a spiritual house (1 Peter 2:5). Your place in Christ is sure; as long as you tarry to abide!

For God's love seals you into Him by the Holy Spirit: "Now he which stablisheth us with you in Christ, and hath anointed us, is God; Who hath also sealed us, and given the earnest of the Spirit in our hearts" (2 Corinthians 1:21-22). Through the operation of this Spirit you are both shaped and guided.

By the loving mortar of the Spirit, God at once lifts you up by the Cornerstone and builds you into the Hall of Faith upon the living courses of stone beneath (Hebrews 12:1-ff.). From there He will raise you up to lift up others! *"God hath...given us the spirit...of power, and of love, and of a sound mind."*

As you walk unto the Spirit, you are a living and moving temple of God's Love. In Christ, you carry an in-dwelling Love

214

that levels mountains (Isaiah 40:4, 45:2; Luke 3:5). Your transgressions, your self-desire, your impurities, your idolatries – every bit of your unrighteousness – cannot get in the way of this Abiding Love. For your dross is drawn out from you and moved as far as the east is from the west as the blood of Jesus flows through you and washes clean everything you set under the Cross (Psalm 103:12).

> "...if we walk in the light, as he is in the light, we have fellowship one with another, and the blood of Jesus Christ his Son cleanseth us from all sin. If we say that we have no sin, we deceive ourselves, and the truth is not in us. If we confess our sins, he is faithful and just to forgive us our sins, and to cleanse us from all unrighteousness."
>
> 1 John 1:7-9

As you accept the legacy of the Spirit and dedicate yourself to the Lord's service as His empty and clean house, the Kingdom of God draws near through you! *"God is love; and he that dwelleth in love dwelleth in God, and God in him"* and *"God hath not given us the spirit of fear; but of power, and of love, and of a sound mind."* Jesus' Love is made visible through you, and Perfect Love "casteth out fear" (1 John 4:18b)!

Prayer of Response: Rising Love!

Please pray aloud with us...

Heavenly Father, You so loved the world and You so loved me that You sent Jesus to finish all that must be done that I might come to You. Though You draw me to Yourself, You do not

215

make me take hold of Your Word – yet I take hold! For Jesus said, "Verily, verily, I say unto you, Whatsoever ye shall ask the Father in my name, he will give it you" and "ask, and ye shall receive, that your joy may be full" (John 16:23-24).

I ask in the Name of Jesus, for an ever-deepening awareness of Your Love rising up in me! The eternal presence of Your Love, by way of the gospel of Jesus Christ, is more than a hard-pressed measure or a feeling of warmth. Father, YOU are love! And YOU receive me in Love as a clay-temple for Your Presence, as it is written that, "He that dwelleth in love dwelleth in God, and God in him," Father, in joy I take up the gospel-testimony that I hereby dwell in Your Love and Your Holy Spirit dwells in me. Thank You, Heavenly Father! I want to know You, and carry Your Love in the earth.

Father, my life is Yours. According to Your will, release Your Love through me. Though I am but clay, I am grateful that You have not given me a spirit of fear...but the gift of a spirit of love! I want to know You and fearlessly demonstrate Your Love in the earth. Let Love rise up in my spirit that I may walk in Your Love alone, now and forevermore.

Thank You, Jesus! Thank You, Father! Thank You for the gift of Love. Holy Spirit, please lead me forward in the Love of God alone, to the praise of the Love of the Father and the Son. Alleluia! In the Name of Jesus, Amen.

Week Five, Day One – Dwell Quietly Without Fear

"Turn you at my reproof; behold, I will pour out my spirit unto you, I will make known my words unto you...for they that hated knowledge and did not choose the fear of the Lord...shall eat of the fruit of their own way, and be filled with their own devices."

"But whoso hearekneth unto me shall dwell safely, and shall be quiet from fear of evil."
Proverbs 1:23, 29-31, 33

God has poured out His *"Spirit unto you."* And as we read yesterday, "...God hath not given...the spirit of fear; but of power, and of love, and of a sound mind" (2 Timothy 1:7). Holding fast to His gift, stir up your spirit to, "...keep by the Holy Spirit which dwelleth in you...That good thing which was committed unto thee" (2 Timothy 1:6, 14). And as you walk in the Spirit, you stand as a living witness to the power of the gospel of Jesus Christ in your own life and beyond.

How shall this be accomplished? By Christ, through the Holy Spirit and by your willingness to empty yourself of ambitious, worldly pursuits and seek first the Kingdom of God (Matthew 6:33). This is not the sort of turning that happens only once; but as you "turn at God's reproof" and "choose the fear of the Lord" – you become less that He may become more (John 3:30).

As you "hearkeneth unto God" and yield your vessel to God's Spirit, He does not crush and shatter you, but turns you round and round and fills you with the Living Water of His Spirit

(John 4:14; Isaiah 64:8)! *"Turn you at my reproof; behold, I will pour out my spirit unto you, whoso hearekneth unto me shall dwell safely, and shall be quiet from fear of evil."*

Are you wondering how dwelling quietly without fear of evil can ever be possible in a world filled with violence and brokenness? Given both the power of the spiritual realities that press against us and the practical manifestations of sickness, hunger, disease, brokenness, heartbreak, loss and division, and every other fiery dart of the adversary – suffering cannot be taken lightly nor merely "spiritualized" away.

Yet God's Word must prevail. It is written, *"But whoso hearekneth unto me shall dwell safely, and shall be quiet from fear of evil."* Therefore the one who turns to God and takes up this Word, must experience a substantial manifestation of safety and quiet. And this has been our personal experience.

Even if your emotions fray under the piling-on evidence of the heartache of life, or if the old watchman-of-the-mind echoes agreement with the natural facts instead of taking up the supernatural Truth, we pray that you will hold fast to the Word of God and "stir up the gift of God, which is in thee" (2 Timothy 1:6). We also add our assurance that we are witnessing to the experience of seeing, hearing and walking in the manifestations of God's power breaking forth in the natural facts of our lives. Nothing about this devotional journey is merely propositional.

As we turned away from interpreting life according to the facts of our circumstances and accepted the authority of God's

Word and the counsel of the Holy Spirit; as we believed more fully what is written about the work of Jesus; as we believed what God has declared to be True – so we have seen this Truth made manifest in the land of the living (Romans 3:4)! Seeing gospel-power followed believing the gospel-truth.

So here in the devotional we bring a more detailed testimony of our experience of the Living God, in hopes that you may know the power of Jesus Christ manifest in our lives. We have prayed that you may believe the impossible is possible and experience the gospel of Jesus "in demonstration of the Spirit and of power;" in the midst of your circumstances, "That your faith should not stand in the wisdom of men; but in the power of God" (1 Corinthians 2:4-5).

Three years ago, as we moved from one side of the nation to the other, we were unaccustomed to witnessing the gospel of power. Listening to Christian radio, and pressing through the deserts, the mountains, and the plains with all we owned packed in a big yellow semi-truck; again and again and again, we heard this word proclaimed:

> This is what the LORD says to you: 'Do not be afraid or discouraged because of this vast army...For the battle is not yours, but God's. Ye shall not need to fight in this battle: set yourselves, stand ye still, and see the salvation of the LORD with you...."
>
> 2 Chronicles 20:15, 17

Here began our practical journey into believing and seeing the manifest power of the Living Gospel of Jesus Christ. As we traveled from everything we had known to a place we had not yet seen; we accepted this scripture as personal guidance from the Holy Spirit to do one thing only – stand-firm on the Word of God – no matter what.

Pressing through on this Word has led to its fulfillment. We have actually seen and continue to see the salvation of the LORD on our behalf! We have seen miracles of healing. We have seen demons manifest and depart. We have seen signs and wonders in the natural. We hear the personal leading of the Holy Spirit in our lives. We have seen the supernatural breaking through in the natural...and all of this is no longer surprising...for God is who HE says He is and substantially does what HE says He will do!

Will you stand with us on God's Word? If you do not yet know the Gospel "in demonstration of the Spirit and of power; That your faith should not stand in the wisdom of men; but in the power of God" (1 Corinthians 2:4-5), will you open your spirit and pray that God would fulfill this word in your life? Will you believe you are God's adopted son or daughter and receive the word of your King and your God as unshakeable; though you may feel your knees shaking and your spirit shaken by the tumult and confusion around you?

If you are resolved to stand-firm in the Word of God; God Himself will fight for you. Yet this is not a name-it-and-claim-it sort of victory. Standing firm in the Word of God requires your life. Jesus said; "For whosoever will save his life shall lose it; but whosoever shall lose his life for my sake and the gospel's, the same

220

shall save it" (Mark 8:35). As you give yourself over to the Gospel of Jesus Christ, then you see the power of God break forth from where you are sitting unto the ends of the earth! And we can testify that this is now the reality of our daily life.

Standing firm the covenant ground is not possible, save through the shed blood of Jesus Christ. For the victorious in Christ, "overcame him [Satan thrown down to earth] by the blood of the Lamb, and by the word of their testimony; and they loved not their lives unto the death" (Revelation 12:11). These words are not merely an allegory.

As you take hold of scripture and walk out life; you will overcome. But all overcoming must be fulfilled in Christ; not as a work apart from God, but by holding fast unto the Promises as both compass point (vector) and covenant ground (place). Jesus won the victory for our every battle as He paid the full price both in heaven and on earth! Every manifestation of the power of God results from Jesus' victory; and your every victory is only in and by Christ alone! *Whoso hearekneth unto me shall dwell safely, and shall be quiet from fear of evil.*

The blood of Jesus Christ ransomed you from sin and death (1 Timothy 2:6; Ephesians 1:7). "Set yourselves, stand ye still" under the Blood of the Lamb. For though you once walked in the world, according to the ways of the world; Almighty God "...hath delivered us [you] from the power of darkness, and hath translated us [you] into the kingdom of his dear Son: In whom we have redemption through his blood" (Colossians 1:13-14a).

221

Do you believe this is true this very moment? Do you believe that you have been transferred from the kingdom of this world to the kingdom of Jesus Christ – today? Do you believe you are delivered unto redemption in his blood – now? Many sons and daughters have received a "gospel" declaring that God's salvation power is only manifest in the "someday" of heaven. But God says: *"whoso heareikneth unto me shall dwell safely, and shall be quiet from fear of evil."* And the Good Shepherd promises safety and abundant life to His Flock:

> Then said Jesus unto them again, Verily, verily, I say unto you, I am the door of the sheep. All that ever came before me are thieves and robbers: but the sheep did not hear them. I am the door: by me if any man enter in, he shall be saved, and shall go in and out, and find pasture. The thief cometh not, but for to steal, and to kill, and to destroy: I am come that they might have life, and that they might have it more abundantly.
>
> John 10:7-10

Though we wander here below, and the thief comes to steal, kill, and destroy; as we turn to Christ, and obediently follow-on in the Presence of our Good Shepherd, we are safely conducted by His Spirit "in and out, and find pasture" unto abundant life (John 10:7-10)! While this picture is ultimately fulfilled in heaven, we are not left without a shepherd to conduct us on earth. Nor are we left here as sheep without a shepherd to be as lambs slaughtered at will by marauding evil. One Lamb was so slain so that the rest of the flock may be set free!

For to this end Christ both died, and rose, and revived, that he might be Lord both of the dead and living.

Romans 14:9

God Himself declares the boundaries for the manifestation of His Lordship. Jesus is Lord "both of the dead and of the living" (ibid). And though we are living in the pastures of this world; yet our "life is hid with Christ in God" (Colossians 3:3).

The lintel of our earthly life has been covered with the blood of the Good Shepherd, also the heavenly Passover Lamb of God – Jesus Christ. Though we walk through the shadowy world; we are hidden in Christ now! Though the forces of sin and death press all around, though the thief comes to destroy in the land of the living (John 10:10) – we conquer by the Blood of the Lamb and the word of testimony (Revelation 12:11)!

Ours is a real victory over real spiritual forces. For we are covered in Christ; therefore, under His blood we *"dwell safely, and...quiet from fear of evil."*

> The LORD is my shepherd; I shall not want. He maketh me to lie down in green pastures: he leadeth me beside the still waters. He restoreth my soul: he leadeth me in the paths of righteousness for his name's sake. Yea, though I walk through the valley of the shadow of death, I will fear no evil: for thou *art* with me; thy rod and thy staff they comfort me. Thou preparest a table before me in the presence of mine enemies: thou anointest my head with oil; my cup runneth over.
>
> Psalm 23:1-5

Our Good Shepherd draws us so nearly under His rod and staff in this shadowy world, that a table of victory is set before us in the very presence of our enemies! Indeed, it is written that those who belong to the Lord will not depart from the protection of His rod and staff to follow the voice of another (John 10:5). And this stranger or worker of evil who comes to steal, kill and destroy; has been defeated by Jesus Christ upon the cross (Colossians 2:14-15). Therefore, the enemy no longer has dominion over us. We are held secure in Christ now, for "...in him we live, and move, and have our being" (Acts 17:28). *"Whoso hearekneth unto me shall dwell safely, and shall be quiet from fear of evil."*

To remain in Christ is to stand firm in the Word of God. For Jesus Christ is the Living Word (John 1:1). While Jehoshaphat stood firm upon the covenant ground of the Promised Land; we stand firm and hold our position upon the Rock, our Lord Jesus Christ (1 Corinthians 10:4; 1 Peter 2:6-7; Daniel 2:34).

> Wherefore also it is contained in the scripture, "Behold, I lay in Zion a chief corner stone, elect, precious: and he that believeth on him shall not be confounded."
>
> 1 Peter 2:6 of Isaiah 28:16

As it was then, so it is today. God's Word is eternal. Will you stand upon God's declaration that you have been "delivered from the power of darkness and been translated into the Kingdom of His dear Son" (Colossians 1:13-14)? Will you refuse to bow to your circumstances and the thief of this world? Will you take up the word of God; "set yourselves, stand ye still, and see the salvation of the LORD with you..." (2 Chronicles 20:17)?

It is written, *"Turn you at my reproof; behold, I will pour out my spirit unto you, I will make known my words unto you...whoso hearekneth unto me shall dwell safely, and shall be quiet from fear of evil."* Amen.

Prayer of Response: Dwell Quietly Without Fear

Please pray aloud with us...

Heavenly Father, please help me to stir up the gift that is within me. I am turning to You that I may hear Your reproof. I am emptying myself before You of what "I think" and of what "I know." I now ask "not to know anything save Jesus Christ, and him crucified" (1 Corinthians 2:2).

Please forgive me for those times where I have not taken You at Your Word. Please forgive me for harboring any belief that You had left me vulnerable and alone in this world. Abba, please pour out Your Spirit upon me and make known Your words unto me. I long to "heareakneth unto You and dwell safely and be quiet from the fear of evil."

Lord Jesus, You have broken every chain. Please release me into the reality of the Gospel in "demonstration of the Spirit and of power," so my "faith should not stand in the wisdom of men; but in the power of God" (1 Corinthians 2:4). I know now that as I stand firm and take up my position in the Body of Christ, by the power of the Holy Spirit and in the Name of Jesus; You will fight for me that I shall dwell safely, and be quiet from fear of evil (Zephaniah 3:17).

I set my life under the Blood of the Lamb. I ask that Your Spirit stir a testimony in me, that I may praise, bless and magnify Your Almighty Name! Thank you, Father for sending Your Son. Thank you, for sending Your Spirit. Thank you, for making me Your own son/daughter. I pray according to Scripture alone, by Faith alone, through Grace alone, by the Holy Spirit alone, in the Name of Jesus alone. Alleluia to the King! Amen.

Week Five, Day Two – Boldly Stand!

And we have known and believed the love that God hath to us. God is love; and he that dwelleth in love dwelleth in God, and God in him. Herein is our love made perfect, that we may have boldness in the day of judgment: because as he is, so are we in this world.
1 John 4:16-17

But thanks be to God, which giveth us the victory through our Lord Jesus Christ.
1 Corinthians 15:57

Have you *"known and believed"* the love of God? Do you know that you know that you know that you are saved? As you will someday stand before the Throne of God, so you may stand today. For *"he that dwelleth in love dwelleth in God, and God in him."* Therefore, you may boldly make a stand now in the perfecting Love of Jesus Christ. *"Because as He is, so are we in this world."*

Jesus is now victorious (Mark 16:19). He has vanquished the foe at the cross (Colossians 2:15). Now you may take up the Victorious Name of Jesus and walk unto the Spirit, looking to the author and captain of your faith alone (Hebrews 2:10, 12:2; Ephesians 2:6). *"...thanks be to God, which giveth us the victory through our Lord Jesus Christ."*

This means that there is no need to set your face against fear – but boldly stand in Jesus Christ. There is no need to set your feet in defiance against the tempter or his demons – but boldly stand in Jesus alone. There is no need to rally against illness, or despair, or anxiety; but rally under the Love of God alone. For *"God is love; and he that dwelleth in love dwelleth in God, and God in him."*

By the love of God, the Holy Spirit Himself dwells in you. Though the world teaches that the natural mind and strength of a man or woman is mighty enough to boldly build a life; in Christ, you know differently. The natural life is but the wisp of pride; "For what is your life? It is even a vapour, that appeareth for a little time, and then vanisheth away" (James 4:14).

Indeed, it is written, that without Christ, you "can do nothing" (John 15:5). Therefore, standing firm in Christ is not accomplished by natural strength. Apart from God, one cannot even say that they stand because Christ stood. Such a self-declaration is as fragile and empty as mist and as insubstantial as dust (Genesis 3:19).

To take God at His Word, is to believe there is nothing in and of man upon which to build a life in this world (John 3:27; James 1:17). Praise God that in Christ there is no need to walk in the wispy strength of the natural mind, the skill of the hand, the discipline of will or the fervency of religion! To boldly stand in Christ is to stand upon more than the pedigrees of education and accomplishment, the wisdom of well-construed arguments and decisions, the honed facility of a professional craft, or the zeal of religious experience! In Christ, we stand up in the love of God alone! *"God is love; and he that dwelleth in love dwelleth in God, and God in him."*

Part of standing in the love of God is emptying the self of every accomplishment. Part of standing in the love of God is taking Him at His Word. Part of standing in the love of God is believing that apart from Him you really are nothing. Part of standing in the love of God is taking up life and death in the mercy and grace of God. *"But thanks be to God, which giveth us the victory through our Lord Jesus Christ."*

Yesterday we described our experience of learning to boldly stand in Christ. We simply took God at His Word and moved from a cycle of powerless defeat in our circumstances, into experiencing the personal presence and power of the Risen Lord. This was not a decision made in or carried out by the strength of our minds or wills – but arose out of falling into the arms of a Father who was gathering us to Himself (Philippians 2:13). Our own education, experience and religious background all conspired against believing that God would directly whisper hope to us or powerfully demonstrate the victory of resurrection power in the circumstances of our lives.

We had experienced so much defeat with Bible's tucked under our arms and with the word of God on our lips, that we could not even imagine experiencing the victory of God! Yet God is love...and God's Spirit bore witness to our spirits that the Word of God is True (John 17:17). On that spiritual impulse, we covered ourselves under God's Word as if we were King Jehoshaphat arrayed for battle.

229

At the time, taking up God's Word felt like a spiritual last stand. And it was. We had come to the end of all of our educational prowess, the end of our natural gifts, the end of our own capability and resiliency, the end of churchly counsel or encouragement, the end of theology and doctrine, and finally; the very end of ourselves. We were stilled at last and fell to our spiritual knees holding onto the Truth of Jesus Christ alone.

> Do not be afraid or discouraged because of this vast army...For the battle is not yours, but God's. Ye shall not need to fight in this battle: set yourselves, stand ye still, and see the salvation of the LORD with you..."
> 2 Chronicles 20:15, 17

Taking hold of the Word of God – no matter what – was only a beginning. Though we raised up the standard of our Bibles, studied the "thus and so's" of God's Word and prayed; though we were applying discipleship models and applying biblical principles that our lives might align with God's Word – we were sinking down, sinking down, sinking down.

We became oppressed, accused and persecuted. We "held firm" for a time, but soon depression, bitterness, confusion, despondence and anger squeezed their way into our minds and hearts. And of course, our reading of the Word of God was brought to bear to justify our oppression. Since Jesus was oppressed, accused and persecuted – we steadfastly believed we would also be. So we were; and our reading of scripture at the time interpreted our suffering as inevitable to fill up Jesus' own (Colossians 1:24).

In taking up and purposing to walk in the word we received, we had only come part way to victory. Taking up the word of God as our rule or standard brought us to the battlefield; yet we had to learn to "stand firm and hold" our position. We believed that was an act of interpretation and application. We did not know we were powerless before the adversary under that paradigm.

Though we recognized Jesus "as whom God hath sent" that "speaketh the words of God: for God giveth not the Spirit by measure unto him" (John 3:34); though we believed in our heart and confessed with our lips that Jesus is the Son of God (Romans 10:9). Though we were baptized a decade before into a church body and "plugged in" to weekly worship, mid-week studies, acts of mercy....then went on to complete a Master of Divinity seminary study; though we bore the fruit of "turned around" lives; though we were sought of many for counsel and led many ministries...

Our children departed from the church, our careers went into a tailspin, we lost a child...finances became thin...lightning (literally) struck our house twice within a year, floods (literally) subsumed our home and basement...our relationship was breaking, the local church was fracturing, chaos seemed to be prevailing; and God seemed absent and silent.

We offer such transparency only in hopes of assuring you that we are not writing out of inexperience. We suspect that this devotional meets you on the battle-front that presses into your own life. It is precisely on this kingdom war-front where we eventually went from believing to knowing God; and "seeing the salvation of the LORD with us!" We then saw the miracle of "the love that God hath to us." That *"God is love; and he that dwelleth in love dwelleth in God, and God in him."*

In the beginning, we came to the spiritual battlefield armed with what we knew about God's word; yet the more we attempted to study, interpret, apply and appropriate it, the more adversity and calamity came upon us and the farther God seemed away. We were holding fast to God's Holy Book and even God's word to us; quite apart from the power of the Holy Spirit.

We pressed on in this manner for two years, then God sent reinforcements. He brought brothers and sisters to testify to the Lord Jesus Christ who walked in Scripture alone, by the Holy Spirit and delivered a gospel in power (1 Corinthians 2:4)! These friends walked impelled and compelled by the Holy Spirit in a pure devotion to Jesus Christ under the liberty of the Gospel. We witnessed first-hand that "... the kingdom of God is not in word, but in power" (1 Corinthians 4:20; 2 Corinthians 11:3).

These friends lived, moved and had their being in Jesus Christ (Acts 17:28). We did not find them in a church, nor do they represent a denomination or particular theology. Crazy as it seems, we met them in a conference room where they walked in the love of God. And we began to experience the miraculous manifest as the *"love that God hath to us."*

232

As we held firm to the Scripture and received "the word of their testimony" (Revelation 12:11), the Lord demonstrated His victory. Through our brothers and sisters, He provided spiritual encouragement and imparted spiritual gifts by the Holy Spirit (Romans 1:11). Indeed, we began to comprehend our decade-ago baptisms as the gift of God Himself!

Instead of taking up Scripture alone by way of our strength alone, we began learning to walk unto the Spirit in all things and at all times, in a pure devotion to Jesus Christ and under the completed fulfillment of scripture in Jesus Christ. We still held firm in faith to the victory given Jehoshaphat in 2 Chronicles; but this by way of being held by the Spirit's hand.

We learned and are still learning to repent and continually turn-away from all natural strength, while continually turning to God's Holy Spirit to lead us step-by-step and moment-by-moment through our everyday lives. *"But thanks be to God, which giveth us the victory through our Lord Jesus Christ."*

Herein began the cycle of walking out the Lord's victory in the 24/7 of our lives! The vast army arrayed before our minds and attacking through our circumstances fell back; and we no longer live and move and have our being apart from Jesus Christ dwelling in and leading us by the Holy Spirit (Acts 17:28). We stand now, in the experienced power of Christ alone, by the Spirit alone and walk in the victory of Jesus Christ demonstrated through us by the Holy Spirit in *"love made perfect...because as he is, so are we in this world."*

Surely we are not perfect, but Christ is! Apart from Jesus Christ, we "can do nothing" (John 15:5). Therefore, "standing firm and holding position" and "seeing the salvation of the Lord" is accomplished of God at work in us. In and of ourselves, anything we do is as fragile and empty as our very lives. Our natural "interpretation" or "application" or "practice" of God's Word is like what we are made of – as insubstantial as vapor (Romans 9:16; 31-32). Yet in Christ, we have the victory!

Now we know that the emptying of self is really not empty at all – because this is the pathway to receiving the fullness of Heaven's gift of Love. "A man can receive nothing, except it be given him from heaven" (John 3:27). For "Every good and perfect gift is from above, coming down from the Father of the heavenly lights, with whom there is no change or shifting shadow" (James 1:17). Therefore, if any spiritual or natural gift is received, it cannot arise of the natural man, but is given by the manifold grace of our Father in Heaven (1 Peter 4:10).

Praise be to God! The Father, by the Spirit has given you a share in the victorious love of Christ! "For we are made partakers of Christ, if we hold the beginning of our confidence steadfast unto the end" (Hebrews 3:14). So the Christ-follower may confess *"God is love"* in the midst of every earthly temptation, adversity, or calamity and look for victory in Jesus alone. For in the New Birth you have received the gift of God Himself! For *"God is love; and he that dwelleth in love dwelleth in God, and God in him."*

Jesus Christ was led of God on earth (John 6:38, 8:29). The Holy Spirit descended upon Him on earth (Isaiah 42:1; Matthew 3:16; John 3:34) and *"so are we in this world."* As you empty yourself of your own understanding and take up the mind of Christ, you are led of God by the presence and power of the Holy Spirit. Indeed, this 40 Day devotional walk unto the Spirit has its very analogue in Jesus' own 40 days in the desert following His Baptism. As He walked, so you walk...not of your own, but by the God that dwells in you.

Standing firm and holding covenant position in Christ is not taking a hold of the scripture and clinging to it like a life-saving rock in the center of a river; rather, it is learning to be swept along by the living water of the Holy Spirit. To be guided, chastened, and carried along in the sweep of the Love of God; in whom you live and dwell, is "to walk, even as He walked" (1 John 2:6). For God's love indwells you now. And *"Herein is our love made perfect, that we may have boldness in the day of judgment: because as he is, so are we in this world."*

So now, the boldness of the day of judgment is already within you. Will you stand in this world, led by the Holy Spirit in Christ the King, unto the Father's will? You do not need to stand with your face against fear. You do not need to stand with your weapons raised against the devil or his demons. You do not need to rise with teary eyes set against illness, or despair, or anxiety....but you may stand impelled and compelled by God's Spirit to stand in Christ who is Heaven's Christus Victor; before

235

whom no weapon may stand (Isaiah 54:17). You may boldly stand as victors in Love *"because as He is, so are we in this world."*

Prayer of Response: Boldly Stand!

Please pray aloud with us...

Heavenly Father, thank You for covering me in the Blood of the Lamb and thank You for stirring a testimony within me. Please forgive me for those times when I stood before Your Word in and of my own intellect. Please forgive me for those times when I looked into scripture but refused to come to You to have life.

I want to know You, Father. I want to come past the gate of scripture and know You. I know that only Jesus Christ crucified has opened this path to me. I know that only You draw me unto Yourself.

Abba, Father! In Christ, You make Your love perfect; therefore in Christ, I receive the Truth that I have boldness in the day of judgment. In Christ, I receive the Truth that in the moment of this prayer and in all time between now and that Great Day, I have the same. So great is Your love Father!

I pray that the Holy Spirit quicken the boldness and love of Jesus Christ in me. Fit me with a spirit of boldness and love according to scripture. So in boldness, as Your Love dwells in me, I stand before You. By Your mercy, I acknowledge the victory of Jesus Christ as a victory won for me.

I acknowledge an end to the cycle of defeat because of my Lord's accomplishment and by His Presence. I declare my praises according to Your Word: "...thanks be to God, which giveth us the victory through our Lord Jesus Christ." Thank You for the amazing grace that Christ dwells in me!

Thank You for the victory of Love! Thank You that Your Love dwells in me. Thank You for making Your Love perfect in me. Thank You that as Jesus is; so in this world I receive and carry the Promise of Your Great Love.

Father, I know that Christ dwells in me; and I am not made to be Him, but am only a humble vessel. I pray release from every stronghold of the mind that had prevented me from stepping into the victory that Jesus secured by His death, resurrection and ascension.

Please lead me by Your Spirit Alone that I may be a vessel overflowing within Your Love to the Glory of God and the Praise of the King. By Grace, through Faith, according to Scripture, by the quickening of the Holy Spirit, in the powerful Name of Jesus. Amen.

Week Five, Day Three – Love Means

"He that loveth not knoweth not God; for God is love."
1 John 4:8

"There is no fear in love; but perfect love casteth out fear: because fear hath torment."
1 John 4:18

Most English-speakers say they love French fries, or chocolate, or hot coffee or some other favorite delight; and that they love a house, job, new device, book or film – and then in the same manner say they love family, God and country. Though in their minds they know that the colloquial use of the word "love" isn't the same in all situations; they say it anyway.

The love of God is filled with power and meaning. *God is love* (1 John 4:8). Therefore, love is an attribute of God that does not depart from Him. Where God is – Perfect Love resides, surrounds, catches up, frees, refreshes, quiets, fills and leads. For God so loved the world, that He sent Jesus, that those who believe in Him have the right to become sons and daughters of Almighty God (John 1:12).

And this is what we are now (1 John 3:1). The Father loved the Son, and with the same love; you are the beloved of God (John 15:9-10; 17:23). You are now free to speak and walk in love as defined in and fulfilled by Christ through your Almighty Father!

Yet by the trick of language, many have come to believe that love is defined as colloquial English suggests. By a trick of

238

the adversary, the definition of "love" is often understood as human-centered feeling; an affection or desire of the heart; or a lateral relationship of employing one language or another to help another person "feel loved." If your desire is to walk in the Love of God alone; then before going farther consider praying with us:

Heavenly Father, please forgive me for my part in accepting and participating in the world's confusing definitions of love. It is written, "God is love;" therefore I believe and confess that love powerfully begins and ends in You.

Please renew my mind by the power of Your Holy Spirit; that "being rooted and grounded in love," I "May be able to comprehend with all saints what is the breadth, and length, and depth, and height; And to know the love of Christ, which passeth knowledge" (Ephesians 3:17-19). Thank You, Father. I pray in Jesus' Name – Amen.

In the fullness of His Love, God sent His son to save you (John 3:16). In the fullness of His Love, the Lamb of God bled and died on the cross to set you free from the bondage and condemnation of sin and death (Romans 8:1-3). In the fullness of Love, the Father sent the Holy Spirit unto you in power (Acts 1:8). In the fullness of His Love, God raised you together with Jesus and has made you sit at His right hand, together in Christ in the Heavenlies (Ephesians 2:6; Hebrews 10:12). In the fullness of His Love, Almighty God has delivered you from the power of darkness, and translated you to the Kingdom of His Son (Colossians 1:13-14a). In the fullness of His Love, God gives you a spirit of love, and of power and of a disciplined mind (2 Timothy 1:7). In the fullness of His Love, God has done all of these things to bring you unto Himself (1 John 4:16-17).

In receiving God's Love, you are delivered from the power of darkness and "and from the power of Satan unto God" (Colossians 1:13; Acts 26:18). Even "sin shall not have dominion over you: for ye are not under the law, but under grace" (Romans 6:14). By the blood of the Lamb shed on the cross and who is now seated on the Throne, a line has been drawn between life and death; between defeat and victory; and between tormenting fear and love! *"There is no fear in love; but perfect love casteth out fear: because fear hath torment."*

"And having spoiled principalities and powers, he [Jesus] made a shew of them openly, triumphing over them in it" (Colossians 2:15). The victory of Jesus Christ the Lamb who was slain, is a victory of Love over the advancing powers of darkness in this world! Your life, as a son or daughter of God, is now hidden in the victorious Christ in the Heavenlies (Colossians 3:3). Can you begin to see that the life you live in Christ, even in this world; extends the victory of the Triumphant Love of Jesus Christ into this realm? Can you see the power of the Love of God and why the tempter is so interested in gutting the meaning of the word in its everyday use?

Is the watchman-of-your-feelings and experiences rising up to protest that the way we speak about love isn't such a big deal? Or do you believe that such triumphant love is only a scriptural ideal but not a present reality? Is the watchman-of-your-mind waking up to join hands with your feelings to cry out that the blood of Christ does not actually free anyone this side of heaven?

Perhaps it seems like circumstantial evidence proves the fact that miracles don't exist and God has abandoned His children in a broken church, a broken marriage, a broken family or a broken natural body. Are you sinking down, sinking down, sinking down in the seemingly overwhelming brokenness? Has the darkness pressed so close that you cannot perceive the Love of God amidst unresolved and untended pain?

God promises to meet you and is healing you. For it is written, "He healeth the broken in heart, and bindeth up their wounds" (Psalm 147:3); and "The LORD is nigh unto them that are of a broken heart; and saveth such as be of a contrite spirit" (Psalm 34:18). Rest assured that the God of Love is mending your war-torn heart, mind, body and soul and is lifting you out of the mire....as *"God is love."*

Will you take up what Love means? It is written in God's eternal word (Psalm 119:9) that the Lord is present with the contrite and brokenhearted. Since it is written – it must be exactly so. *"God is love"* and the miraculous love of God does not waver nor change:

> God is not a man, that he should lie; neither the son of man, that he should repent: hath he said, and shall he not do it? or hath he spoken, and shall he not make it good?
> Numbers 23:19

241

And though God's Word stands as its own witness, we can testify to the miraculous Love of God breaking forth in our lives. You already know some of what we experienced as we took up the word to Jehoshaphat "to stand firm, hold your position, and see the salvation of the Lord with you" (2 Chronicles 20:15, 17); but we have more to share.

Shortly after our drive across the nation and our move to the old 1850's homestead, my wife's health failed. From August to October of 2016, she was continually pressed down with relentless chest-pain. Her brother had just been diagnosed with a congenital heart-valve defect, and given her past-history and continuous pain, she was prepared for the same news.

The chest-pain had come upon her suddenly while pushing our daughter in a wheelbarrow up a small rise in the yard. The symptoms were continuous, except we noticed they diminished as she sang hymns and praise songs or read scripture aloud. Amazingly, they did not worsen with physical exercise. Considering this unusual evidence, we chose to defer medical testing for a time and take-up the matter in the manner of Jehoshaphat.

During this time of continual pain and sleepless nights, my wife learned that every breath was a gift from God. She learned to entrust the raising of our youngest daughter to her Father in Heaven. She learned to believe God alone would and could cover me in love. The Lord gave her strength to continue running the homestead and to continue in the community she was involved in; but I watched her slowly fail.

Finally, in late October, she tearfully took hold of me in the kitchen and asked me to take her to the emergency room. Waking and sleeping, she had been battling and struggling for months. She was exhausted and beyond relief. Her faith wavered with her strength.

Though my heart was crying out and I was angry in my spirit; I was led to encourage her to keep pressing. I refused to take her to the hospital, but told her that she could drive herself if she wanted to. I knew that she seriously doubted that I loved her or had any sense of the terrible, searingly real burden she was carrying.

Yet as a scientist and engineer, I knew there was clear evidence that she was not dealing with a natural issue. Cardiac pain does not decrease with exercise. Nor did I believe that the simple reading or singing of God's Word could eliminate cardiac dysfunction.

Two days later, as she sat reading God's word aloud in her favorite window-chair; the deliverance of the Lord came on her behalf! As she prayed aloud Psalm 147:3, "He healeth the broken in heart, and bindeth up their wounds;" her prayer changed from desperately asking God to take the pain away....to asking God to fulfill this word in her life NOW.

As she prayed these words aloud, the pain was lifted from her. Months of searing, tearing breathing ended within a moment of what felt like radiating heat moving within her rib-cage. In that moment, she experienced the power of Perfect Love and rose rejoicing and testifying to what God had done!

The next day though, the pain returned as powerfully as it had come as she was pushing the wheelbarrow back in midsummer. Instead of accepting it, she immediately prayed aloud, "Jesus Christ has healed my broken heart and bound my wounds; therefore, I stand healed." And the pain left.

We began seeing the salvation of the Lord on our behalf; and this from the valley filled with pain and dark shadows. We began learning that standing firm and holding covenant position in Christ is not taking a hold of the scripture and clinging to it like a life-saving rock in the midst of a roaring river. Seeing the salvation of the Lord begins with believing His Word is fully capable of commanding the flood of life's circumstances.

At the time, my wife had no idea the difference this would make in our lives. We had never clearly experienced the direct supernatural power of God (Luke 7:7; Matthew 8:8). This was the first time she had pressed so far in simple faith and the love of God poured forth, not of her doing, but through God's power-filled Word. Christ's Victorious Love delivered her and we learned first-hand that:

> God is not a man, that he should lie; neither the son of man, that he should repent: hath he said, and shall he not do it? or hath he spoken, and shall he not make it good?
> Numbers 23:19

244

Here we leave our personal testimony and trust the Holy Spirit to weave a thread back into today's leading scripture: *"There is no fear in love; but perfect love casteth out fear."* How can this be that love casts out anything? The answer is pure and beautiful for every Believer: ***"God is love"*** (emphasis ours).

There is now no power in the universe that can separate you from the power-filled manifestation of God's Love (Romans 8:38-39); even in the here and now, even in the midst of apparent defeat, or what "feels like" hollow victory. In whatever circumstance that now assails you, Jesus Christ has already delivered you from fear as a son or daughter of the Kingdom (Romans 8:15).

> Who shall separate us from the love of Christ? shall tribulation, or distress, or persecution, or famine, or nakedness, or peril, or sword?...Nay, in all these things we are more than conquerors through him that loved us.
>
> Romans 8:35

Though no power can separate you from the power of God's Love, our Heavenly Father will not force His Love upon you. No power in the universe except for your "yes and amen" to receiving and holding fast to Jesus Christ alone, by Grace alone, through Faith alone, according to Scripture illumined by God's Holy Spirit alone...will open the door of your life to all that God has prepared for you.

You are the only one in the universe who can, by believing, receive the manifesting victory of the love of Jesus Christ. This is what my wife learned sitting at home in that maroon window-chair. And that was only the beginning...

Perhaps you remember that once Jesus came to His own hometown and the people "were offended at him" (Mark 3:6b; Matthew 13:55-58)? Do you remember when Perfect Love Himself was walking in their midst with the supernatural power to deliver them from every natural captivity? Yet Jesus...

> ...could there do no mighty work, save that he laid his hands upon a few sick folk, and healed them. And he marveled because of their unbelief. And he went round about the villages, teaching.
>
> Mark 6:5-6

The testimony of scripture has not changed; nor has the world changed. Christ is victorious and has sat down "on the Right Hand of God" (Hebrews 1:3). All authority in heaven and earth has been given to Jesus (Matthew 28:18); for "The Father loveth the Son, and hath given all things into his hand" (John 3:35).

Perfect Love delivers you "out of the hand" of your enemies that you "might serve him without fear" (Luke 1:74). As you run to Jesus by the Holy Spirit of God, the Lord Himself will not despise your broken-heart or ignore your broken life...but will draw near.

Do you really believe this supernatural word? In believing, not only shall you see the Hand of God at work in the battles of your life, but you will also begin hearing the voice of the Holy Spirit leading you deep within your spirit (Isaiah 30:21, 48:17; 1

John 2:27). For the Shepherd King does not leave His sheep without His voice, nor does He leave them in the mouth of the world (John 10:27).

The victory of Jesus Christ the Lamb who was slain, is a victory of Love over the advancing powers of darkness in this world. Your life, as a son or daughter of God, is now hidden in the victorious Christ in the Heavenlies (Colossians 3:3). Can you begin to see that the life you live in Christ, even in this world, extends the victory of the Triumphant Love of Jesus Christ over you?

A line has been drawn between life and death; between defeat and victory; and between tormenting fear and love! Will you ask Father to manifest the power of His Love in your life? Jesus has made a way for you. The Holy Spirit of God will lead you. For now, *"There is no fear in love; but perfect love casteth out fear: because fear hath torment."*

Prayer of Response: Love Means

Please pray aloud with us...

Heavenly Father, having heard Your Word, I receive Your Love and turn away from fear. Father, please forgive me for harboring fear in the past. Thank You that I may take up Your infallible word, "There is no fear in love; but perfect love casteth out fear!"

I believe Your Word is fulfilled in my life. I confess in the Spirit and by the authority of the Risen Jesus Christ that "There is no fear in love; but perfect love casteth out fear." Therefore, I am now free to live unto God alone by the purifying Blood of Jesus Christ poured out in Love for me (Hebrews 9:14, 10:10). In the Name of Jesus Christ, I now close my heart to any spirit of fear.

For it is written, "Herein is love, not that we loved God, but that he loved us, and sent his Son to be the propitiation for our sins" (1 John 4:10).

Jesus, your Love means life without fear. Thank You for so great a Love. In Jesus' name, Amen.

Week Five, Day Four – Transformed

"Who shall separate us from the love of Christ?
shall tribulation, or distress, or persecution, or famine, or
nakedness, or peril, or sword?

As it is written, For thy sake we are killed all the day long; we are
accounted as sheep for the slaughter. Nay, in all these things we
are more than conquerors through him that loved us.

For I am persuaded, that neither death, nor life, nor angels, nor
principalities, nor powers, nor things present, nor things to come,
Nor height, nor depth, nor any other creature, shall be able to
separate us from the love of God, which is in Christ Jesus our
Lord."
Romans 8:35-39

Like you, St. Paul and the disciples faced real peril, yet they walked in the *"love of Christ...as more than conquerors."* Though life is an up-hill battle in a fallen world, their eyes of faith were fixed firmly on their Good Shepherd as true sheep of Jesus Christ. Though the world targeted them for death; Jesus Christ held them fast as His own.

"Who shall separate" a person from Christ? Only the sheep who choose to run away from Jesus to find their own pasture, or to hide themselves from the wolves, or take up self-care or self-help, may distance themselves from Jesus. Though the fullness of life is in proximity to Jesus, yet nothing in heaven or earth can separate them out of the Flock (John 10:10).

If you know anything about sheep, they are not particularly bold in and of themselves. Even Jesus' disciples were shaky-kneed in the face of the present and pressing evil that came against them. Peter denied Jesus three times (Matthew 26:34). The others fled in fear and went into hiding as Jesus went from the ground of Gethsemane to the tree of Golgotha (Matthew 26:56). Only the women and the young apostle John stood the ground beneath the cross and the jeering, mocking world, as the Good Shepherd bled and gave His life for His sheep (John 19:25-26).

Yet only a matter of fifty days later, these same shaky-kneed disciples and those who joined them in prayer, were indwelled with the power of God in the Upper Room (Acts 2:1-4). They received the Holy Spirit and were transformed from fearful hiding into bold witnessing in words of power! The doors to their waiting were flung wide and they broke out into the streets proclaiming the gospel in ways and in languages they could never have imagined; even unto performing miracles in the Name of Jesus (Acts 2-4)!

In boldness, Peter stood before the condemning crowd and preached the gospel (Acts 2:13 ff.). In boldness, the apostles defied the religious authorities in Jerusalem and proclaimed salvation in the Name of Jesus alone (Acts 4:1ff). And this was just the beginning of the transforming work of the Holy Spirit in the Flock of Jesus Christ! Jesus' Sheep were no longer weak-kneed and in-hiding, but were indwelled and established in Christ with power from on High (Acts 2:4). Under the anointing of the Spirit, these sheep confidently stood-fast in the midst of the very real and present powers who had set themselves against Jesus (1 John 2:20, 27; Psalm 2).

These witnesses did not believe that the power of God was reserved for some heavenly realm alone. These brothers and sisters, in the very shadow of the cross, took up the song of the victory of Jesus Christ. For after the cross – after the battle – the victory was won, and they witnessed the King ascending as they took up His command to wait for the coming of the Holy Spirit (Acts 1:4; Mark 16:19; Luke 24:48-49).

These were not hearers of the word alone. They did not walk in deception; but were doers also (James 1:22). These went to the Upper Room and waited in prayer as the Lord commanded. And it is written, "whoso looketh into the perfect law of liberty, and continueth therein, he being not a forgetful hearer, but a doer of the work, this man shall be blessed in his deed" (James 1:25).

And those who believed and obeyed received the blessing of power from on High, not to hide in defeat or to fulfill a ministry of words alone; but to walk in the realized Love of Jesus Christ. These transformed witnesses obeyed Jesus by proclaiming His Name and manifesting the power received of the Holy Spirit in word and deed. These Sheep went forth in the certainty of the power of God poured out through the Holy Spirit in that Upper Room.

Just as the Dove descended upon Jesus at His baptism; so in like manner, does the Holy Spirit come upon all who are baptized into the Name of the Lord Jesus (Acts 19:5-6). And it is written, "...if the Spirit of him that raised up Jesus from the dead dwell in you, he that raised up Christ from the dead shall also quicken your mortal bodies by his Spirit that dwelleth in you" (Romans 8:11). So now, the mortal body of each Christ-follower is quickened in the presence of the Holy Spirit!

Two millennia after the life and death of our Lord, you receive the same Spirit that raised up Jesus from the dead (Romans 8:11; Ezekiel 37:14). This same Holy Spirit dwells within you (2 Timothy 1:14). This same Holy Spirit quickens your natural bodies in the new birth and makes it possible for you to boldly witness to the resurrection of Jesus Christ (Ezekiel 11:19, 36:27; Romans 8:11; Acts 1:8). As a finished matter of the Spirit you are transformed and transforming in this world by your baptism and belief in the Name of the Lord Jesus Christ (Acts 2:38-39; Titus 3:5).

Since there is no shadow of turning in the Godhead, the Holy Spirit is the same yesterday, today and tomorrow (Malachi 3:6). Is it then reasonable to see manifestations of the power of the resurrected Jesus Christ in the Christian life? Is it spiritually logical that the Holy Spirit you received in your baptism can breakthrough into this worldly realm that you may be *more than conquerors through him that loved us"*?

May the infallible word of scripture be received deep in your spirit. It is written:

> Wherefore henceforth know we no man after the flesh: yea, though we have known Christ after the flesh, yet now

252

henceforth know we him no more. Therefore if any man be in Christ, he is a new creature: old things are passed away; behold, all things are become new.

2 Corinthians 5:16-17

But ye are not in the flesh, but in the Spirit, if so be that the Spirit of God dwell in you.

Romans 8:9a

And if Christ be in you, the body is dead because of sin; but the Spirit is life because of righteousness...Therefore, brethren, we are debtors, not to the flesh, to live after the flesh.

Romans 8:10,12

...Walk in the Spirit, and ye shall not fulfil the lust of the flesh.

Galatians 5:16

If we live in the Spirit, let us also walk in the Spirit.

Galatians 5:25

But the manifestation of the Spirit is given to every man to profit withal. For to one is given by the Spirit the word of wisdom; to another the word of knowledge by the same Spirit; To another faith by the same Spirit; to another the gifts of healing by the same Spirit; To another the working of miracles; to another prophecy; to another discerning of spirits; to another divers kinds of tongues; to another the interpretation of tongues: But all these worketh that one and the selfsame Spirit, dividing to every man severally as he will.

1 Corinthians 12:7-11

Verily, verily, I say unto you, He that believeth on me, the works that I do shall he do also; and greater works than these shall he do; because I go unto my Father.

John 24:12

253

On the basis of the testimony of the Word you who are in Christ may no longer walk in the flesh as a shaky-kneed present-day follower of Jesus, but walk "in the Spirit" with the very supernatural Holy Spirit dwelling within!

The love of the Lord is such that transformation is not reserved for the someday of heaven, but is received here below as you walk the pavement of this earth. Even life does not stand in the way of being in Christ: *"neither death, nor life...Nor height, nor depth...shall be able to separate us [you] from the love of God, which is in Christ Jesus our Lord."* So this side of heaven, surely you are *"more than conquerors through him that loved us."*

Your spiritual transformation by the Spirit of the Lord from glory unto glory – is happening in the present-tense. You "are changed into the same image" as your Lord Jesus now; though as beholding but dimly His glory. One day you will see Him face to face as He is (1 Corinthians 13:12; Revelation 22:4)! Yet even now there is nothing that separates you from *"the love of God, which is in Christ Jesus our Lord."*

Though you are as clay, you are now filled with the abiding presence of God (1 Corinthians 6:19). You are no longer a debtor to the flesh to live in merely natural ways, by your own strength, or according to the world's leading. Now you may walk in the transforming presence and liberty of the Spirit of Life (John 6:63; Romans 8:2)!

> Now the Lord is that Spirit: and where the Spirit of the Lord is, there is liberty. But we all, with open face

beholding as in a glass the glory of the Lord, are changed into the same image from glory to glory, even as by the Spirit of the Lord.

2 Corinthians 3:17-18

Walking in the spirit is walking in the powerful Love of God, to the glory of the Lord, by the very power and presence of God's Spirit! The nature of this walk is demonstrated by the great cloud of witnesses who have gone before us, who in the face of present and pressing *"tribulation, or distress, or persecution, or famine, or nakedness, or peril, or sword"* walked as *"more than conquerors through him that loved us."* Those who walk by the Spirit, walk in Christ, and through His Love, receive the power to walk in victory.

And having spoiled principalities and powers, he [Jesus] made a shew of them openly, triumphing over them in it.

Colossians 2:15

And ye are complete in him [Jesus], which is the head of all principality and power.

Colossians 2:10

The enemy has no legal hold over you. Your position, place and empowerment is **complete** in Christ now. In this earthly life you overcome the onslaught of evil by testifying to the victory of the cross (Revelation 12:11). The victory is never your own; but belongs solely to Jesus Christ. "...Thanks be to God, which giveth us the victory through our Lord Jesus Christ" (1 Corinthians 15:57)!

In Christ, and by the Holy Spirit, it is your legacy to walk as a son or daughter who is *"more than a conqueror;"* being fully

255

"persuaded, that neither death, nor life, nor angels, nor principalities, nor powers, nor things present, nor things to come, Nor height, nor depth, nor any other creature, shall be able to separate" you *"from the love of God, which is in Christ Jesus our Lord."*

Prayer of Response: Transformed

Please pray aloud with us...

Abba, Father! Thank You for complete victory in Jesus Christ! Thank You for the seal of the Holy Spirit and for receiving me as Your son/daughter. I glorify You and give thanks that no power in heaven or earth can sever the power of the bond of Love of Jesus Christ!

Heavenly Father, let me walk in Jesus' Victorious Love! Let me join the great cloud of witnesses who saw the power of Love manifest in the 24/7 of their natural lives. Let me take up Your Overcoming Love by the Blood of Jesus Christ and the Holy Spirit working in me. Please bring forth Your Glory through my clay vessel that I might walk unto your Holy Spirit all my days.

Moment-by-moment please let me receive and demonstrate the Perfect Love of Jesus unto Your Glory, by Grace, through Faith, by the power-filled presence of the Holy Spirit alone. In Jesus Name, Amen.

Week Five, Day Five – Who are You?

"For we wrestle not against flesh and blood, but against principalities, against powers, against the rulers of the darkness of this world, against spiritual wickedness in high places. Wherefore take unto you the whole armour of God, that ye may be able to withstand in the evil day, and having done all, to stand."
Ephesians 6:12-13

How is it we know with certainty that *"we wrestle not against flesh and blood, but against principalities, against powers, against the rulers of the darkness of this world, against spiritual wickedness in high places?"* That moment by moment in the spiritual walk, the wrestling is not a factor of our own flesh? The answer comes in knowing who you are, who you are becoming and who you belong to. The answer forms the basis for standing successfully in spiritual battle.

Do you know "who" the Bible says you are now? As a Believer, you are "...a new creature: old things are passed away; behold, all things are become new" (2 Corinthians 5:17). You belong to Jesus whose blood has ransomed you from the law of sin and death (1 Peter 1:18-20; Titus 2:14). You are now seated with Him in the heavenlies (Ephesians 2:6) and your life is hidden in Christ in God (Colossians 3:3). Therefore, you are in the world, but no longer of the world (John 15:19; 17:11). Almighty God has delivered and translated you, "...from the power of darkness...into the kingdom of his dear Son" (Colossians 1:13-14a). In Christ, you now "...live, and move, and have your being" (Acts 17:28, pronoun change ours).

Will you take God at His Word that this is who you are now? By the power of God's Holy Spirit, will you receive the scriptural testimony about your identity in Christ? If you will believe what is written, then press forward with this devotion....

Even if there is whispering and pressing doubt that rises up to accuse you of not being worthy, or of not believing enough, or of having failed too often; or of having been too selfish, or broken, or worn; or that you are caught in a relationship or situation where you cannot follow or believe God. You may even feel plagued by internal "voices" with questions akin to: "Who do YOU think you are? And why would God say these things about YOU?" Ask God to deliver you from the enemy, forgive any sin, and then keep pressing on with a similar question...

Who are you becoming? Perfect Love has driven and is driving out all fear (1 John 4:18). And as you take God at His Word and take up the Word of God, you are being transformed from glory unto glory in your spirit by the quickening presence of the Holy Spirit (Romans 12:2; 2 Corinthians 3:18; Ephesians 4:23-24). As Jesus is, so you are now becoming (1 John 4:17; Romans 8:29; 2 Corinthians 3:18).

You are in Christ and as you receive the gift of the Holy Spirit, you shall move into the work that God has prepared for you from before the world began (Ephesians 2:10). As it is written, He shall "worketh in you both to will and to do of his good pleasure;"

that you may complete that which is "pleasing in His sight" (Philippians 2:13; Hebrews 13:21); even unto the "greater works" of the Lord Jesus Christ (John 14:12).

Will you take God at His Word? Do you believe that your legacy in life is completely revealed in Christ, through the Holy Spirit as found in the Scriptures? Do you believe Jesus is the Word-made-Flesh?

If you will believe God at His Word, then press forward with this devotion. Even if anxiety, fear or confusion begin an assault on your mind in an attempt to persuade you that you are getting this walk unto the Spirit all wrong; or that your scriptural understanding is flawed or fanatical; or that your pride is rising up to make you think you could ever be such a man or woman of God; or that your life simply cannot be the platform from which God might reach into the world; or that you are out-of-your-right-mind for believing what you are hearing; or that your family, pastor, or church will not believe what God is saying to you; or any other assault which simply echoes this question: "...did God REALLY say this about YOU?" Ask God to strengthen your inner spirit, then take up the next question...

Who do you belong to? You are no longer your own, but have been bought with a price as an adopted son or daughter of God "to the praise of His glorious grace" (1 Corinthians 6:19-20; Ephesians 1:4-6). You have been drawn by the Father and have received Jesus Christ as your Lord and Savior, your King and your God (John 6:65; Romans 10:9; Revelation 17:14; Isaiah 9:6). By your confession, you have received the gospel of Jesus Christ and the New Birth of the Holy Spirit.

You are a son or daughter of glory (John 17:22; Romans 8:30); one beloved by and rescued "from this present evil world" by Jesus Christ (John 15:9; Galatians 1:4). You are a fit member, belonging in His great Body (1 Corinthians 12:27). You are of Heaven's fold; the Good Shepherd's sheep whom He has separated unto Himself (John 10:16).

You are His witness (Acts 1:8), His ambassador to the nations (2 Corinthians 5:20), His workmanship (Ephesians 2:10), His Temple (1 Corinthians 3:16-17) and a servant of the Gospel, "according to the gift of the grace of God" and "the effectual working of his [God's] power" (Ephesians 3:6-7).

If you believe all that is testified to, you are a member of Christ's body – the Church. You are a minister of the Gospel of Jesus Christ and have a share in the commission of the King! This Kingdom mission does not depart from Christ's very own:

> The Spirit of the Lord is upon me, because he hath anointed me to preach the gospel to the poor; he hath sent me to heal the brokenhearted, to preach deliverance to the captives, and recovering of sight to the blind, to set at liberty them that are bruised. To preach the acceptable year of the Lord.
> Luke 4:18-19

Our Lord Jesus forevermore preaches a gospel of power, not of man – but of God. In Christ, by the Spirit of the Lord, is healing, deliverance, the recovery of sight to the blind and liberty for the bruised. As this gospel is proclaimed, the supernatural power of the Kingdom of God works in the natural world to demonstrate the greatest miracle of all in the supernatural: that of reconciliation unto eternal life in God.

If you will accept it, Jesus Himself confirms and extends this full mission to you as a member of His Great Body. As you are led of the Holy Spirit, and proclaim the gospel, the supernatural power of the Kingdom of God breaks forth. Can you hear the echo of the King's mission extended to you in the Gospel Commission as recorded by St. Mark?

> "Go ye into all the world, and preach the gospel to every creature. He that believeth and is baptized shall be saved; but he that believeth not shall be damned. And these signs shall follow them that believe; In my name shall they cast out demons; they shall speak with new tongues; They shall take up serpents; and if they drink any deadly thing, it shall not hurt them; and they shall lay hands on the sick, and they shall recover."

> So then after the Lord had spoken unto them, he was received up into heaven, and sat on the right hand of God. And they went forth, and preached every where, the Lord working with them, and confirming the word with signs following. Amen.
>
> Mark 16:15-20

We pray that you might receive this gospel-word for your own life. We pray that even now you are rooted in Christ, fully exercising the Faith of Jesus Christ, and believing that you may see! If you are "saved" – you have already experienced the supernatural power of the salvation of the Lord! And to your own miracle of salvation, we can add our personal experience of God teaching us who we are and who we are becoming in Jesus Christ. Though we once believed that we could not see the miraculous power of God in the land of the living; our old belief systems no longer stand.

We have seen the Word of God fulfilled in our lives (Luke 4:21). And the miracles of God have confirmed the leading edge of His Word breaking forth every day and everywhere into this present darkness through those working with the Lord (Mark 16:20). It is now "normal" for us to perceive the power of the Gospel in the 24/7 nitty-gritty of life (Romans 1:16b; 1 Corinthians 2:4, 4:20). And we have learned that the term "spiritual warfare" is nothing more or less than the Gospel of Jesus Christ breaking forth into the natural world.

The work of the gospel is not the natural work of man but the supernatural work of God (Romans 1:16; 1 Corinthians 1:22-24; 1 Thessalonians 1:4-6). You enter into this gospel work, not by human might, natural power, or the wisdom of this age; but by the Spirit of God alone (1 Thessalonians 1:4-6). Therefore, as workers for the gospel and Jesus' own followers, you no longer battle alone and according to this world against the flesh, and the natural causes assailing natural man (2 Corinthians 10:4).

The warriors of God do not take up any mission or armor apart from that of Jesus Christ the Risen Lord. And if you will receive it, herein lies the fullest answer to the original question: How is it that we know with certainty that *"we wrestle not against flesh and blood, but against principalities, against powers, against the rulers of the darkness of this world, against spiritual wickedness in high places"*? That now, even now, *"we wrestle not against flesh and blood"* – even our own?

According to scripture, you do not battle sin by your own natural strength in your own flesh and blood (Romans 6:6, 7:25). For you are buried in your baptism and risen in Jesus through faith in God and can now say (Colossians 2:12); "I have been crucified with Christ, and I no longer live, but Christ lives in me. The life I live in the body, I live by faith in the Son of God, who loved me and gave Himself up for me" (Galatians 2:20). So you take up your personal battle against sin by taking up your place in Jesus Christ; knowing fully who you are – whose you are – and who you are becoming by the transforming power of God at work in you!

For it is "the word of his grace, which is able to build you up, and to give you an inheritance among all them which are sanctified" (Acts 20:32). And your weapons are not of this world, "For though we walk in the flesh, we do not war after the flesh: (For the weapons of our warfare are not carnal, but mighty through God to the pulling down of strong holds)" (2 Corinthians 10:3-4).

By grace through faith in and of Jesus Christ, through the quickening power of the Holy Spirit, you are a warrior for the Gospel of Jesus Christ. And should you choose, God will fit you with the spiritual weapons to stand for, in, by and to the Gospel of Jesus Christ in this world. *"Wherefore take unto you the whole armour of God, that ye may be able to withstand in the evil day, and having done all, to stand."*

What is this armor that you may take up? Looking to the original Greek, *"the armour of God"* is in the possessive case. This means by way of the grammar of scripture itself, that *"the armour of God"* is "God's own armor." This armor is a possession of God; therefore, it is both spiritual and supernatural (2 Corinthians 10:4).

This unseen spiritual armor is received by your spirit and is available upon your asking the High King to cover and dress you. The natural man cannot take up what is supernatural (1 Corinthians 2:14; Romans 8:7); so God's own armor is fit only upon the man or woman whose life is hidden in Christ. This armor is received by faith (Hebrews 4:2, 12:2).

Will you take up the mantle of the Holy Spirit and be a servant of the gospel and a worker for Jesus Christ? Will you, impelled by the Spirit of God, ask for God's armor and take your stand in the supernatural commission of the Gospel of Jesus Christ? Jesus Christ has delivered you into the light of the Kingdom of God and made you a light in a dark world (Philippians 2:15). Brother or sister, "The night is far spent, the day is at hand...therefore cast off the works of darkness...put on the armour of light" (Romans 13:12).

For we wrestle not against flesh and blood, but against principalities, against powers, against the rulers of the darkness of this world, against spiritual wickedness in high places. Wherefore take unto you the whole armour of God, that ye may be able to withstand in the evil day, and having done all, to stand.

Prayer of Response: Who are you?

Please pray aloud with us...

Heavenly Father, I confess that Your Kingdom mission is beyond my complete comprehension, yet I praise and bless You for what I do understand. Through the power of the gospel, You have worked the supernatural miracle of transferring me from the kingdom of darkness to Your Kingdom. In Christ and by Your Love, I have become Your own adopted son/daughter (Ephesians 1:5). Thank You, Father.

Thank You for empowering me to take my place as a witness and servant of the Gospel (Acts 1:8). Thank You for Your grace and the working of Your power (Ephesians 3:6-7). Though I am nothing, You have made me Your own. Father, this is almost too much for me; for what can I give in return for such amazing love?

Please forgive me for every time that I have forgotten that I am redeemed in Christ. Please forgive me for forgetting that my life is hidden in God. Please forgive me for any hesitation in believing that You would confirm Your Gospel with healing, release from bondage, and the restoration of liberty – all through the working of Your power! I glorify You and exalt Your Name! Alleluia!

Heavenly Father, thank You that today I may confirm my commitment to be a servant of the Gospel of Jesus Christ. Please reveal to me the ministry that You have for me. Please show me

265

how I may be Your witness. Please free me and cover me with Your armor, that I may be able to stand as a soldier for Jesus Christ, commissioned unto carrying Your gospel in power to the lost.

These things, I ask in Faith. For they are too great for me, except for the testimony of Scripture. Thank You for Your grace, mercy and love. Thank You for Your healing and deliverance. I love You and glorify You in the Name of Jesus, Amen.

Author's Note: In preparation for tomorrow's devotion, please ask the Father for the "armor of God" and an especially protected time of meeting in the Spirit. You may be led to tarry for a time before taking up this next day...

Week Five, Day Six – Under Authority

"And what is the exceeding greatness of his power to us-ward who believe, according to the working of his mighty power, Which he wrought in Christ, when he raised him from the dead, and set him at his own right hand in the heavenly places,

Far above all principality, and power, and might, and dominion, and every name that is named, not only in this world, but also in that which is to come:

And hath put all things under his feet, and gave him to be the head over all things to the church, Which is his body, the fulness of him that filleth all in all."
Ephesians 1:19-23

In taking up the confession of Jesus as Lord and Savior, every Believer is fixed firmly into Christ as a living member of the Church. This Church is not defined by a physical building, nor is it merely a denomination, mission or local congregation. The Church *"is his body, the fulness of him that filleth all in all."* Being in the Church is identified with being in Jesus Christ who *"according to the working of his mighty power...to us-ward who believe"* is *"the head over all things to the church."* So your place now is in Christ and you are caught up and made complete in Him (Colossians 2:10).

Indeed, Almighty God *"hath put all things under his [Jesus'] feet."* While there are earthly structures to local churches and denominational bodies, these subordinate to Jesus Christ that the visible church may be caught up in His invisible Body. If and when an individual, local church or denominational body prefers its own structure, doctrinal foundations, or theological interpretations over and against the pure scriptural revelation of the One whom God *"set...at his own right hand in the heavenly places"* – this natural organization, by its own decision, departs from a firm-mooring in Jesus Christ.

Grave as this is, the individual Believer need not despair; for their life is hidden in Christ that they might "live and move and have their being in Him" in the midst of the fallen and falling structures of the world (Acts 17:28). God's adopted sons and daughters are joined into the Body of Christ as a living member and given gifts for the building up of His Body (1 Corinthians 12:27-28; Ephesians 4:11-13). As they walk in Christ, they are held firm and complete in Jesus as they minister to others in vigilant faithfulness to their Lord. For it is written:

> As ye have therefore received Christ Jesus the Lord, so walk ye in him: Rooted and built up in him, and stablished in the faith, as ye have been taught, abounding therein with thanksgiving.
>
> Beware lest any man spoil you through philosophy and vain deceit, after the tradition of men, after the rudiments of the world, and not after Christ. For in him dwelleth all the fulness of the Godhead bodily. And ye are complete in him, which is the head of all principality and power.
>
> Colossians 2:7-10

The scriptural imperative for the Believer is to first take hold of his or her place in Christ as revealed by God, then walk unto the Spirit in whatever local body of Believers that the Lord Jesus Christ calls them to serve within. The ultimate identity for Christ's own son or daughter is not in the local congregation or fellowship; but in Christ alone (Colossians 2:7,10). And Jesus Christ dwells within every Believer's heart and by faith each one has access to God (Ephesians 3:11,17; Galatians 2:20).

As a Believer, will you follow Jesus, take hold of your place in Him and deny yourself (Matthew 16:23b-25)? Will you take up your position in the family of God over and above any position in a worldly family or structure (Ephesians 3:15; Galatians 4:6-7; Colossians 2:7)? Jesus Himself confirms your adopted place in His Family. As it is written, "My mother and my brethren are these which hear the word of God, and do it" (Luke 8:21b).

All authority has been given to Jesus Christ; therefore, all godly submission is first to Jesus, then through Him, to the authorities established by God in the family, church and world. Christ-centered submission is rooted in God, impelled by the power of the Holy Spirit and defined by scripture. Therefore, a Believer is free to walk under the authority of Jesus Christ, led of the Holy Spirit, for there is One Lord of heaven and earth who is *"far above all principality, and power, and might, and dominion, and every name that is named, not only in this world, but also in that which is to come...."*

While Believers are charged to respect the authorities God appoints and live peaceably in subjection to them (Romans 13:1; 1 Timothy 2:2; Titus 3:1; Hebrews 13:17); we are to do so as unto the Lord Jesus Christ and not according to men (Colossians 3:17, 23; Ephesians 6:7). There is a tremendous distinction between walking in Christ and thereby submitting to others; and replacing or substituting worldly authorities for Jesus Christ, following them wherever they go, all the while asking for Jesus to bless leadership that is of the world and not of Him.

Unfortunately, many Believers have been discipled to walk in the name of a local assembly or under a gifted leader, without much regard for their position in Christ. In these situations, the Christian sees themselves first as a member of this or that ecclesial tradition, denomination, congregation or mission. The authority of a particular teacher, liturgy, priest, pastor or religious leader, sacrament or ecclesial teaching becomes accepted alongside, or sometimes even in place of, a pure devotion to the Lord Jesus Christ as revealed of scripture (2 Corinthians 11:2-4).

If a Believer prefers the authority of their natural or church family over their place in the Body of Christ as revealed in scripture; by their own decision, they forfeit a firm-mooring in Jesus Christ. It is here where we begin to tremble. For there is only One Name in Heaven and Earth to which all knees will bow (Philippians 2:9-11; Romans 14:11). There is only one King for the Throne (Mark 16:19). There is only One to Whom the Father has given all authority, power and dominion (Matthew 28:18; Ephesians 1:22-23).

And there is only One through Whom the power of God is extended to *"us-ward who believe"* – Jesus Christ, the Son of God,

270

born of Mary, crucified, died, risen, ascended, and sitting at the Right Hand of God! In Christ, we receive every spiritual blessing and experience the in-breaking of the Father's miraculous love (Ephesians 1:3). Outside of Christ, we not only can do nothing (John 15:5b) – but we also receive nothing.

Scripture testifies that the double-minded man cannot "receive any thing of the Lord" (James 1:7-8b). So it can be no surprise that those who confess Christ, while at the same time giving primary authority over their life to something or someone else, do not "receive any thing of the Lord" (James 1:8b). When a person chooses to set themselves under any other primary authority, how can they expect to directly experience the manifest power of God? "Know ye not, that to whom ye yield yourselves servants to obey, his servants ye are to whom ye obey" (Romans 6:16)?

The power of Almighty God works through Jesus Christ and manifests in the Church by the quickening power of the Holy Spirit. Apart from Christ, the miraculous work of God does not flow into the body. Under the authority of God alone, we receive the Holy Spirit; salvation, life abundant, spiritual blessings and armor, miracles of healing and deliverance, as well as the authority to witness the gospel in power and not merely with winsome words of man's wisdom (1 Corinthians 2:4, 4:20).

The Body of Christ can do nothing apart from Jesus (John 15:5); therefore, a man and woman apart from God can do nothing of Kingdom importance or spiritual value. Jesus says, "...apart from Me you are able to do nothing" (John 15:5). It follows that

271

apart from Christ, the miraculous work of God shall not manifest itself in the world.

Yet it is written that "...the gospel of Christ...is the power of God unto salvation to every one that believeth..." (Romans 1:16). Do you believe the power of the gospel? Do you believe that the Head, or Crown of the Church is Jesus Christ, King of Kings and Lord of Lords? Do you believe that your Living Head, as the adopted son or daughter of God, is Jesus Christ alone?

If you believe, do not give authority to the things of man – but to the things of God (1 Corinthians 2:11-13). Do not let your crown be a parish, congregation or denomination or its pastoral leadership team, liturgy, worship style, unity, theology, strength of purpose, orthodoxy, history, wealth of facilities, abundant resources, or thriving ministries. Let the Risen Lord Jesus Christ be your living authority!

Then you will be caught up in knowing and understanding God through the revelation of Christ Jesus as you experience *"the exceeding greatness of his power to us-ward who believe, according to the working of his mighty power."*

> Thus saith the LORD, Let not the wise man glory in his wisdom, neither let the mighty man glory in his might, let not the rich man glory in his riches: But let him that glorieth glory in this, that he understandeth and knoweth me, that I am the LORD which exercise lovingkindness, judgment, and righteousness, in the earth: for in these things I delight, saith the LORD.
>
> Jeremiah 9:23-24

Taking up your place in Christ under the mantle of the Holy Spirit, may or may not look like pouring yourself into the ministries of your local fellowship. Walking unto the Spirit will, however, set you firmly in Christ, be rooted in Scripture and lead to the outpouring of "lovingkindness, judgment, and righteousness, in the earth; for in these things I delight, saith the LORD" (Jeremiah 9:24b). Taking your place in Christ, under the mantle of the Holy Spirit will edify the spiritual Body of Christ; wherever their location and position (Ephesians 4:12).

Walking unto the Spirit is glorying in understanding and knowing the LORD, through Christ Jesus by the power-filling Holy Spirit (Jeremiah 9:23-24); for "...he that receiveth me [Jesus] receiveth him [the Father] that sent me" (Matthew 10:40b). Taking up your place in the Church brings you into the proximal glory of understanding and knowing your Abba, the Almighty God; who has given all power and authority in heaven and earth unto Jesus (Matthew 28:18).

Taking up your place in the Church brings you under the veil of the authority of Jesus Christ. In Christ, God demonstrates through your life:

> ...what is the exceeding greatness of his power to us-ward who believe, according to the working of his mighty power, Which he wrought in Christ, when he raised him from the dead, and set him at his own right hand in the heavenly places. For you have been raised from the spiritually dead, by the working of God through Christ, and are now seated with Him in the Heavenlies.
>
> Ephesians 2:6

Though you are merely a pilgrim in this world; though your earthly body occupies the workman's chair, or the manager's chair, or the homemaker's chair, or the teacher's chair, or the businesswomen's chair, or the inventor's chair, or the scientist's chair, or the operator's chair, or the servicemen's chair, or doctor's chair, or student's chair, or the minister's chair; though you are part of an earthly family as mother, father, daughter or son; your spirit is abiding in Jesus Christ who is sitting on Heaven's Throne. Walking unto the Spirit is living, moving and having your being in this Risen Christ (Acts 17:28)!

It is written that, already "ye are risen with him [Jesus] through the faith of the operation of God" (Colossians 2:12b). And by His Grace, God "...hath raised us up together, and made us sit together in heavenly places in Christ Jesus" (Ephesians 2:6). As a member of the Church, you are part of this spiritual, substantial, invisible, power-filled Body of Christ in *"the fulness of him [Jesus] that filleth all in all."*

By your confession of Jesus as Lord and Savior, you are fixed firmly into Christ as a living member of *"his body, the fulness of him that filleth all in all!"* Being a member of the Body of Christ sets you under the authority, power and might of the Lord Jesus Christ in so far as you abide in the Counsel of the Holy Spirit (Romans 8:1). And under the authority of Christ, you are miracle-worker and foot-washer to the world (John 13:14; Mark 12:17).

Will you allow your spirit to die to all other spiritual authorities and rise in Christ, by the quickening, guiding and comforting leadership of the Holy Spirit? Will you take God at His Word? Will you ask Jesus to raise you up to a full understanding and knowledge of your place in His Church?

Will you ask for the power of the gospel to be made manifest through you? Will you invite Jesus to work through you as a witness to His Resurrection? If you will so pray, then you are simply asking God to bring you into an understanding of what is already true about your position as a member of the Body of Christ. Ask Jesus and He will not deny His own (Luke 11:10; 2 Corinthians 3:5-6).

Prayer of Response: Under Authority

Please pray aloud with us...

Heavenly Father, I fall on my knees crying out for Your mercy. Please forgive me. I confess that Your word is true (John 17:17) and that "all authority in heaven and earth has been given" unto Jesus (Matthew 28:18); therefore I am to submit to Your Son alone and through Him, by the Holy Spirit and according to Scripture – to the authorities that You have placed in my life. Please forgive me for exalting any worldly authority; let me walk under the authority of Jesus Christ alone and demonstrate the power of the gospel in my life.

Heavenly Father, You have demonstrated the "...exceeding greatness of Your power to us-ward who believe" through the resurrection of Christ and You have set Him at Your "own right hand in the heavenly places, far above all principality, and power, and might, and dominion, and every name that is named, not only in this world, but also in that which is to come: And hath put all things under his feet, and gave him to be the head over all things to the church, Which is his body, the fulness of him that filleth all in all" (Ephesians 1:19-23, pronoun changes ours).

Thank You Lord Jesus for receiving me into Your Body – the Church. Thank You for giving me the ability to accept You as my Living Head. Thank You for freeing me to walk under authority, led of the Holy Spirit, unto demonstrating Your power-filled gospel. Please fulfill my petition according to scripture to the glory of the Father's Love! I ask all of this in Jesus' Name; Amen.

Week Six, Day One – God With You

"Let us therefore come boldly unto the throne of grace, that we may obtain mercy, and find grace to help in time of need."
Hebrews 4:16

Dear brother or sister, what ails your heart? Are you weighed down with difficulties? Has disease come upon you? Do wounds, addictions or voices plague you? Are your relationships shattering? Are you hungry, cold, naked, worn, imprisoned, utterly without hope? Does sin press upon you? Or loneliness or death draw near? Have you found yourself for who you are in Christ, yet mourn in grief a besetting weakness which seems to keep you from drawing near unto Him?

Call upon the Name which powerfully cuts as a laser through the darkness. Jesus is Immanuel or "God with us" (Matthew 1:23)! The Lord is personally present in this very moment for those who call upon Him (Psalm 91:15; John 6:37). God is with you by His indwelling Holy Spirit (1 Corinthians 3:16). This is not some mechanical or psychological presence, but the personal presence of God Himself.

You are not forsaken. Your God is with you and is a covering (Psalm 91:1, 4). He is your Comforting Comfort, your Healer, your Sustainer and your Friend (Matthew 11:28-29; 2 Corinthians 1:4; Isaiah 53:5; Psalm 54:4; John 15:14). For as you have received the Son, you have received the Father that you are made one in God (John 17:21). Jesus says, "Abide in me, and I in you" (John 15:4). And see how near Jesus is – for as you are in need and afflicted, so the Bible teaches – is He:

> For I was an hungered, and ye gave me meat: I was thirsty, and ye gave me drink: I was a stranger, and ye took me in: Naked, and ye clothed me: I was sick, and ye visited me: I was in prison, and ye came unto me. Then shall the righteous answer him, saying, Lord, when saw we thee hungry, and fed thee? or thirsty, and gave thee drink? When saw we thee a stranger, and took thee in? or naked, and clothed thee? Or when saw we thee sick, or in prison, and came unto thee? And the King shall answer and say unto them, Verily I say unto you, Inasmuch as ye have done it unto one of the least of these my brethren, ye have done it unto me.
>
> Matthew 25:35-40

The Lord Jesus hungers with you, thirsts with you, is naked, estranged, sick, even imprisoned...for as the King sits on the Throne; His Spirit also dwells within each of His own (1 Corinthians 3:16). In this manner, the Lord by the indwelling Holy Spirit, bears with your disease, your iniquity, your transgression, your afflicting wounds. If this were not so – it would not be recorded that every act of love brought to you, would be as if unto Jesus Himself. "Verily I say unto you, Inasmuch as ye have done it unto one of the least of these my brethren, ye have done it unto me" (Matthew 25:40). What comes upon you...touches Him.

If it is too much to hear that the Comforter is with you in these sorrows (2 Corinthians 1:3-4); raise your eyes to the cross! For surely our Lord Jesus walked this earth "despised and rejected of men; a man of sorrows, and acquainted with grief" (Isaiah 53:3). Surely Jesus...

> ...hath borne our griefs, and carried our sorrows...he was wounded for our transgressions, he was bruised for our iniquities: the chastisement of our peace was upon him; and with his stripes we are healed.
>
> Isaiah 53:4-5

What is true at the Cross is true now. There is nothing too small to bring nor anything too great. For all sorrow was borne and all healing was attained by His stripes (1 Peter 2:24). He is the God who hears your cry and takes every tear in a bottle (Psalm 56:8, 66:19-20). Since Jesus Christ has borne and carried your grief, sorrows, wounds, bruises, chastisement and stripes; in bringing your every sorrow to Him, you thereby take up the power of what Jesus has already accomplished and give glory to God (Psalm 50:15; 1 Corinthians 1:17-18).

And you are a member of His body now and He is your head. "And whether one member suffer, all the members suffer with it; or one member be honoured, all the members rejoice with it" (Colossians 1:18; 1 Corinthians 12:26-27). Isn't the head of the body the most capable in sensing, understanding, and responding to the needs of its members? So it is with Jesus Christ. *Let us therefore come boldly unto the throne of grace, that we may obtain mercy, and find grace to help in time of need.*

And what help may be found at the throne of grace by the mercy of God? Once again, let us look to the Cross. At the Cross,

Jesus Christ rescued you from sin and death and made you righteous in Him (2 Corinthians 5:21). Christ died that you may be reconciled and restored unto a full relationship with God; indeed, Believers are one in Him and share in His Glory (Colossians 1:20; John 17:22).

Through the power of the cross of Jesus Christ and the quickening of the Spirit, God loves you and receives you as His own (John 1:12, 15:9; 1 John 3:1-2). In Christ you are an adopted daughter or son of God. You are raised up together with Jesus and made to sit "together in heavenly places in Christ Jesus" (Ephesians 2:6).

All authority in heaven and earth belongs to Christ the King – the One who is seated on the Throne – the One in whom you are seated – the One who loves you! In Christ, the full help and authority of heaven, by the love of the Father, is available to you now (John 3:16). And it is written: "He that spared not his own Son, but delivered him up for us all, how shall he not with him also freely give us all things?" (Romans 8:32). *Let us therefore come boldly unto the throne of grace, that we may obtain mercy, and find grace to help in time of need.*

In the midst of any trial, you have the ear of the High King of Heaven along with an invitation to pour out your heart; "Casting all your care upon him; for he careth for you" (1 Peter 5:7). And as you bring before Him your needs you may look for the good-gifts of God! For Jesus says:

...Ask, and it shall be given you; seek, and ye shall find; knock, and it shall be opened unto you. For every one that asketh receiveth; and he that seeketh findeth; and to him that knocketh it shall be opened.

Luke 11:9-10

What shall be given from the Throne? The first gift of God is: Himself. Jesus says, "If ye...being evil, know how to give good gifts unto your children: how much more shall your heavenly Father give the Holy Spirit to them that ask him?" (Luke 11:13)

And where God is, all of His attributes are present (Deuteronomy 6:4, Colossians 2:9). So with the Holy Spirit abides Divine counsel, comfort, healing, wisdom, strength, peace, love; abundance, provision; life; indeed all that is of God! And herein, may the ears of your spirit hear the Holy Spirit speaking to you...

For the helps of God are known by the Holy Spirit, as is your deepest personal need (Matthew 6:8; 1 Corinthians 2:10-11). The Holy Spirit counsels and comforts you deep in your spirit; this counsel you receive in your mind as intuition through a pure conscience (see Week One and Four, Day Five). If and as you ask the Father for help according to the Holy Spirit's leading within; then what you ask is under the authority and direction of God Himself.

And whatever is asked according to the will of the Father is completed on earth as it is in heaven (1 John 5:14-15). And the Holy Spirit does not counsel prayers before the Throne unto your spiritual demise or bondage, nor unto physical or mental illness, brokenness or captivity; but unto the liberty and victory won by the

Lord Jesus Christ at the cross! For it is written, "And whatsoever ye shall ask in my name, that will I do, that the Father may be glorified in the Son" (John 14:13). *"Let us therefore come boldly unto the throne of grace, that we may obtain mercy, and find grace to help in time of need."*

Jesus Christ is the pathway of prayer; for "no man cometh unto the Father, but by me" (John 14:6b). The way to the Throne is not a liturgy, or form, or ritual, or dance, or song, or circlet of beads; but Jesus Himself! In Christ, we come at once to Heaven's Gate and Calvary's Cross and the Father's Throne....for heaven came down...and pours down its mercies by and through every drop of Jesus' Blood shed for you that you may enter into the joy of your salvation (John 10:9, 11:25-26, 14:6, 17:13).

So let us come in Faith "unto the throne of grace, that we may obtain mercy, and find grace to help in time of need." Come to the Throne in the Faith of Jesus Christ (see Week Three, Day Two); taking hold of Him, and believing all truth, taking hold of every word of healing and supplication in scripture without hesitation or doubt. For just as faith the size of a mustard seed moves mountains making "nothing...impossible unto you" (Matthew 17:20b); so one little seed of doubt rends the mountain of belief and casts a man into the sea of double-mindedness. Such a one misses the blessing of God. For it is written:

> But when you ask, you must believe and not doubt, because the one who doubts is like a wave of the sea, blown and

282

tossed by the wind. That person should not expect to receive anything from the Lord.

James 1:6-7

Yet you are in Christ, so take heart dear brother or sister and press on in faith to the Throne! It is not upon merit or by the measure of your faith that heaven's blessings flow down! Since you have the Faith of Jesus Christ, you have all that is needed if you receive what is written and refuse to be moved by circumstances, emotions, thoughts or even the terrors of pain.

Do not fret that you do not have enough faith, or enough knowledge about God, or enough experience about healing, or enough experience about prayer. All you need is to be held fast in Jesus Christ. *"Let us therefore come boldly unto the throne of grace, that we may obtain mercy, and find grace to help in time of need."*

Have no fear! For the Perfect Love of the Father has opened the Throne of Grace and Jesus intercedes continually for you, even as the Holy Spirit cries out with words too deep to be spoken (Romans 8:26, 34; Hebrews 7:25)! Take hold of the God-with-you! With Jesus as your intercessor, follow the counsel of the Holy Spirit and cast your concerns and cares and supplications before the Throne in your weakness (1 Peter 5:7). Rejoice that your prayers are borne from your spirit unto God as "...the Spirit itself maketh intercession for us with groanings which cannot be uttered" (Romans 8:26).

For it is by Grace alone that you receive the provisions of God (Acts 14:17; Psalm 145:9,16). Jesus won the victory at the cross for your eternal salvation and that your present life may be filled to abundance! (John 10:10; Psalm 23) And this is also the vanquishing blow to the adversary. For it is written, "For this purpose the Son of God was manifested, that he might destroy the works of the devil" (1 John 3:8). As surely as the devil was defeated at the cross, every time a Believer takes up the power of Grace, that victory of Jesus Christ is made manifest in the earth.

But the first work of the tempter is to barrage your spirit with the question, "Yea, hath God said...?" (Genesis 3:1b) And similar questions swirl after..."Will you really receive any benefit from the King's Throne? Haven't you asked before and been left without? Surely the miracle-power of God ended with the apostles?" And on the barrage goes. Yet today...if you press through this reading...a line will be drawn in your spirit that the enemy will not be able to transgress (Ephesians 6:16).

But if and as you allow the flak from the adversary to penetrate your spirit, the fall away from the word of God and the fall from blessing begins. Scripture openly declares that a double-minded man or woman receives nothing from God (James 1). The problem is not that God will not bless; but that Believers do not single-mindedly receive God's blessing.

If the enemy's question "Yea, hath God said...?" causes anyone to question whether the word of God stands firm, or causes them to look to natural circumstances for some proof that scriptures are true; a measure of doubt has already entered in. This seed yields the produce of natural eyes looking for heavenly results and sets natural human judgment above the supernatural. Unfortunately, miracle proof is never found because Believers are looking for evidence instead of wholly accepting the divine assurances of God Himself. Trust is ripped from its mooring in faith and is given over to natural eyes, natural ears and natural circumstances.

In this situation Doubt instructs the natural hand to reach for and take hold of natural provision and directs the spirit to stand down and forget the supernatural provision of God. Doubt captains the plucking of and tasting of the fruit of the tree of knowledge, over and above obedience in faith to the word and provision of God. The loud voice of doubt fills the ears with the wisdom of man about God: "Yea, hath God said..." thus draws the son or daughter of God away from hearing and following the still, small voice of God (1 Kings 19:2).

The tactic of the enemy is to cultivate doubt. A spirit of doubt continuously creates the suspicion that a Christian cannot take God at His Word; but that faith is best placed in what the world says about God. "Know ye not, that to whom ye yield yourselves servants to obey, his servants ye are to whom ye obey" (Romans 6:16a)? If a Believer turns aside to doubt; it is doubt that is served. If a Believer turns aside in fear; it is fear that is served. If a Believer turns aside to the gospel as interpreted by the world, or according to the wisdom of man; it is this gospel which is served.

> Ye ask, and receive not, because ye ask amiss, that ye may consume it upon your lusts. Ye adulterers and adulteresses, know ye not that the friendship of the world is enmity with God? whosoever therefore will be a friend of the world is the enemy of God. Do ye think that the scripture saith in vain, The spirit that dwelleth in us lusteth to envy?
>
> James 4:3-5

Yet Christian, take heart! What is written in scripture is not to condemn you (John 3:17). It is for your edification and training in the faith, for your instruction and hope, (2 Timothy 3:16; Romans 15:4) and for the defeat of the devil and his lies (Revelation 12:11)! St. John explicitly writes his gospel, "that ye might believe that Jesus is the Christ, the Son of God; and that believing ye might have life through his name" (John 20:31).

Dear brother and sister, take up unwavering belief and take up life! Lay aside every doubt, every fear, every condemning spirit, every voice of the world that says God cannot or will not act; and hold fast to the Word of God in Jesus' Name:

> Having…boldness to enter into the holiest by the blood of Jesus, By a new and living way, which he hath consecrated for us, through the veil, that is to say, his flesh; And having an high priest over the house of God; Let us draw near with a true heart in full assurance of faith, having our hearts sprinkled from an evil conscience, and our bodies washed with pure water. Let us hold fast the profession of our faith without wavering; (for he is faithful that promised;)
>
> Hebrews 10:19-23

No matter what has happened in your personal past, are you ready to "draw near with a true heart in full assurance of faith" (ibid)? Will you believe what God has to say is available to you as you *"...come boldly unto the throne of grace...obtain mercy, and find grace to help in time of need?"* For as you take up what is written, you fulfill these words...

Bless the LORD, O my soul, and forget not all his benefits:

Who forgiveth all thine iniquities; who healeth all thy diseases;

Who redeemeth thy life from destruction; who crowneth thee with lovingkindness and tender mercies;

Who satisfieth thy mouth with good *things; so that* thy youth is renewed like the eagle's.

The LORD executeth righteousness and judgment for all that are oppressed.

He made known his ways unto Moses, his acts unto the children of Israel.

The LORD *is* merciful and gracious, slow to anger, and plenteous in mercy.

He will not always chide: neither will he keep *his anger* for ever.

He hath not dealt with us after our sins; nor rewarded us according to our iniquities.

For as the heaven is high above the earth, *so* great is his mercy toward them that fear him.

As far as the east is from the west, *so* far hath he removed our transgressions from us.

Psalm 103:1-12

Dear brother or sister, what ails your heart? Are you weighed down with difficulties? Has disease come upon you? Do wounds, addictions or voices plague you? Are your relationships shattering? Does sin press upon you? Or loneliness or death draw near? Are you hungry, cold, naked, worn, imprisoned, utterly without hope? *"Come boldly unto the throne of grace...obtain mercy...find help in time of need."*

Prayer of Response: God With You

Please pray aloud with us...

Dear Heavenly Father, in my need I cry out for the provision of Your Hand. In the Name of Jesus and with boldness; I plead mercy. I plead that every benefit of the Throne of Grace be imparted unto me. For I am weighed down and have walked for so long thirsting for You in this parched, dreary land (Psalm 63:1). Comfort me, Father! Pour out Your provision. (Take time to specifically present your needs to Father).

Thank You for pouring Your power into my life and for meeting my many needs. In the Name of Jesus, I tell any form of doubt, double-mindedness, fear, worldly teaching, unworthiness and pride to depart from me now.

In the Name of Jesus, I entrust my prayers to the Holy Spirit's intercession. *(Take time to praise and thank God as you are led of the Holy Spirit for His many benefits).* *I pray all of this in the NAME of Jesus Christ who is King of Kings and Lord of Lords. Amen.*

Week Six, Day Two – In the Arms of the I AM

"Behold, what manner of love the Father hath bestowed upon us, that we should be called the sons of God...Beloved, now are we the sons of God, and it doth not yet appear what we shall be: but we know that, when he shall appear, we shall be like him; for we shall see him as he is. And every man that hath this hope in him purifieth himself, even as he is pure."
1 John 3:1-3

"Remember ye not the former things, neither consider the things of old. Behold, I will do a new thing; now it shall spring forth; shall ye not know it?   I will even make a way in the wilderness, and rivers in the desert."
Isaiah 43:18

"Beloved, now are we the sons of God." Yes dear brother and sister, let your spirit rejoice for we are God's children – now! Does your heart cry out – NOW?

There is not a time when God is not, nor is there a place where God is not. For it is written, "I am Alpha and Omega, the beginning and the ending, saith the Lord, which is, and which was, and which is to come, the Almighty" (Revelation 1:8). And our Father's very Name is I AM; now and then, today and forever. For "God said unto Moses, I AM THAT I AM" (Exodus 3:14) and "I am the LORD" (Exodus 6:2). Because our Father is the great "I AM" – we are.

When are we God's children? Now. Where are we God's children? Now. Can you hear the lingual relationship between "I

AM" and "we are"? Can you hear the contingency? Sounds philosophical: "God is; therefore, we are." But this relationship is more than an idea. It is an insoluble connection. The profound, substantial reality is the presence of God with you – now!

Surely, God was yesterday. Surely God will be tomorrow. Yesterday is already gone, tomorrow has not yet come. The past and future are both out of reach. Therefore we are not to be bound by the past, though we feel its circumstantial results. Nor are we bound to future worries, for our eternal and present hope is in God working with and through us. It is written:

> Remember ye not the former things, neither consider the things of old. Behold, I will do a new thing; **now** it shall spring forth; shall **ye not know it**? I will even make a way in the wilderness, and rivers in the desert (emphasis ours).
>
> Isaiah 43:18

Does your heart still cry out – NOW? Does your mind leap to surveying the wilderness of your present circumstances or retort that Isaiah was surely talking about what God was doing or might someday do?! Ah, how we have been taught to see the work of God in the past and the hope of God in the future, all the while missing the new thing of God in the present.

The Holy Spirit is making a way for you in this present wilderness and is providing rivers in the desert. Lest God did a new thing through your New Birth, where today, would you be? Is not Christ the way in the wilderness and the Holy Spirit the river in the desert?

God's Name is "I AM." Though you live among a people of unclean lips, though you live among a people devoted to their own means and ends; though you live in the hard press and push and pull of this present generation of the world's bondage: *"Remember ye not the former things, neither consider the things of old. Behold, I will do a new thing; **now** it shall spring forth; shall ye not know it?"*

Surely Christ is the way in the wilderness of your present sufferings and the Holy Spirit is the water well for this parched day! Jesus said, "I am the way, the truth, and the life" (John 14:6). Jesus said, "...whosoever drinketh of the water that I shall give him shall never thirst; but the water that I shall give him shall be in him a well of water springing up into everlasting life" (John 4:14).

Surely, in the New Birth the old has gone and the new has come (2 Corinthians 5:17). Once you were a child of the world, now you are a son or daughter of God (1 John 3:1-3)! NOW are you in Christ, and a temple of the Holy Spirit as an adopted child of the Most High God. Therefore, *"Remember ye not the former things, neither consider the things of old."* And *"Behold, what manner of love the Father hath bestowed upon us...we are children of God now."* And the children are heirs, "heirs of God, and joint-heirs with Christ; if so be that we suffer with him, that we may be also glorified together" (Romans 8:17).

Suffer? Yes. "For we that are in this tabernacle do groan, being burdened" (2 Corinthians 5:4). For though we are in Christ, we are yet walking in this wilderness land in the midst of a culture devoted to pocket books, career goals, calendars, technologies, accomplishments, fitness, personal goals, families, entertainments and personal networks; "we have turned every one to his own way" (Isaiah 53:6).

Suffering comes as devotion to God languishes and the things of the world captain life. Where selfish idolatry abounds, love and charity dissolve. The tender mercies of God are overshadowed as the people of God turn unto the pursuit of fulfilling worldly, instead of Kingdom priorities.

Yet as the people of God return unto Kingdom priorities, they embody the forgetting of "the former things" and personally look to the "new thing" springing forth. In the midst of suffering the pain of personal and inter-personal captivation, outright sin or woeful neglect; Believers who continually turn to God are held fast in the love of God in Jesus Christ.

Holding fast in the love of God is holding fast to God Himself; who is love, compassion and tender mercy. Nothing in all of creation including your own weakness, can separate you from God's Love. Indeed, the Potter's Hands are covered in the water and mud of your life as you cry out for Him to transform you from what you have been, and conform you to who you are becoming in Jesus Christ (Romans 8:29). As you ask and are willing to receive, the new thing of God will spring forth. And the Father's blessing, through Christ, will manifest in the things of this life (John 14:13).

To suffer in the midst of this present darkness is not a lone wilderness journey. For God takes your suffering to Himself as you lay it upon Him; for it is written, "Surely he took up our pain and bore our suffering" (Isaiah 53:4a). Therefore, Jesus knows your pain intimately because all you endure and will endure in this life, has fallen upon His shoulders.

Herein lies the comfort and tender mercies of God. Even as Believers cry out with open and gaping wounds of pain, the balm of the Spirit comes through the Word and substantial spiritual and natural healing follows (Isaiah 66:14; Proverbs 3:8, 4:20-22). Such is the ongoing suffering and healing of the Christ-follower in the land of the living. Such is the operation of the cross in the wilderness of this world.

In the midst of suffering, will you take up the provision of Jesus' cross as your very own (Matthew 10:38)? Each member of Christ's Body is "sanctified through the offering of the body of Jesus Christ once for all" (Hebrews 10:10b). Since you are sanctified and Jesus Christ offered Himself "once for all" there is no conditional requirement that you take up a cross apart from Him.

Though you are touched by suffering in this world; you are freed from pursuing suffering as an end. For Jesus' sacrifice was offered "once for all." You are freed from a spirit of suffering; unto the love of your Lord Jesus Christ.

Practically then, what is a child of God to do? Jesus says - "Take therefore no thought for the morrow: for the morrow shall take thought for the things of itself" (Matthew 6:34). Even in matters of great importance, in life-and-death situations before leaders and powers, Jesus says, "...take ye no thought how or what thing ye shall answer, or what ye shall say" (Luke 12:11). In the simpler matters of daily need and sustenance, Jesus says, "...Take no thought for your life, what ye shall eat; neither for the body, what ye shall put on" (Luke 12:22).

So in the midst of life-or-death suffering, in great matters or small, does a child of God really "take no thought" of life? And what exactly does this mean? Jesus says: "Fear none of those things which thou shalt suffer...be thou faithful unto death, and I will give thee a crown of life" (Revelation 2:10). And Brother Paul exhorts: "...be thou partaker of the afflictions of the gospel according to the power of God" (2 Timothy 1:8).

Herein lies the power-filled distinction of the gospel: there is a difference between filling our minds with thoughts of our suffering and filling our minds with Christ in the midst of suffering. Taking thought of Jesus Christ in the midst of suffering brings to bear the manifest power of God; in leading healing and unto attaining the sustaining measure of God's comfort and strength in the midst of the trial (Mark 10:30; 1 Peter 2:21-25; Isaiah 51:12; 2 Corinthians 1:4). Taking heed of suffering itself, whether in walking in the midst of the brokenness of this generation or in the breaking frame of our physical bodies, turns the child of God round about on themselves and away from the heavenly helps of God (Genesis 4:7; 1 Samuel 15:24; Isaiah 51:13; 1 Peter 3:14).

Brother and sister, what need have you this day? What decision presses upon you? What burden of the world weighs you down? What ailment tears at your frame? What poverty leaves you indebted, dependent and anxious?

Does fear of irrelevance captain? Does worry or want lead your spirit? Does purpose demand its fulfillment? Does performance and production raise their measure as your rule?

"Behold, what manner of love the Father hath bestowed upon us, that we should be called the sons of God...Beloved, now are we the sons of God." Dear brother and sister take your seat in Christ with your Father in Heaven. Confess that you believe that Almighty God really is "I AM;" and that all good gifts come from and through Him unto your hand (James 1:17). Ask for direct help from the Holy Spirit.

Is the watchman-of-your-mind surging up? Tell this watchman that you have the mind of Christ – now (1 Corinthians 2:16). Is your pain surging up? Tell the pain that the Holy Spirit of God and the Lord Jesus Christ intercede for you; therefore living water will pour forth in this wilderness. Tell your mind and your suffering the gospel-truth: in Christ you live and move and have your being – now (Acts 17:28). Come, Holy Spirit...in the Name of Jesus!

Will you take God at His Word – in the now? For the Great I AM is Eternal and Present. Or will you be captained by the sufferings of life or by your own mindful experience? Our problem is that we have lived in a land devoted unto the things of this world, instead of the riches of God (Luke 13:20-21).

"Remember ye not the former things, neither consider the things of old. Behold, I will do a new thing; now it shall spring forth; shall ye not know it? I will even make a way in the wilderness, and rivers in the desert."

God the Father has made very clear that He knows of your need in life-and-death matters outside your home and within it (Matthew 6:8). As you seek Heaven's Provision, the Father has promised that He will provide. For it is written:

> For all these things do the nations of the world seek after: and your Father knoweth that ye have need of these things. But rather seek ye the kingdom of God; and all these things shall be added unto you. Fear not, little flock; for it is your Father's good pleasure to give you the kingdom.
>
> Luke 12:30-32

The provisions of the Kingdom exceed the riches of the world, for they are given of God. The Promise of God is not for earthly pastures of poverty and heavenly pastures of wealth; as many have taught. Nor is the Promise of God the "name it and claim it" wealth of worldly provision apart from the "riches of God" (Luke 13:20-21).

Jesus died that you might, "go in and out, and find pasture" in this world. And though the thief come "for to steal, and to kill, and to destroy," Jesus came that in Him you "might have life" and "...have it more abundantly" (John 10:9-10).

> I am the door: by me if any man enter in, he shall be saved, and shall go in and out, and find pasture. The thief cometh

297

not, but for to steal, and to kill, and to destroy: I am come that they might have life, and that they might have *it* more abundantly.

John 10:9-10

Instead of operating out what you have been taught *about* the scriptures, or what you have been taught *about* biblical futures; will you receive what is written? The sheep are first saved and they DO transverse a door from earth to heaven to "go in and out, and find pasture" – and His Name is Jesus Christ! Surely the thief is not a present threat in Christ!

As before so again, you are standing at a crossroads. Will you release yourself and your life and your livelihood unto the riches of God? Will you take up a pure pursuit of the Kingdom of Heaven? For it is written that, "...He [God] is a rewarder of them that diligently seek him" (Hebrews 11:6b).

> And Jesus answered and said, Verily I say unto you, There is no man that hath left house, or brethren, or sisters, or father, or mother, or wife, or children, or lands, for my sake, and the gospel's, But he shall receive an hundredfold now in this time, houses, and brethren, and sisters, and mothers, and children.

Mark 10:29-30a

More than all of this, God has given you Jesus Christ, the fullness of Heaven's Provision! *"And every man that hath this hope in him purifieth himself, even as he is pure."* Will you take on the purity of the mind of Christ, that you may receive that which God has prepared for you?

Will you release yourself unto Jesus Christ and the full provision of living, moving and being in Him? Will you give over every single decision in matters great and small? Give over the decision, and you will receive the provision...

For there is a great Promise for the child of God who will come in their full need to the Father. Such a son or daughter will not be given a stone; but will be given the Holy Spirit (Luke 11:11-13). By the Holy Spirit comes all counsel, all comfort, every spiritual gift and the armor of God to stand fully arrayed against the schemes of the devil unto victory in this life (Ephesians 6:13; 2 Corinthians 10:4; James 4:7).

For, "No weapon that is formed against thee shall prosper" - whether suffering, or poverty, or want (Isaiah 54:17a). "And every tongue that shall rise against thee in judgment thou shalt condemn" - whether accusation, diagnosis or curse (Isaiah 54:17b). "This is the heritage of the servants of the LORD, and their righteousness is of me, saith the LORD" (Isaiah 54:17c).

Prayer of Response: In the Arms of the I AM

Please pray aloud with us...

Heavenly Father, Thank You for calling me Your son [daughter]. Thank You for making every provision for me in Jesus Christ to receive Your good gifts and to defeat the devil. I ask that You purify me that I may have the mind of Christ.

In the Name of Jesus I take up my inheritance as Your son [daughter] now, and take hold of Your loving provision in the

299

midst of the wilderness of my present circumstances. Please refresh me by Your Holy Spirit. Per Your scripture, I know that You will give me all that is needed in this life and the world to come; therefore, I pray for the restoration of life in the Name of Jesus. For what is written is what must be.

I now turn away from any teaching and any circumstance that has led me to believe that You are not with me, nor caring for me with gospel power [Take time for personal prayer as the Holy Spirit leads]. Thank You that I am not captained by the past, nor the future. Thank You for making a way in the wilderness and overflowing the desert of my life with rivers of life! Let me know of the new thing that You are doing! In Jesus' Name, Amen.

Week Six, Day Three – Yoked in Faith

"Even so faith, if it hath not works, is dead, being alone. Yea, a man may say, Thou hast faith, and I have works: shew me thy faith without thy works, and I will shew thee my faith by my works. Thou believest that there is one God; thou doest well: the devils also believe, and tremble. But wilt thou know, O vain man, that faith without works is dead?"
James 2:18-20

"And every man that hath this hope in him purifieth himself, even as he [Jesus] is pure."
1 John 3:3

To have the faith of the Lord Jesus Christ is to have a living faith. To believe God is both to hear and obey, to both pray and fulfill that prayer in taking up the word of the Lord as a personal command for the heart, will, soul, mind and spirit. To walk in the faith of Jesus Christ is to walk in the Spirit without departing from the leading will of the Father (Philippians 2:13). What does this mean?

Faith holds together belief and trust as *"...faith, if it hath not works, is dead, being alone."* The word behind "faith" may be translated from Greek as "I believe" or "I have faith in" or "I trust;" depending on the context. This is actually helpful in perceiving that faith cannot remain purely cognitive, but leads to action.

In English there are three different shades of meaning for the Greek word "faith." This is not uncommon in matters of translation as language not only signifies meaning, but also carries along the story and life of a particular people within a particular time and culture. Language merely points to the reality behind a word and the substance that underpins or follows on from it.

The reality of "faith" manifests the invisible ideas of believing, having faith in, and the action of trusting. Having "faith" is a matter of believing God, and then entrusting oneself in and through every decision to act; completely to Him. The inclination or internal mooring of a human heart is known through the audible words and visible deeds of the body (Luke 6:45).

Faith, being of Jesus Christ, moves from incarnate word to incarnate action in the one hearing and doing the word (Revelation 14:12). So it is that the apostle writes, "I will shew thee my faith by my works." It is by this faith that you may walk as Christ walked (1 John 2:6), glorify God in all things (John 17:4), take captive all thoughts (2 Corinthians 10:5) and thereby function in your place as a member of the Body of Christ.

In Faith there is no gap between hearing and doing the word of God by means of being personally conducted by the Holy Spirit of God Himself – if you but take Him in faith as if by the hand (Psalm 73:23). Then, by the hand of faith, are you led in the whole of your mind, heart, soul and strength to do God's will (Mark 12:30).

To be conducted by the Spirit within is to invite the purification of the heavenly coal upon your lips; that you may submit in Christ to speak as God alone gives you means to speak and to do what God alone shows you to do (1 Peter 4:11; Psalm 24:3-5; Philippians 2:13). Taking up the faith of Jesus Christ is

302

taking up the heavenly vision of the Holy Spirit. As Isaiah was before the Throne and Seraph, so you are now standing in the presence of the Holy Spirit deep within (1 Corinthians 6:19).

Taking up the Faith of Jesus Christ is accepting the Word of God Himself as the guard and guide for your tongue (1 Peter 4:11; Psalm 32:9; Psalm 141:3). Faith becomes hearing and answering the divine question of, "Whom shall I send, and who will go for us? Then said I, Here am I; send me" (Isaiah 6:8). Responding in faith glorifies and honors the One sending (John 17:18). Therefore, before the Holy Spirit of God, the operation of faith ends in doing the will of God:

> I beseech you therefore, brethren, by the mercies of God,
> that ye present your bodies a living sacrifice, holy,
> acceptable unto God, which is your reasonable service. And
> be not conformed to this world: but be ye transformed by
> the renewing of your mind, that ye may prove what is that
> good, and acceptable, and perfect, will of God.
>
> Romans 12:1-2

As you present yourself to God in full Faith, you become a walking sacrifice of praise proclaiming the hope of Jesus Christ and proving or demonstrating in all that you do and say "that good, and acceptable, and perfect, will of God" (Romans 12:1-2). Faith proclaims Jesus as Lord and your body as the vessel of God via the Holy Spirit; that He may be known to the world. For it is written:

> And the glory which thou [Father] gavest me [Jesus] I have
> given them; that they may be one, even as we are one: I in
> them, and thou in me, that they may be made perfect in one;

303

and that the world may know that thou hast sent me, and hast loved them, as thou hast loved me.

John 17:22-23

Are you asking – what does this practically mean? Take hold of the biblical examples of what it means *to "shew thee my faith by my works"* and to *"purifieth himself, even as he is pure."* According to the Bible, taking on the faith of Jesus Christ involves completely accepting the Lordship of Jesus Christ and being led of Him in all praising and all purposing, all thinking, and all praying and all doing, that He may be to you that which He is – "Christ is all, and in all" (Colossians 3:11b; Ephesians 4:5)! By faith you substantially proclaim Jesus unto the world in all you say and in all you do.

Jesus invites every Believer to, "Take my yoke upon you, and learn of me; for I am meek and lowly in heart: and ye shall find rest unto your souls" (Matthew 11:29). Be yoked with the yoke of the faith of God through Jesus. Place your head through the girdle of the yoke. Accept Jesus Christ as Lord and be set as one with Him. "Be made perfect in one...that the world may know...thou hast loved" (John 17:23). "Faith" manifests the invisible love of God as you believe God and then entrust every spoken word and decision to act; completely to Him.

For just as a physical yoke connects two laboring animals thereby making their purpose, direction and strength to be as one – so to have the faith of Jesus Christ is nothing less than receiving the leading yoke of God Himself! This spiritual yoke makes one purpose, one effort and one end from the efforts of two laboring together. As you walk in the Faith of Jesus Christ, you walk in Him; and as He is, so you are becoming in this world...one step after the other (1 John 4:17; Romans 8:29). *"And every man that hath this hope in him purifieth himself, even as he is pure."*

To walk in faith is to be yoked to the perfection of Jesus Christ. How can this perfect yoke be easy? Because our Lord and Savior bore the wood of the cross, that we might be freed unto the liberty of Christ from the bonds of sin and death (Romans 8:2; Colossians 2:14-15).

"Stand fast therefore in the liberty wherewith Christ hath made us free, and be not entangled again with the yoke of bondage" (Galatians 5:1). We are freed from walking under the yoke of bondage to sin and its captaining powers (Romans 6:14; Colossians 2:14-15) to walking in Faith unto living in the freedom of the quickening Holy Spirit of God (John 8:36; 2 Corinthians 3:17). *"And every man that hath this hope in him purifieth himself, even as he is pure."*

So be purified under the liberating yoke of the faith of Jesus Christ! Jesus is calling, "Come unto me, all ye that labour and are heavy laden, and I will give you rest" (Matthew 11:28). "Come unto me, all"! There is no pre-qualification for being received into this yoke. There is not a training period through which you must pass; indeed, there is not even a requirement of strength of purpose or passion or past purity. There is but one requirement and end – to come unto Jesus as your Lord!

Yet many who yearn for the yoke of Jesus have not yet attained it because they have confessed Jesus as Savior apart from confessing Jesus as Lord. For it is written: "That if thou shalt confess with thy mouth the Lord Jesus, and shalt believe in thine heart that God hath raised him from the dead, thou shalt be saved" (Romans 10:9). It is the Lord Jesus whom must be confessed with our lips. Confessing Jesus as Savior is not the same as receiving the word of God as the Rule of Life.

Believing in the facts of the Lordship of Jesus Christ apart from taking His yoke upon your neck to lead you and guide you, is merely a beginning. It is fact that Jesus is King of Kings and Lord of Lords from whom salvation comes (Revelation 19:16; Philippians 3:20). It is a fact that "Jesus saves," yet receiving Jesus Christ requires more than believing the facts. *"Thou believest that there is one God; thou doest well: the devils also believe, and tremble. But wilt thou know, O vain man, that faith without works is dead?"*

In the English language, having "faith" or "believing" can merely mean accepting something as a fact, apart from making that fact a guiding and immovable principle in life. The English word "trust" brings us closer to this idea of giving ourselves over to that which we believe to be so; yet even this can be worked out as more of a confessional ideal than a constitutional principle or operational reality from which to move in all matters of living and being.

Therefore it is possible for persons to receive the gospel of our Lord Jesus Christ; say they believe in the facts of the matter, accept the salvation of Jesus, even be devoted to the study of the facts of and attestations of scripture, confess all this through baptism before the church – and all the while be apart from having the Faith of Jesus Christ. *"Even so faith, if it hath not works, is dead, being alone."*

Perhaps you are asking, how can this be? Perhaps you yourself accept the facts of scripture, have been baptized, are devoting yourself to studying and living Christian principles – indeed even working through this devotional. Perhaps you have seen the fruit of a changed life as you have moved from outright sin, to a Christian life reflecting what God's written word says is so – *"thou doest well! But wilt thou know, O vain man, that faith without works is dead?"*

If you confess Jesus as Savior and Lord without setting yourself under his Lordship, there is yet the grave need of the Spirit's yoke. It is by the observation of Jesus Himself that those who are near, but not yet firmly yoked, are beset with weariness, are carrying heavy burdens and are filled with unrest in their souls (Matthew 11:28-29). For the reality is that they work alone, by human resolve, decision and strength. Those who are weary, drawn-thin, weighed down with the sins of others and the oppression of the world; those anxious and shaking and wondering where the strength of God, the love of God and their soundness of mind is...do well to pray for the facts of the scripture to be transformed into life (2 Timothy 1:7)!

For though these are led by the facts of salvation, they may have retained their own lordship and may do what they do apart from the Spirit's leading. They may demonstrate an overtly Christian language of belief, a certain interpretation of that belief, and even act upon that belief. Yet the visible outcome of all these seem to appear during worship or Bible study, yet dissolve under the pressures of the world. "Belief" becomes worldly and natural works, sustained with worldly and natural powers, unto worldly and natural ends.

Scripture confirms that faith is to lead our every action; as it is written that "...everything that is not from faith is sin" (Romans 14:23). Jesus confirms that the work of faith can only be what He Himself is doing. "Verily, verily, I say unto you, He that believeth on me, the works that I do shall he do also; and greater works than these shall he do; because I go unto my Father" (John 14:12). These are grave words to the man or woman who loves God and has confessed Jesus as Savior and Lord! *"Yea, a man may say, Thou hast faith, and I have works: shew me thy faith without thy works, and I will shew thee my faith by my works."*

We know this place of works, apart from faith...for once we walked in the counsel of scriptures insofar as we could digest their meaning and work out our life to match what we read. These were the years we spent doing Christian works according to our own heart's leading. There were no healings, few if any miraculous answers to prayer, no manifestations of the resurrection power of

308

Jesus Christ – and we could not and did not perceive the direct leading of the Holy Spirit.

These were arduous years. We knew we were missing something. We knew our lives didn't reflect what we "read about" the power of God. We explained it all away as a matter of theology and the unfolding dispensations of the history of God's work in the church.

All the while, our lives fractured and we spent our time engaging the same helps that the world brings to bear. When we were sick, we went to the doctor first. When we were tired or anxious, we sped down to the local health food store for herbal remedies. We accepted every worldly diagnosis for our problems and picked up the appropriate self-help book for everything from raising our children to communicating better with one another.

That is no longer our story.

So do not despair if you are moving from a similar place, for your faithfulness need only be caught up in the Spirit's yoke under the Lordship of Jesus Christ! And the change is not difficult! Simply receive into the depths of your spirit, the words of the Most High God: "This is my beloved Son, in whom I am well pleased; hear ye him" (Matthew 17:5). "Hear ye," dear brother and sister, "Him!"

"Hear ye him!" As we began listening past words on the page to Jesus as Lord, we moved from a confession of "Jesus as Savior;" and gave Lordship to Jesus in every matter of our lives. We moved from the work of interpreting and applying scripture, to

309

being coupled unto Jesus by the yoke of the Holy Spirit. This change happened in the space of a prayer to be released from any bond which kept us from being apart from our Lord Jesus. Now we are being transformed in practice by God's Holy Spirit in all thinking, all purposing, all praying, all living, all moving and all being!

Accepting Jesus as Lord is the life-long, life-giving work of faith! This is confirmed by Jesus, the author and finisher of faith (Hebrews 12:2). A people seeking the bread of life asked, "What shall we do, that we might work the works of God? Jesus answered and said unto them, "'This is the work of God, that ye believe on him whom he hath sent'" (John 6:28b-29).

If the work of God is belief; is that not also the first and continuous work of our faith?

So we have found that under the yoke of the Spirit, we moved and continue to be moving from weariness and heavy burden, to ease unto rest of soul in Jesus Christ (Matthew 11:28-29). We move now to an ever more continuous voice saying; "This is the way, walk ye in it" (Isaiah 30:21). And now instead of just going to church on Sunday and doing Christian works of our own design, we continually walk in faith under a spiritual yoke. There is a highway "...called The way of holiness; the unclean shall not pass over it; but it shall be for those: the wayfaring men, though fools, shall not err therein" (Isaiah 35:8).

Those who walk this highway walk by the leading of the Holy Spirit "into all truth" (John 16:13). As the Holy Spirit "shall teach you all things, and bring all things to your remembrance, whatsoever I [Jesus] have said unto you" (John 14:26b). We remain fools, but now we are fools only for Jesus Christ (1 Corinthians 4:10).

So NOW we come to what it means to fully say: *"I will shew thee my faith by my works."* In Christ, the "works" of faith are not the carrying of a heavy burden to determine how to live Christ in this world. For if we are in the Faith of Jesus, we are impelled and compelled by the Spirit of God. And God working through us, demonstrates the power-filled evidence of His presence as we do only what the heavenly Father shows us to do, and to speak only what we hear Him speak – all by way of the guiding yoke of the Holy Spirit; our very real connection unto unity in Jesus Christ.

As Jesus did only what His Father showed Him to do, and said only what His Father showed Him to say; so yoked to Him we become ambassadors of the Kingdom of God (2 Corinthians 5:20). This is why James says, *"I will shew thee my faith by my works."* Everything James said or did showed forth Jesus Christ! For it is written that the Lord Jesus Christ Himself is "the author and finisher of our faith" (Hebrews 12:2). So the Faith of Jesus Christ is the basis for and end of all of our works in Christ!

By believing, we take up the Lordship of Jesus Christ and are led of the Holy Spirit in all thoughts and in all things; we are even led of God to will and work according to His good pleasure (Philippians 2:13). Therefore what we do and say is not of our own work, by our own strength, or to our own glory – for all is said and done through Christ to the glory of God (Ephesians 2:10; Romans 11:36).

"And every man that hath this hope in him purifieth himself, even as he is pure." Indeed, as you take up the yoke of Christ, you do so in the supernatural Kingdom of God. That yoke holds you fast even unto the Throne of Grace in all prayer and supplication. Your spirit is led of His Holy Spirit to pray as you ought (Romans 8:26-27). The Lord Jesus Christ himself intercedes for you; and thereby are you led into the unique destiny and the victory that the Lord has prepared for you in Christ Jesus (Romans 8:34,37; Ephesians 2:10).

Yea, a man may say, Thou hast faith, and I have works: shew me thy faith without thy works, and I will shew thee my faith by my works.

Prayer of Response: Yoked in Faith

Please pray aloud with us...

Abba, Father! Thank You for sending Jesus as my Savior and Lord! Thank You for sending Your Holy Spirit that I may be led into all truth! Thank You for sending your Holy Spirit to teach me all things! Thank You that I have such a treasure in my clay jar and for the Scripture which witnesses such great truths!

Please forgive me for anything that I have accepted or done apart from faith. Please deliver me from the world's understanding of "having faith" unto having the Faith of Jesus Christ Alone. (Take time to for personal repentance, supplication and praise as the Spirit leads). *I confess and believe with my heart that Jesus Christ is Lord of all.*

Jesus, I take up Your spiritual yoke. By the Faith of Jesus Christ, I set the 24/7 living and doing of my life under the leading of God's Spirit. Thank You Father for not leaving me alone and orphaned in this world to work alone. Thank You for being with me always, that Your purposes may become my own and the world may know You through me.

Alleluia to my Lord and King, Jesus! Alleluia to the Father! May Your Kingdom come and Your will be done through me...by Your Spirit...on earth, as it is in heaven! In the Name of Jesus, Amen.

Week Six, Day Four – Uncommon Common Good

"But the manifestation of the Spirit is given to every man to profit withal."
1 Corinthians 12:7

"Now the Lord is that Spirit: and where the Spirit of the Lord is, there is liberty."
2 Corinthians 3:17

The Lord has appointed spiritual gifts to man for the common good. The appointment of these spiritual gifts is manifest; that is, made present and visible in the Body of Christ, as each member takes their place according to God's design and will. Where the gift of the Spirit is, there is the Giver of the Gift. Just as the Faith of Jesus Christ does not depart from its Giver and the Love of God is God's Love itself manifest; so then *"the manifestation of the Spirit is given to every man to profit withal!"*

Unity in the Body of Christ is maintained through *"the manifestation of the Spirit"* insofar as each member takes up the gift and measure given by God "For the perfecting of the saints, for the work of the ministry, for the edifying of the body of Christ" (Ephesians 4:12). The perfecting of the Body is the movement of each individual part into its proper design and alignment that the whole may fully stand upright by the Spirit, under Jesus Christ.

The world with its logical, analytical, empirical self-aware words, wars against *"the manifestation of the Spirit...given to every man.*" "For the flesh lusteth against the Spirit, and the Spirit against the flesh: and these are contrary the one to the other: so that ye cannot do the things that ye would" (Galatians 5:17). A man caught in the midst of the desires of the Spirit and the desires of what is of the world becomes paralyzed and does not know what to do. He looks to human frailty and failing and takes up the work of self-purification according to the logic of the world; which is not of God. It is as if the flesh says, "I will train myself and press forward in good works;" as the Spirit says, "I would fill you with the glory of Jesus Christ, if you would give yourself over."

The opposition between what is natural and supernatural is a churning storm-front within the soul; this is why "A double minded man is unstable in all his ways" (James 1:8). Though the heart of this member may be alive in Christ, a pure devotion is lacking. In one moment the world is master, and he speaks, moves and has his being in accordance with the pattern of its teaching. This one remembers his training in the secular schoolroom of science, philosophy, business, art or craft and walks in one accord to produce the natural products each calls forth. This is the pattern of the world operating within him; it is as a crystalline spiritual labyrinthian structure designed to return him always to himself.

This secular man divides the world based upon the evidence of what the eyes see, unto the virtual exclusion of the supernatural origin and direction of all things. A war-front runs through the soul as the secular man works out of a paradigm rooted in self-esteem, self-production, self-actualization and self-preservation. Unknowingly, these dear brothers and sisters are given over to the rebel teachers who say, "How doth God know? and is there knowledge in the Most High?" (Psalm 73:11); even as they cry out for the Good Shepherd to lead them out of this internal and spiritual Egypt.

The world calls, "If you do what you love, eat what you love, take what you love – satisfaction will follow!" And from the beginning, scorecards are given for accomplishing and achieving. Make the grade. Make the report. Get the prize. Make the product. Make your living. Buy what you need. If you want to be a good citizen and have a good life, be productive. Take care of yourself, take care of your family and with what is left over; pay it back or forward to help others so they can have as much as you.

The structures of the world shape a man "to will and to work" according to and for its pleasure. If this were not so, the new man in Christ would not be directed to turn-away from being led by the conforming world, to being led by a transforming God! "And be not conformed to this world: but be ye transformed by the renewing of your mind, that ye may prove what is that good, and acceptable, and perfect, will of God" (Romans 12:2).

There is in the world a religious spirit. The root of religion is found in the origins for the word itself. "Religion" carries both an etymological sense of "binding" and "obligated seeking." A religion in modern terms is defined primarily as "the service or worship of God or a supernatural being" or "a personal set or institutionalized system of religious attitudes, beliefs, and practices"

316

(https://www.merriam-webster.com/dictionary/religion accessed 3/1/2018). Both the root of religion and its present manifestations are to be held before the light of God's leading Spirit.

The manifestation in the world of "religious" structures, including patterns for living, moving and being in accordance with "religion" are often not moored in the "manifestation of the Spirit." For the Holy Spirit glorifies Jesus Christ. And Jesus Himself declares, "The wind bloweth where it listeth, and thou hearest the sound thereof, but canst not tell whence it cometh, and whither it goeth: so is every one that is born of the Spirit" (John 3:8). The leading yoke of the Spirit is as free as the moving of the wind!

As Believers take up the yoke of the Spirit, the authority of God's word confirms they are freed unto unity in the Love of God in Jesus Christ (John 17:26). For it is explicitly written: *"Now the Lord is that Spirit: and where the Spirit of the Lord is, there is liberty."* With the charge: "Stand fast therefore in the liberty wherewith Christ hath made us free, and be not entangled again with the yoke of bondage" (Galatians 5:1).

The Child of God is not bound to natural rituals, or churchly or ritual patterns of behavior, or even patterns of living based on achieving or demonstrating a level of "goodness" or piety; nor do they take up a yoke of works. And these are not led by worldly or religious patterns or pathways; but are led of God Himself. For it is written:

> For as many as are led by the Spirit of God, they are the sons of God. For ye have not received the spirit of bondage

again to fear; but ye have received the Spirit of adoption, whereby we cry, Abba, Father. The Spirit itself beareth witness with our spirit, that we are the children of God: And if children, then heirs; heirs of God, and joint-heirs with Christ.

Romans 8:14-17a

The Lord Jesus Christ does not bind God's children, but calls them. He does not drive His sheep, nor appoint dogs to bite at their heels to keep them. He invites them from the sheep fold into open pastures; but does not make them come. Jesus Christ is the Good Shepherd who gives His life for the sheep (Psalm 23; John 10).

The religious spirit is often hidden in language that sounds heavenly; though it is thoroughly not. Many religious practices and values really find their root in a spirit of "binding" and "obligated seeking," rather than in the liberty of following the leading of Jesus Christ.

So now we have uncovered the root of the matter and can address the deep structures that war against the *"manifestation of the Spirit...to every man to profit withal."* These deep structures are not neutral, as the world itself is in rebellion against God. For it is written, "all that is in the world, the lust of the flesh, and the lust of the eyes, and the pride of life, is not of the Father" (1 John 2:16).

The deep structures that war against the Spirit are of the flesh (Galatians 5:17). Many Believers have not been trained up in the "nurture and admonition of the Lord" (Ephesians 6:4b) but

318

were trained up to either pursue the things of the world; or to deny the things of the world. On the one extreme is the life of the prodigal and on the other, that of the religious.

Both the prodigal and the religious are concerned about the things of the world: one unto the succor of the flesh, the other unto the denial of the flesh. The biblical picture of this bipolar attachment to the world is the Parable of the Prodigal Son, or as it is also known, the Parable of the Two Brothers. Both captain themselves toward worldly ends; one to promiscuous living (Luke 15:12-24) and the other to sacrificial living (Luke 15:25-30).

The younger brother squandered his inheritance in wanton relationships, the elder squandered his relationships in wanton obedience. The younger took the resources of the father and squandered them, the older forsook the relationship with the father by his diligent attention to those resources. As the Loving Father restores the prodigal to Himself, He lovingly entreats the obedient son to receive all that He has and celebrate His love; "Son, thou art ever with me, and all that I have is thine" (Luke 15:31).

The Father celebrates the movement of the younger son from lawlessness into His loving-kindness even as He invites the elder son past the perfection of lawfulness into His arms. Therein is the picture of the wanton and the legalist; the Gentile and the Pharisee; both caught in different manifestations of the world's training - one promiscuous and worldly, the other perfectionistic and religious.

Our loving Father sent His Son to free us from the bondage of achievement. For it is written, "Wherefore henceforth know we no man after the flesh...if any man be in Christ, he is a new creature: old things are passed away; behold, all things are become new" (2 Corinthians 5:16-17). The child of the world is embraced as a child of God.

The enemies of God are buried in the deep structures of the heart. The world champions prodigals and perfectionists who pursue the pride of life (networks and positions of influence or the heroic and all that elevates a person above the work of others); the lust of the eyes (the well-appointed things of life or the perfection of never being wrong); and the lust of the flesh (the satisfaction of experiencing safety, sensuality and outcomes which prove and uphold personal value) (1 John 2:16-17). The "pride of life" or "lust of eyes" or "lust of flesh" are unseen. They are passing remnants buried in the thought-ground of the mind.

Though these deep structures that war against the Spirit are of the flesh (Galatians 5:17), they have a supernatural foundation and power. Worldly patterns of behavior are not neutral or powerless, but manifest the counterfeit spirit through their conforming powers (Romans 12:2). For the "prince of the power of the air" imitates the Spirit of God and beckons all who will be deceived into walking "according to the course of this world," and is presently at work "in the sons of disobedience" (Ephesians 2:2). If you accept what is written in the following excerpts from Ephesians, walking according to the conforming powers of the world is walking out the work of the "prince of the power of the air" in this realm.

> And you hath he [God] quickened, who were dead in trespasses and sins; Wherein in time past ye walked according to the course of this world, according to the prince of the power of the air, the spirit that now worketh in the children of disobedience: Among whom also we all had our conversation in times past in the lusts of our flesh, fulfilling the desires of the flesh and of the mind; and were by nature the children of wrath, even as others.
>
> Ephesians 2:1-3

> But God, who is rich in mercy, for his great love wherewith he loved us, Even when we were dead in sins, hath quickened us together with Christ, (by grace ye are saved;) And hath raised us up together, and made us sit together in heavenly places in Christ Jesus: That in the ages to come he might shew the exceeding riches of his grace in his kindness toward us through Christ Jesus. For by grace are ye saved through faith; and that not of yourselves: it is the gift of God: Not of works, lest any man should boast. For we are his workmanship, created in Christ Jesus unto good works, which God hath before ordained that we should walk in them.
>
> Ephesians 2:4-10

It is written, "in time past ye walked according to the course of this world" but now "God, who is rich in mercy, for his great love wherewith he loved us...hath quickened us together with Christ...And hath raised us up together with Christ" (Ephesians 2:1, 4). In this transformation, the New Birth is displayed as the bondage of the world is rent by the Quickening Spirit. *"Now the*

Lord is that Spirit: and where the Spirit of the Lord is, there is liberty."

As we are transformed in Christ, we move from walking in the realm of the world and according to the patterns of the "prince of the air" to walking in the realm of the Spirit. The old enemy of sin is vanquished in our death in Christ and our resurrection in Him unto being seated "together in heavenly places in Christ Jesus!" (Ephesians 2:6) The cross of Jesus Christ and His Victory over hell publicly displayed the penultimate defeat of the enemy who will finally be cast down in the lake of fire at the culmination of the age (Revelation 20:10).

Since Jesus Christ has defeated sin and death, and we are quickened by the Holy Spirit and our life is now hidden in Christ; we are no longer fleshly men or women captained by the world's conforming powers of sin or death. Believers no longer conform to the patterns of the world and are the transformed and transforming Children of God in Jesus Christ (Romans 12:1-3)! Believers are overcoming ambassadors of the High King who have been rescued from the invisible structures of death and transferred from the stronghold of the enemy unto life in Christ.

Our Lord and King Jesus confirms, "A good man out of the good treasure of the heart bringeth forth good things: and an evil man out of the evil treasure bringeth forth evil things" (Matthew 12:35). Whether these words are attached to world-views, cognitive pathways or neural structures, they arise from significant structures within each person. As it is written:

They are of the world: therefore speak they of the world, and the world heareth them. We are of God: he that knoweth God heareth us; he that is not of God heareth not us. Hereby know we the spirit of truth, and the spirit of error.

1 John 4:5-6

The strong hold of the world upon a man or woman is demonstrated by what they say and by what audience gathers to listen. For the formation of the thoughts of a man are the man. We cannot think one thing and be another. We cannot be at once formed of the world and informed by God's Spirit. This is why the Christian is "in the world" but no longer "of the world" (1 John 4:5-6).

The Believer's battle is not against sin or death for Our Lord Jesus destroyed these enemies and they no longer captain our service (1 Corinthians 15:57; Romans 6:6). Our battle is for the mind, as it is written: "For as he [a man] thinketh in his heart, so is he" and "As in water face answereth to face, so the heart of man to man" (Proverbs 23:7, 27:19). The strongholds raised against God are built in the mind, then manifest in the words of the mouth and the movements of the body. For the mouth and body follow the design and direction of the mind.

Yet the Sons and Daughters of the High King are armed with more than natural weapons! "Blessed be the God and Father of our Lord Jesus Christ, who hath blessed us with all spiritual blessings in heavenly places in Christ!" (Ephesians 1:3). *"But the manifestation of the Spirit is given to every man to profit withal."*

323

Thus are you given the Spirit not only unto your blessing, but also to the benefit of all peoples.

To the Believer, you are an instrument of exhortation and encouragement over the noisy confusion of insistent, worldly thoughts which continually war against the Spirit. To the prodigal or religious, you are an ambassador of the King sent to proclaim the freedom of the gospel of Jesus Christ. *"Now the Lord is that Spirit: and where the Spirit of the Lord is, there is liberty."*

> For though we walk in the flesh, we do not war after the flesh: (For the weapons of our warfare are not carnal, but mighty through God to the pulling down of strong holds;) Casting down imaginations, and every high thing that exalteth itself against the knowledge of God, and bringing into captivity every thought to the obedience of Christ.
> 2 Corinthians 10:3-5

According to scripture then, the spiritual battle is not against the heathen or the sinner or the backsliding or even against your own flesh. *"But the manifestation of the Spirit is given to every man to profit withal."* If you are willing, take up the mighty weapons of warfare against the schemes of the deceiver unto freeing the chained and the lost. The manifestation of the Spirit is for the uncommon, yet common good: *"Where the Spirit of the Lord is, there is liberty."*

Prayer of Response: Uncommon Common Good

Please pray aloud with us...

Heavenly Father, thank You for being a God who purposes within Himself and completes all that is purposed (Isaiah 46:9-11)! The world is filled with its own agendas and designs-for-life. In the Name of Jesus, I put down every thought, every pattern-of-thinking, every indulgent, perfectionist or achieving spirit, every imagination; indeed, every habit of the flesh that departs from Your Word or stands in the way of the Holy Spirit working freely in and through me.

I turn away from what is in the world and of the world; even from what is of the world yet rooted in religion. (As you are led of the Spirit, name each thing and declare in the Name of Jesus that you are putting it behind you and taking up the mind of Christ on these matters).

Thank You Jesus for both saving me from being captained by sin or being lost in death! Thank You Jesus that You have bled, died and rose again to secure my freedom from death and have given the manifestation of the Spirit to me and to all who follow You; that all men and women may profit! Thank You that where You are, there is liberty in the life of the Spirit!

Thank You for inviting me to walk in freedom! I take-up a refreshed walk in You today. May I stand fast in Your Name forevermore without ever again submitting to the yoke of slavery (Galatians 5:1); in accordance with Your Word alone, by Your

Grace alone, in Faith alone, led by Your Holy Spirit alone, to the glory of Your Name alone! Alleluia! Thank You, Lord Jesus!

Author's Note: Please ask the Heavenly Father to dress you for spiritual battle. Tomorrow we take up victory and triumph in Jesus Christ. The Lord may lead you to pray through the day in two parts. We have marked the text where a pause may be of some help.

Week Six, Day Five – Victory and Open Triumph!

"The law and the prophets were until John: since that time the kingdom of God is preached, and every man presseth into it."
Luke 16:16

"For God, who commanded the light to shine out of darkness, hath shined in our hearts, to give the light of the knowledge of the glory of God in the face of Jesus Christ."
2 Corinthians 4:6

"For we wrestle not against flesh and blood, but against principalities, against powers, against the rulers of the darkness of this world, against spiritual wickedness in high places."
Ephesians 6:12

Christ is Victorious! In and by His Spirit you walk in the victory of the High King of Heaven who has sat down at the Right Hand of the Father (Hebrews 10:12). You are seated in Him in the heavenlies and the laurel crown of glory is set upon you already; for the victory of the cross pierces through the nether regions and rends powerless the enemy's strongholds in the lives of the heirs of heaven (Ephesians 2:6; Revelation 12:11).

Walking in the *"light of the knowledge of the glory of God in the face of Jesus Christ"* is as circling Jericho; with a shout the walls fall and you press into the promised land of the kingdom of God this side of glory (2 Corinthians 4:6). You do not take down the stonewalling deceptions of the enemy, thief and destroyer of your own strength, for the Lord is your "strength and shield" (Psalm 28:7)!

How can this be so? Is the watchman-of-your-mind rising again to defend a special anointing or season for the supernatural work of walls falling and the Kingdom advancing? Then let us deal with the mind and look at the grammar of scripture and see what design of God is fixed in the phrase: *"since that time the kingdom of God is preached, and every man presseth into it."*

The dividing line of the Good News of the Kingdom of God is John the Baptist. For John the Baptist fulfilled Isaiah's prophecy in preparing the way of the Lord as the Elijah to come (Isaiah 40:3; Luke 1:17)! Jesus confirms:

> And from the days of John the Baptist until now the kingdom of heaven suffereth violence, and the violent take it by force. For all the prophets and the law prophesied until John. And if ye will receive it, this is Elias, which was for to come. He that hath ears to hear, let him hear.
> Matthew 11:12-15

Since the time of the Baptist, there is not one human being that comes into the supernatural kingdom of God except that it be pressed or violently taken hold of by force. *"The law and the prophets were until John: since that time the kingdom of God is preached, and every man presseth into it."* Is this hard-press a work of natural man? The unraveling answer begins with the Father drawing His chosen unto Himself through His Son (John 6:44) and ends in the revelation that Jesus is the only way unto the Father (John 14:6).

328

By His victory at the cross, the vanquishing of hell, and His resurrection and ascension to the Throne as the Reigning King: Jesus won your victory. There has never been such a force-filled campaign, nor will ever there be again! Jesus' victory was not accomplished with natural warfare.

A merely natural effort could only lead to natural ends because supernatural spiritual relief and nurture abides only in God (Psalm 91). Yet supernatural relief came in the flesh: *"For God, who commanded the light to shine out of darkness, hath shined in our hearts, to give the light of the knowledge of the glory of God in the face of Jesus Christ."* Therefore your press into the Kingdom is not by your own natural strength or power, but in the power of God!

Said another way, if and only if Christian effort begins in the supernatural light of the Almighty, will it shed about the glory of the Kingdom and demonstrate the power of God. For only what is wrought in the light of Christ shining in your heart extends the Kingdom of God. Only what is divinely wrought casts down the invisible spiritual forces arrayed against you (Ephesians 6:12). And that which is divinely wrought is now in us; for the stone has been rolled away from your dead spirit and the *"light of the knowledge of the glory of God in the face of Jesus Christ"* now shines within your heart!

> For though we walk in the flesh, we do not war after the flesh: (For the weapons of our warfare are not carnal, but mighty through God to the pulling down of strong holds;)

Casting down imaginations, and every high thing that exalteth itself against the knowledge of God, and bringing into captivity every thought to the obedience of Christ.

2 Corinthians 10:3-5

Before the *"light of the knowledge of the glory of God"* shown within, what could you do but rely only upon natural strength and human thinking? These old thoughts were formed and fostered apart from Christ and by their very nature are as the walls of a stronghold. Some Believers think there is no power in the thoughts and imaginations of man; yet there is, or God would not bother to fashion divine spiritual weapons to take them down!

"For God, who commanded the light to shine out of darkness, hath shined in our hearts;" therefore the laser-sharp light of God presses from within. Yet where dead thoughts stand as walls in a Believer's mind, the light and power of God cannot break forth. Jesus did not die on the cross to take the minds of His sheep or drive their thoughts into His own captivity. Yet every thought not impelled by "the obedience of Christ" (2 Corinthians 10:5c) is by definition not of God, *"who commanded the light to shine out of darkness."* And what is darker than the human mind and heart?

Even the world celebrates efforts to "enlighten" the human heart and mind with knowledge and thereby affect the darkness of human "thought-worlds." So in education, or by self-help strategies, or by positive self-speak, or cognitive behavior therapy processes, or in developing new coping skills and the like; even the

330

world takes on confusion in the mind and heart with efforts to move man toward intelligent thinking, mental health and a balanced, successful life. Many go to the doctor's and counselor's chairs in hope of inner light; and perhaps there is some value in this physical training of repatterning the mind through human guidance and effort (1 Timothy 4:8).

The Bible more than confirms the need for inner darkness to be dispelled; for it is written: "...the carnal mind is enmity against God: for it is not subject to the law of God, neither indeed can be" (Romans 8:7) and "The heart is deceitful above all things, and desperately wicked" (Jeremiah 17:9). And "whatsoever is not of faith is sin" (Romans 14:23). Confused thinking is a grave threat; for deceit, wickedness, lawlessness and enmity with God all move within the mind from thought...to decision...to act. And the Lord's teaching is clear that an evil thought is as heinous as a manifest act (Matthew 5:22, 28, 39).

Yet God has fashioned and provided divine weapons to bring to bear upon the war front in the mind! These "weapons...mighty through God" cast down "every high thing that exalteth itself against the knowledge of God" (2 Corinthians 10:4-5)! These weapons of God operate within the deepest place of a Believer's inner thoughts.

The tempter cannot defeat these weapons; so he lies. And these lies can become patterns-of-thoughts which stand as walls obscuring what is penetratingly clear. Many Believers suspect that the veil was never torn – at least not in their very own spirit. Yet if you can begin to perceive that the spiritual war-front is in your mind and that upon that field you *"wrestle not against flesh and blood, but against principalities, against powers, against the rulers of the darkness of this world, against spiritual wickedness in high places?"* All praise to God for providing Jesus Christ to light these inner thoughts and enlighten every follow-on step (Psalm 119:105! Praise God for the open triumph of Jesus Christ!

Praise God that the saints lay down the strength of their own lives and take up this open victory by the blood of the Lamb and the word of testimony (Revelation 12:11). Every Believer dies to the "old man" in the New Birth of the Holy Spirit. In the New Birth, the tomb of your dead spirit was quickened with the Light of life (John 1:4, 8:12)! And as you walk in the Faith of Jesus Christ, the grave of your spirit and the tomb of your heart are filled with the laser-sharp, darkness-defeating *"light of the knowledge of the glory of God!"*

Even the veil to the Holiest of Holies was torn! Though once you were a tomb, now you are a temple. In you, Light shines in the darkness, and the darkness cannot overcome it (John 1:5). And "...God is light and in Him there is no darkness at all" (1 John 1:5)!

As with the Temple, so now with you – for upon you and within you, does His light so shine! For the Bride of Christ is not to be conducted by the lamps of the world; but by the light of the Bridegroom Himself. For it is written, "Now is the judgment of this world: now shall the prince of this world be cast out. And I, if I be lifted up from the earth, will draw all men unto me [Jesus Christ]" (John 12:31-32).

The matter of spiritual warfare from a biblical standpoint, is not a matter of overwhelming defeat, but of standing in the open victory of Jesus Christ! Walking in the Spirit is the militant march of the heirs of the kingdom resisting the devil by again and again declaring the victory of the King. For those covered in Christ are set apart for and sealed by the Holy Spirit unto God for the good works of the Kingdom (Ephesians 2:10, 4:30; 2 Timothy 1:9).

"Now shall the prince of this world be cast out" (John 12:31). Now let your every thought; let your every emotion; let your very hearing and doing; "draw all men unto me [Jesus Christ]" (John 12:32). For the work of God is the Faith of Jesus Christ (John 6:29) that draws all people unto the person of our Lord Alone – unto the Light of the World – Jesus Christ (John 8:12)! And Jesus is not somewhere out there to be found out by you; but the Light of the World is already found within you (Matthew 5:14; John 14:16).

Our Lord Jesus cast out the "ruler of this world" thereby destroying the strong-hold of the enemy's bondage over you (John 12:31; 8:36). For it is written, "For this purpose the Son of God was manifested, that he might destroy the works of the devil" (1 John 3:8). And "Having spoiled principalities and powers, he [Jesus] made a shew of them openly, triumphing over them in it" (Colossians 2:15).

An open triumph, in ancient terms, is the military parade celebrating the victory of the conquering king! So all spiritual battles are complete triumphs in Jesus Christ; for the devil has been destroyed and the day of victory already declared. Therefore as we submit to God and stand in resistance, Satan may not captain our service; though the devils roar as if to devour (James 4:7; 1 Peter 5:8-9).

The matter of spiritual warfare, from a biblical standpoint, is not a matter of pressing into a natural Promised Land at Jericho. Nor is it a press reserved only unto the twelve apostles. But it is a press into the spiritual reality of the Reign of God – that the world may know and believe in Jesus Christ (John 17:20-21, 20:29). *"The law and the prophets were until John: since that time the kingdom of God is preached, and every man presseth into it."*

Author's Note: Those who are led to work through today's devotion in two parts may find it profitable to pause here. We encourage you to pray as you are led...

As you walk in the Spirit, you take up the open victory won by Jesus' death, resurrection and ascension over *"principalities, against powers, against the rulers of the darkness of this world"* and *"against spiritual wickedness in high places."* For God purposed in this victory that the "ruler of this world" be cast out and his works destroyed (John 12:31, 8:36; 1 John 3:8). And Jesus openly triumphed over him (Colossians 2:15)!

334

As you walk in the Spirit, you are filled with the light of the knowledge of the glory of God by the leading presence of the Counselor Himself, to will and work according to God's good design for your life (Philippians 2:13; Hebrews 13:21). As you walk in the Spirit, you are comforted by the Comforter Himself. *"For God, who commanded the light to shine out of darkness"* is with you and the darkness is overcome; so the tactics of the adversary need not prevail in you and through you (2 Corinthians 10:5). As you walk in the Spirit, and are guided by the Paraclete Himself unto the power of God in, by and through the victory of the cross and the resurrection of Jesus Christ; you press into the supernatural Kingdom of God (Luke 16:16).

And how do you declare Jesus' victory and press the Kingdom of God in this world? By virtue of "bringing into captivity every thought to the obedience of Christ" (2 Corinthians 10:5). You become a light to the world *"to give the light of the knowledge of the glory of God in the face of Jesus Christ"* so others may see Jesus and be saved. The Light of Jesus Christ breaking forth in you and through you IS His Light shining in victory; that the world may see your good works and glorify your Father in Heaven (Matthew 5:16)!

Jesus Christ the Victorious, the very Light of the World (John 8:12), is now seated upon Heaven's Throne (Hebrews 10:12). All authority in heaven and on earth has been given unto Him (Matthew 28:18). The defeated powers are cast down, the Victorious King has begun His Reign.

335

So now as you walk in the Spirit, what is defeated in heaven may be defeated on earth. So now in Christ, your spiritual battle is won and you may "conquer by the blood of the Lamb" and by the "word of testimony" (Revelation 12:11). And what now must bow under the authority of the High King of Heaven are the defeated forces: those unseen spiritual "things in heaven and things in earth, and things under the earth" (Philippians 2:10b), the *"principalities...powers... rulers of the darkness of this world"* and *"spiritual wickedness in high places."*

> Wherefore God also hath highly exalted him, and given him a name which is above every name: That at the name of Jesus every knee should bow, of things in heaven, and things in earth, and things under the earth; And that every tongue should confess that Jesus Christ is Lord, to the glory of God the Father.
>
> Philippians 2:9-11

Let us take yet one more deep breath in the Spirit for an even deeper plunge into the depths of God's Word. Before going farther, we unfurl the standard upon which this book is written: that we are to walk in the Word of God, by Grace, through Faith of and in Jesus Christ alone, by the leading of the Holy Spirit, to the Glory of God on earth as it is in heaven! Lead on into Truth, dear Holy Spirit...

As we consider the open triumph of Jesus Christ, many ask "when" is this victory achieved? Let us once again go to the grammar of the Greek behind the English translation to find out just what it means that "every knee should bow" and "every tongue confess" the victorious Lordship of Jesus. Surely we note that scholars dedicate pages to what we will give one sentence; and they prove to the world what is true. May God, through these brief words, prove in our hearts what is of His Holy Spirit.

The answer to the question of "when" the power of Jesus' victory manifests is brought forth in the Greek grammatical construction of "the bowing of the knee" and "the confessing of the tongue." In the original language, the form of the verb (aorist subjunctive) is concerned more with the action to be performed, than when the action occurs. As you perceive, the full import of this verbal form does not always translate easily into English as it emphasizes "that" -- not "when" – the simple act of bowing and confessing follows as a direct response to Jesus' Name.

While the King James comes near to this idea with the translations of "should bow" and "should confess;" these must be considered in modern terms. Today, we do not say that a person "should live" at birth and "should die" at death; but express what happens as a result of these completed actions as – a person "shall live" at birth and "shall die" at death.

Jesus has all authority in heaven and earth. Jesus has defeated the foe. So "every knee shall bow" and "every tongue shall confess" Jesus is Lord! As a result of what Jesus has already completed, the powers of darkness are already defeated and must bow in subjection under the authority of Jesus' Victorious Lordship (Colossians 2:15).

Herein is the spiritual Victory of Jesus Christ, which is your spiritual legacy in Christ...if you would walk in it. Herein is the explanation that undergirds the imperatives to: "**Submit** yourselves therefore to God. **Resist** the devil, and he will flee from you" (James 4:7). Can you begin to perceive your victory in submitting to Christ through actively resisting the devil? As you take every thought captive to Christ, you declare the victory of Jesus Christ and the devil must flee (2 Corinthians 10:5; James 4:7).

For Scripture testifies that Jesus Christ was lifted up to "draw all men unto me [Himself]" (John 12:31-32). And it is written that your life is now hidden in the Risen King; where He is, seated on the Throne (Colossians 3:3)! And it is again testified that "...God, who is rich in mercy, for his great love wherewith he loved us...hath raised us up together, and made us sit together in heavenly places in Christ Jesus" (Ephesians 2:4,6).

So, by the mercy and love of God, are you rescued from the powers of this world as you are set under the authority of the Throne of Jesus! As you walk in the Spirit and learn by the leading of the Counselor Himself to will and work according to God's good design; you walk in the power of the Reigning King and unto the NAME of Jesus Christ!

So it is that the weapons of our warfare are not natural, or of this world; the weapon is of the Word of God delivered through His ambassadors and under the power of His Name! All authority in heaven and earth has been given to Jesus Christ; therefore all authority in heaven and on earth is in the NAME of the Reigning King! (Matthew 28:18).

There is not a word **you** speak, prayer **you** utter, or discipleship strategy, ministry outreach effort, or any other work **designed by man** that will break the stronghold of the adversary and build the kingdom of God! Only what is undertaken in every thought "to the obedience of Christ" (2 Corinthians 10:5) is in accordance with, and extends the authority of Christ Himself.

For in submitting every thought to Christ, the devil will flee and you shall vanquish this present darkness by the Name of Jesus Christ; both in your home and in other relationships where God gives you authority (James 4:7). "Wherefore take unto you the whole armour of God, that ye may be able to withstand in the evil day, and having done all, to stand" (Ephesians 6:13). And remember that, by Faith, not one fiery dart of the enemy goes unextinguished (Ephesians 6:16).

Can you perceive the logic of the Holy Spirit? Can you see that you are released from operating under your own authority, to walking under the leading authority of the Word of God? Can you see that your enemy is God's enemy now? Can you see that your mind is the stormed front between two kingdoms? Can you see that as you are led of the Spirit of God and take every thought captive, you speak the life of God into this world? The matter of spiritual warfare is not a power encounter with the devil; that violent work has been finished. Your victory is only a matter of taking up the open triumph of Jesus Christ – today.

The law and the prophets were until John: since that time the kingdom of God is preached, and every man presseth into it.
Luke 16:16

Prayer of Response: Victory and Open Triumph!

Please pray aloud with us...

Heavenly Father, Holy is Your Name! "Thine, O LORD, is the greatness, and the power, and the glory, and the victory, and the majesty: for all that is in the heaven and in the earth is thine; thine is the kingdom, O LORD, and thou art exalted as head above all" (1 Chronicles 29:11). I praise and bless You for establishing Your Kingdom in Victory!

Father, please forgive me for all of the times I have lifted up my own thoughts and followed them in opposition to Your will and Your ways. Please teach me to take every thought into captivity to obedience to Christ by the power of Your Holy Spirit working in me. Thank You for rolling away the stone over my dead spirit and filling me with Light! How great is Your Love; that You commanded the light to shine out of darkness into my heart. How great is Your Love; that I may have the light of the knowledge of the glory of God in the face of Jesus Christ!

Alleluia, Father! My Lord and God, help me to take up the open victory of Jesus Christ! Teach me to understand my place in Your Kingdom and take up the victory of the NAME of Jesus by the leading of Your Holy Spirit. Please train me in matters of spiritual warfare. Please teach me to speak what You

would have me speak and do only that which You would have me do! Let Your Victory break forth through me that You may be exalted among men.   Alleluia!   To King Jesus!   Alleluia, Amen.

Week Six, Day Six – Steadfast Weapon?

"I am he that liveth, and was dead; and, behold, I am alive for evermore, Amen; and have the keys of hell and of death."
Revelation 1:18

"Death is swallowed up in victory. O death, where is thy sting? O grave, where is thy victory? The sting of death is sin; and the strength of sin is the law. But thanks be to God, which giveth us the victory through our Lord Jesus Christ. Therefore, my beloved brethren, be ye stedfast, unmoveable, always abounding in the work of the Lord, forasmuch as ye know that your labour is not in vain in the Lord."
1 Corinthians 15:54b-58

The stakes are high. You will soon see that to walk in the Spirit in the fear of the Lord is to walk as a heavenly weapon (Romans 6:13); but to walk in the fear of human wisdom and by its ways is to significantly deny the Lordship of Christ and the leading of the Holy Spirit. Of those who walk according to the world, it is written: "There is a way which seemeth right unto a man, but the end thereof are the ways of death" (Proverbs 14:12).

Eternal life weighs in the balance as each person decides, "Which way shall I go? The way of God or the way of the world?" And there are only those in Christ and those outside of Christ, there are only those who are covered in the Blood of the Lamb and those who are covered in the iniquity of rebellions.

As your ears are open and your eyes are wide, hear the Holy Spirit and walk in the fear of the Living God who says, "I will instruct thee and teach thee in the way which thou shalt go: I will guide thee with mine eye" (Psalm 32:8). *"I am he that liveth, and was dead; and, behold, I am alive for evermore, Amen; and have the keys of hell and of death."*

So who or what do you fear? Violence shakes our nation as students open fire in schools, citizens massacre Christians in their churches, and malevolence spills forth upon innocents in American homes and marketplaces. A spirit of violence rips at our hearts and shakes the foundations.

In the midst of this churning darkness, where does help come from? Better security systems? Expedited emergency evacuation plans? Contingency studies? Investment in human factors? Surveillance systems? The tumult of these days puts into sharp focus the question, "whom shall I fear...of whom shall I be afraid" (Psalm 27:1a, c). This is not a new dilemma:

> Thus saith the LORD, Stand ye in the ways, and see, and ask for the old paths, where is the good way, and walk therein, and ye shall find rest for your souls. But they said, We will not walk therein. Also I set watchmen over you, saying, Hearken to the sound of the trumpet. But they said, We will not hearken. Therefore hear, ye nations, and know, O congregation, what is among them. Hear, O earth: behold, I will bring evil upon this people, even the fruit of their thoughts, because they have not hearkened unto my words, nor to my law, but rejected it.
> Jeremiah 6:16-19

Will you come to the Lord "ask for the old paths, where is the good way, and walk therein" that you "shall find rest for your souls" (Jeremiah 6:16)? Will you "Hearken to the sound of the trumpet" (Jeremiah 6:17)? To do so is to take up the fear of God alone and to declare immediate release to any spirit of fear which binds your heart. For the Comforter is with you even now...

> I, even I, am he that comforteth you: who art thou, that thou shouldest be afraid of a man that shall die, and of the son of man which shall be made as grass. And forgettest the LORD thy maker, that hath stretched forth the heavens, and laid the foundations of the earth; and hast feared continually every day because of the fury of the oppressor, as if he were ready to destroy? and where *is* the fury of the oppressor?
>
> Isaiah 51:12-13

In the midst of this present darkness, the Lord sees your comings and goings and perceives your innermost thoughts and loves. The Lord moves in the earth to gather a people unto Himself (Jeremiah 23:3). *"I am he that liveth, and was dead; and, behold, I am alive for evermore, Amen; and have the keys of hell and of death."*

"The fear of the LORD is the beginning of wisdom: and the knowledge of the holy is understanding" (Proverbs 9:10). To fear the Lord is to set the eyes of your mind and the affections of your heart upon Him; it is to look to Him for all guidance, all provision, all work and all sustenance even unto life itself. To fear the Lord is to acknowledge that all riches, all life, all holiness, all power, all judgment, all victory and all authority reside in Him and pour forth from Him (1 Chronicles 29:11; Matthew 6:13). To fear the Lord is to trust in the leading of His Spirit alone and to walk in footsteps patterned according to prayer unto "THE LORD OUR RIGHTEOUSNESS" (Jeremiah 23:6).

344

Walking in the Spirit is walking in the fear of the Triune God in the obedience of love; for as the Father loves the Son; so the Son says and does only what His Father commanded Him to do; and so the Spirit calls to mind everything that Jesus has said that you may keep the Risen King's commands (John 14:21,23; John 15:10). Walking in fear is walking in the living Word of God according to Divine design, purpose and plan. And Jesus says, "If ye love me, keep my commandments. And I will pray the Father, and he shall give you another Comforter, that he may abide with you for ever" (John 14:15-16).

Therefore the fear of the Lord is the only path for the people of God; it is the one purposed in, designed by, and leading into the perfection of the Living God. "As for God, his way is perfect: the word of the LORD is tried: he is a buckler to all those that trust in him" (Psalm 18:30). It is the path of Jesus Himself as "the way, the truth and the life" (John 14:6). *"I am he that liveth, and was dead; and, behold, I am alive for evermore, Amen; and have the keys of hell and of death."*

"Where is the fury of the oppressor?" (Isaiah 51:13b) God, in His mercy, does not leave us in this life to be devoured by heaven's rebel. Jesus Christ, the Righteous has vanquished this foe! Yet where and when THE LORD OUR RIGHTEOUSNESS is not feared; the fear of the world and the tactics of the world prevail upon God's people. "Know ye not, that to whom ye yield yourselves servants to obey, his servants ye are to whom ye obey;

whether of sin unto death, or of obedience unto righteousness?"
(Romans 6:16)

The world commands obedience to its natural ways and
promises results. To the extent that the Church of the Lord Jesus
Christ accepts the worlds' training and tactics; the power of the
cross is overshadowed and the people of God walk in bondage to
fear apart from walking in the freedom of Jesus Christ. Why?

The training and tactics of the world focus the mind and
heart of many in this generation on natural solutions and natural
authorities. This is a modern picture of Rabshakeh, commander of
the fearsome armies of Assyria, standing on the walls of Jerusalem
calling out to the people in a language they understand, saying:

> ...hearken not unto Hezekiah, when he persuadeth you,
> saying, The LORD will deliver us. Hath any of the gods of
> the nations delivered at all his land out of the hand of the
> king of Assyria? Who are they among all the gods of the
> countries, that have delivered their country out of mine
> hand, that the LORD should deliver Jerusalem out of mine
> hand?
>
> 2 Kings 18:33,35

The ambassadors of the world are quick to tell you that the
LORD our God has no power and no concern for His people. Do
modern Believers face this veiled provocation as the men on the
walls of Jerusalem did in Hezekiah's day? That cloud of witnesses
"held their peace, and answered him [Rabshakeh] not a word" (2
Kings 18:36). Then King Hezekiah took the matter before the
Lord:

Of a truth, LORD, the kings of Assyria have destroyed the nations and their lands, And have cast their gods into the fire: for they were no gods, but the work of men's hands, wood and stone: therefore they have destroyed them. Now therefore, O LORD our God, I beseech thee, save thou us out of his hand, that all the kingdoms of the earth may know that thou art the LORD God, even thou only.

2 Kings 19:17b-19

And Jerusalem was saved by the miraculous hand of God as the enemy was drawn to another front and disaster overtook the standing forces of fear (2 Kings 19:32 ff.).

Is the watchman-of-your-mind asking what this has to do with our modern fears or being a steadfast weapon? Is the watchman-of-your-mind doubting that believing in Jesus has anything to do with believing that God is a miracle-working God? Is the watchman calling to mind all of the times you have cried out to God and not seen a miracle working in your own life?

Are you therefore justified in saying that a biblical worldview is to be abandoned in matters that are better handled by the surer methods of locked doors, gated communities, back-ground checked volunteers, church security cameras and systems, and whatever other methods will dissuade violence and protect the people of God from the invasion of violence and fear?

Remember Rabshakeh did encounter the security forces of Jerusalem on its walls. The city was defended with the resources available to it – but in the face of the presenting annihilation, the people posted their watchman and stood their ground trusting not in themselves – but in God. At least this time, the people of God

347

remembered the Name of their God and set all of their hope before Him.

Fast-forward to today. Are you standing against whatever invades the walls of your heart, your home and your church with the weapons formed of man, or of God? In the face of the fear and violence shaking our nation in the language it understands, what is your response? How will you prevail?

> Death is swallowed up in victory. O death, where is thy sting? O grave, where is thy victory? The sting of death is sin; and the strength of sin is the law. But thanks be to God, which giveth us the victory through our Lord Jesus Christ. Therefore, my beloved brethren, be ye stedfast, unmoveable, always abounding in the work of the Lord, forasmuch as ye know that your labour is not in vain in the Lord.
>
> 1 Corinthians 15:54b-58

There is victory over the darkness in one Name in heaven and upon earth – in the Name of the King of kings and the Lord of lords – Jesus Christ! For God has "delivered us from the power of darkness, and hath translated us into the kingdom of his dear Son" (Colossians 1:12); therefore He did not die on the cross only to leave us defenseless against the marauding enemy who "as a roaring lion" walks the earth "seeking whom he may devour" (1 Peter 5:8 b).

You are delivered unto the Kingdom of God! Rejoice that your name is written in the Book of Life; for once this occurs, the spirits shall flee from you as you walk in obedience in the love and power of the Risen Lord! Jesus said:

I beheld Satan as lightning fall from heaven. Behold, I give unto you power to tread on serpents and scorpions, and over all the power of the enemy: and nothing shall by any means hurt you. Notwithstanding in this rejoice not, that the spirits are subject unto you; but rather rejoice, because your names are written in heaven.

Luke 10:18-20

Their rejoicing was not in earthly authority, but in heavenly victory made manifest through them over the thief who comes "but for to steal, and to kill, and to destroy" (John 10:10b). And what now for you...will you take up the "sword of the spirit, which is the word of God?" (Ephesians 6:17b) Will you speak a word from heaven or a word from earth?

Just as words pour forth from heaven's throne; words pour forth from the realm of darkness (Psalm 19; John 8:44; Revelation 12:10b). Just as blessing is a substantial word spoken in accordance with God-given position and authority; so lies and curses are substantial words pouring forth from the father of lies. For it is written: "Death and life are in the power of the tongue" (Proverbs 18:21a). The unbridled tongue, "...is a fire, a world of iniquity...that it defileth the whole body...setteth on fire the course of nature; and...is set on fire of hell" (James 3:6); "it is an unruly evil, full of deadly poison" that man cannot tame (James 3:8).

Brother Paul acknowledges that we are either instruments of righteousness or unrighteousness (Romans 6:13). Once again, if we peel back the English and look at the Greek word for "instrument"; it is hoplon, which Strong's defines as "an instrument, arms, weapons." (Strong's 3696). So Paul is right-on.

In our living, moving and having our being – we either are weapons of righteousness or weapons of unrighteousness. We either wield "the sword of the spirit, which is the word of God" (Ephesians 6:17b) or we take up worldly, idle speech for which we will someday give a reckoning (Matthew 12:36).

As we speak, we are either weapons of the kingdom of God as ambassadors of reconciliation manifesting the Light of God in a lost and dying world – or we are weapons of open rebellion speaking in concert with a world at enmity with God (2 Corinthians 5:20; Matthew 5:14-16). For what is of the flesh, wars openly against matters of the Spirit of God (Galatians 5:17). And we may choose to be a weapon of righteousness or unrighteousness with every word we speak.

"Though sticks and stones may break bones," it is a lie that words "shall never hurt me." For Jesus declares that words spoken lead to life or condemn unto death.

> A good man out of the good treasure of the heart bringeth forth good things: and an evil man out of the evil treasure bringeth forth evil things. But I say unto you, That every idle word that men shall speak, they shall give account thereof in the day of judgment. For by thy words thou shalt be justified, and by thy words thou shalt be condemned.
> Matthew 12:35-37

And how does the treasure of a good or evil word break forth in this world? From the lips of man. Creation fell and man was deceived by the twisting power and promise of Satan's words. In the beginning, the hiss of the snake in the garden drew Eve into discourse with open evil; so today the lion's roar throughout the world draws people into open discourse with the same predator.

The Lamb-Who-Was-Slain, whose blood set us free from sin and death, has defeated the roaring and hungry lion. Most Believers lift up the cross and perceive that Jesus is seated-on-the-throne. Do they also believe or even know to believe that Jesus is the Christus Victor; the one who has defeated Satan in triumph both on earth and under the earth? Do they know that Jesus died and death is defeated?

Jesus descended to hell for three days whereupon the cup of God's wrath continued pouring out; that the punishment that was to be ours, would be His:

> Forasmuch then as the children are partakers of flesh and blood, he [Jesus] also himself likewise took part of the same; that through death he might destroy him that had the power of death, that is, the devil...For verily he took not on him the nature of angels; but he took on him the seed of Abraham. Wherefore in all things it behoved him to be made like unto his brethren, that he might be a merciful and faithful high priest in things pertaining to God, to make reconciliation for the sins of the people.
>
> Hebrews 3:14,16-17

The wrath of God is poured out unto Christ on the cross and unto "the pains of death" (Acts 2:24). The "pains of death" describe the righteous judgment of God fulfilled in the eternal wages of sin. Yet, Jesus paid it all – even in descending to hell to take upon himself the curse of death. And hell is now defeated, for the resurrection is proof that death could not defeat Heaven's King! As it is written, "He [David] seeing this before spake of the resurrection of Christ, that his soul was not left in hell, neither his flesh did see corruption" (Acts 2:31).

From that which Jesus Christ assumed, we are redeemed: Christ took on flesh, Christ endured sin, Christ was accused of Pilate, crucified, died and buried...Christ descended to hell. And what did Christ do there? The same that Christ did on earth. Jesus proclaimed and heralded the victory of the cross; which is the victory of God; "that through death he might destroy him that had the power of death, that is, the devil" (Hebrews 2:14).

> For Christ also hath once suffered for sins, the just for the unjust, that he might bring us to God, being put to death in the flesh, but quickened by the Spirit: By which also he went and preached unto the spirits in prison.
> 1 Peter 3:18-19

And this preaching was to what end? The end of the gospel: "to make reconciliation for the sins of the people" (Hebrews 2:17b). And how did Jesus do this? By taking upon Himself our punishment...even unto death and Hades: "But he was wounded for our transgressions, he was bruised for our iniquities: the chastisement of our peace was upon him; and with his stripes we are healed" (Isaiah 53:5). For the Lord said, "...I looked, and there was none to help; and I wondered that there was none to uphold:

therefore mine own arm brought salvation unto me; and my fury, it upheld me" (Isaiah 63:5).

And in the fury of God and by the arm of God, salvation has come. For the keys of victory over death and Hades are no longer in the hands of the foe, but in the hands of our God. *"I am [JESUS] he that liveth, and was dead; and, behold, I am alive for evermore, Amen; and have the keys of hell and of death."*

> Death is swallowed up in victory. O death, where is thy sting? O grave, where is thy victory? The sting of death is sin; and the strength of sin is the law. But thanks be to God, which giveth us the victory through our Lord Jesus Christ.
>
> Therefore, my beloved brethren, be ye stedfast, unmoveable, always abounding in the work of the Lord, forasmuch as ye know that your labour is not in vain in the Lord.
>
> 1 Corinthians 15:54b-58

In Christ, dear brother or sister, you do not labor in vain. Since Jesus Christ has overcome death and the world (John 16:33); you are delivered from the evil one (1 John 2:13). As you live and move and have your being in this world, you may defeat the menacing and roaring foe; as in Christ you take up what Jesus has given you in His Victorious Name.

For it is written that the saints of God overcame the devil "...by the blood of the Lamb, and by the word of their testimony; and they loved not their lives unto the death" (Revelation 12:11). This is a victory accomplished this side of heaven by the speaking of "the word of...testimony" (ibid). This is a victory accomplished this side of heaven by loving Jesus Christ, for the Perfect Love of the Lamb drives out all fear (1 John 4:18b). This victory is accomplished this side of heaven at the cross by our Lord Jesus Christ.

Thanks be to God that by the Blood of the Lamb, Believers are now weapons made fit to proclaim the Kingdom of God. Let us bring to bear the words of life. Let us die to the fear of man and take up the fear of God Alone and cast off all darkness...

> ...knowing the time, that now it is high time to awake out of sleep: for now is our salvation nearer than when we believed. The night is far spent, the day is at hand: let us therefore cast off the works of darkness, and let us put on the armour of light.
>
> Romans 13:11-12

Taking up the armour of light...let us walk in the open victory of our Lord Jesus Christ!

Prayer of Response: Steadfast Weapon?

Please pray aloud with us...

Heavenly Father, You created the heavens and the earth out of nothing. From chaos You bring creation, from darkness – light. From the death of Jesus Christ, You bring new life! And the life You give is eternal; from this time on and forevermore! For the keys are now in the hand of the King of kings and Lord of lords! Alleluia! All praise to You, Elohim! God of heaven and earth!

354

In the name of Jesus, I renounce the training and tactics of this world. In the name of Jesus, by the Blood of the Lamb and according to scripture, I acknowledge that my citizenship has been transferred from the world unto the Kingdom of God. In the name of Jesus, I now hearken to the sound of the trumpet and take up the ancient paths and walk therein!

I confess and believe that Jesus Christ has defeated death and hell; therefore I am not only released from fear, but am also given the armor of light that I may be a weapon of righteousness! And so I am – not by my own strength – but by taking up the victorious cross of my Lord! So now, I lift high the cross with the shout of Alleluia to the King of kings and Lord of lords! Thank you, Jesus, for giving Your life that I might live in the victory You secured unto all eternity, from this day forth and forevermore!

I pray that by Your Holy Spirit I may walk in the fear of God alone in the obedience of love. For as the Father loves the Son; so the Son says and does only what His Father commands Him to do. Please Holy Spirit, call to mind everything that Jesus has said that I may keep the Risen King's commands (John 14:21,23; John 15:10).

Please forgive me for every worldly, idle word that I have spoken. Please teach me to take up "the sword of the spirit, which is the word of God," that in all I say and do, I speak the word of life. Come, Holy Spirit! Lead me in the ancient paths...as confirmed in the Scriptures, to the Glory of God alone, by Grace, through Faith, by the leadership of the Holy Spirit in the NAME of Jesus! Amen.

Week Seven, Day One – War Inside

"But all things that are reproved are made manifest by the light:
for whatsoever doth make manifest is light."
Ephesians 5:13

"For ye were sometimes darkness, but now are ye light in the Lord:
walk as children of light: (For the fruit of the Spirit is in all
goodness and righteousness and truth;) Proving what is acceptable
unto the Lord. And have no fellowship with the unfruitful works of
darkness, but rather reprove them."
Ephesians 5:9-11

The war-front of light and darkness is the collision of two kingdoms. The battle between these two powers is evidenced by what men and women do and say, though the front itself is hidden and invisible. For the divine weapons of warfare are not appointed against flesh and blood or against what is seen – but against what is unseen, undercover and kept in secret (2 Corinthians 10:4).

The ground where the powers of heaven and hell collide is not the external landscape of the battlefield; but the internal ground or "inscape" of the mind and heart. This spiritual line cuts through the mind of every Believer as what is of the world works against the Word of God as proclaimed "on earth as it is in heaven" (Matthew 6:10). The mind can be likened to a war room where the Spirit of God breaks forth in words and counsel set in accordance with the High King of Heaven; even as the Deceiver breaks in with whispers of dark deceptions and temptations set to thwart the Word of God and steal, kill and destroy (John 10:10).

Many Christians believe they go to the bedroom prayer closet to battle the enemy and this is not forbidden – but the spiritual war room is not limited to a physical space behind closed doors or to the quiet, open place of a park or garden. The war room is the secret place of your very own mind where two-kingdoms under two opposing and undiluted standards; battle to command your thoughts. And in your thinking, you either take up the standard of the world or the standard of God – for His glory and your life.

The war between heaven and hell is for more than your salvation after you die; it is for your mind, heart, soul and body this side of heaven. The enemy would hijack everything you say, everything you do, everything you think and thereby influence all that you have. Jesus Christ, Heaven's High King has died that you may live, move and have your being in Him – forever (John 17:3; Acts 17:28). And forever begins the moment that you know Him (Psalm 90:1). Forever is now.

Jesus Christ has given His life-blood to forever set you free from being the bond-servant of the world and its captaining darkness. By His victory and your word-of-confession, your citizenship is transferred to heaven, and you are sealed with the presence and power of the Holy Spirit (Romans 3:24; Colossians 1:13-14; Ephesians 1:13). Now a substantial line is drawn over you by the blood of Jesus Christ and by God's power you are sheltered as a redeemed of the Lord!

The power of Jesus' Blood is the basis for overcoming victory (1 Corinthians 11:24-30)! Though the battles wage; the war is won! *"For ye were sometimes darkness, but now are ye light in the Lord: walk as children of light: (For the fruit of the Spirit is in all goodness and righteousness and truth;) Proving what is acceptable unto the Lord."*

The Deceiver is overcome "by the blood of the Lamb, and by the word of...testimony" (Revelation 12:11). So what Christ has accomplished in His death and resurrection is attested to and confirmed by your witness – and in Christ you press back the enemy – even unto the secret war room of your mind. Then as you live out the faith of Jesus Christ, the NAME of the Lord is glorified on earth (2 Corinthians 4:13-14). *"Walk as children of light: (For the fruit of the Spirit is in all goodness and righteousness and truth;) Proving what is acceptable unto the Lord."*

What is at stake in your witness of "living, moving and having your being" in Christ is the glory of God manifest in the 24/7 NOW of life (Acts 17:28). As you submit every thought to the power of the Holy Spirit unto the praise of His NAME, then begins the overcoming victory in the war room of your mind as every stronghold, presumption, opinion, high proud word or thought raised against the knowledge of God is defeated and taken into captivity to Christ (2 Corinthians 10:4-6)! As you bring your thoughts to Christ, you take up the witness-mantle and *"all things that are reproved are made manifest by the light: for whatsoever doth make manifest is light."*

Our Lord Jesus did not win a partial victory over Satan at the cross. He did not win your eternal life and your living damnation. He did not establish His NAME in heaven, and withdraw His power and dominion from earth. The King won your eternal life and "exalteth the horn of his people" in this creation (Psalm 148:14). The King established His NAME forever and is seated on the Throne and He has exalted you to be His ambassador in the earth. Therefore, the banquet table of the King is not only to be set in the heavenlies, but also in the midst of the powers on earth. "Thou preparest a table before me in the presence of mine enemies: thou anointest my head with oil; my cup runneth over" (Psalm 23:5, 35).

And how is this table of the King established? How is the NAME of Jesus manifest in the earth? First – by your setting every thought, word and deed under His rod and staff, which are His dominion, His headship, His leadership, His protection, His provision; indeed His very Presence, by the Holy Spirit. Second – by His Word accepted and proved by your following on after Him in all you believe in your mind, heart and soul. And third – by you manifesting the will of God with your body through spoken words and the doings of your hands. In essence, you become a living sacrifice of praise declaring: "But thou art holy, O thou that inhabitest the praises of Israel" (Psalm 22:3)!

360

...all people; princes, and all judges of the earth: both young men, and maidens; old men, and children; let them praise the name of the Lord for his name alone is excellent; his glory is above the earth and heaven.

Psalm 148:11-14a

As you glorify Jesus, you continually reprove fear, human wisdom, passions, and all attentions even unto death – and run toward Christ alone. Your life substantially declares, "Yea, though I walk through the valley of the shadow of death, I will fear no evil: for thou art with me; thy rod and thy staff they comfort me" (Psalm 23:4).

So then, dear friend, can you perceive the leading word for today's devotion is established in your spirit? *"For ye were sometimes darkness, but now are ye light in the Lord: walk as children of light: (For the fruit of the Spirit is in all goodness and righteousness and truth;) Proving what is acceptable unto the Lord. And have no fellowship with the unfruitful works of darkness, but rather reprove them."* Do you see how this is not an ephemeral or insubstantial word, but is tried and true of the King Himself? As it is written:

And Jesus answered him, The first of all the commandments is, Hear, O Israel; The Lord our God is one Lord: And thou shalt love the Lord thy God with all thy heart, and with all thy soul, and with all thy mind, and with all thy strength: this is the first commandment.

Mark 12:29-30

361

Then saith Jesus...it is written, Thou shalt worship the Lord thy God, and him only shalt thou serve.

Matthew 4:10

Scripture is clear. We are to follow the Good Shepherd alone, we are to worship and serve God alone, we are to "love the Lord" with all of our heart, soul, mind and strength" (paraphrase of Mark 12:29). In so doing, we *"have no fellowship with the unfruitful works of darkness, but rather reprove them."*

Take hold of these words and the war-front in your mind will resolve and your life will be transformed. For it is the world and its captain that have diluted the pure devotion to Jesus Christ by deluding the sons and daughters of light into believing they first serve people, systems, organizations and communities – then the NAME of Jesus. This is an inversion which divides heaven and earth asunder in that the power of God is not manifest.

With the confession that Jesus is Lord; a Believer sets all matters of "living, moving and having their being" under Him. Thereby a Christian thinks all things and does all things to honor and glorify the NAME of the Lord Jesus (1 Peter 4:11); and by the leading of His Holy Spirit shines with the light of the glory of God wherever they walk (John 16:13-16). The Christian walking in light, serves Jesus alone, and is led by His Spirit alone according to the Word alone in all they do and say. As they are so led, the light of heaven shines in the darkness. So "Let your light so shine before men, that they may see your good works, and glorify your Father which is in heaven" (Matthew 5:16).

So now it is time for some difficult questions, for the spirits that are in the world must be reproved that light may be made manifest. And reproof comes only through conviction and conviction is the work of the Holy Spirit. For it is written that when the Advocate comes, "He will reprove the world of sin, and of righteousness, and of judgment" (John 16:8).

What says the Holy Spirit of God to these questions: Is it possible to serve personal goals alongside Jesus? Or health and fitness, and then the Kingdom? How about a career or family; and Jesus? Or church and Jesus? Or a country and Jesus? What about recreation or "fun" – and Jesus? Religion and Jesus? Doctrine and Jesus? Spiritual warfare and Jesus? Or any other craft or art, and then Him? Or even your own needs, then Jesus? Can you love yourself, or love others...and then love Jesus? (Deuteronomy 11:1; 1 Corinthians 16:4; Romans 12:9).

Most voices in the world teach you to do all of these. Yet in first serving any other power, person or thing in heaven or earth: we reprove the Good Shepherd and His dominion, His headship, His leadership, His protection and His Word. We choose another rod and staff as our comfort and guide. We glorify the things of man, or ourselves, or even our families or religion – above God. *"But all things that are reproved are made manifest by the light: for whatsoever doth make manifest is light."*

Are you ready to establish victory in your war room? Reprove any thought contrary to the Word of God. *"Proving what*

363

is acceptable unto the Lord." For what is brought to light is made light!

As you turn to Jesus alone, the light of heaven shines upon you and in an instant, you are made light. As you look to Jesus, and reprove all devotion of mind, heart, body and soul to created things or powers; you move from darkness to light. Transformation in the Lord takes place as darkness is made light. Freedom in Christ is tied to the cross and Throne of heaven; not to personal reflection, self-improvement, penance or therapy. For it is written:

For ye were sometimes darkness, but now are ye light in the Lord: walk as children of light: (For the fruit of the Spirit is in all goodness and righteousness and truth;) Proving what is acceptable unto the Lord.

Is the watchman-of-the-mind saying this is impossible? Is a voice crying out in you that it is reasonable and practical to make your life about your work, your church and your family? Is your experience exclaiming that miracles died with the apostles so the paths of therapy, penance and self-help are the best pathways toward walking in freedom and light? Are you hearing a whisper that all this about what is dark being made light is so heavenly it is no practical good? Or maybe, the tears are falling or hope is rising...

Tell the watchman-of-the-mind to stand down; "...as it is written, Eye hath not seen, nor ear heard, neither have entered into the heart of man, the things which God hath prepared for them that love him" (1 Corinthians 2:9). "For ye were sometimes darkness, but now are ye light in the Lord!"

The world measures wealth in providing currency, goods, status, and influence. The "abundant life" is the fashionable, well-fed, well-dressed, well-appointed life of personal success and fulfillment, of "being all you can be" and of bringing home the prize of luxurious living. The design of the world is for productivity, efficiency, accomplishment and recreation; toward overflowing homes and extended vacations; less labor and better technology; more personal time, more hobby time, more play time, more idle time and all in all accordance with "making your dreams come true" or "living into your gifts." Clearly, all of these can arise from service to the heart and mind of man.

What God has prepared extends beyond what man imagines. What God has prepared extends beyond what man can accomplish. What God has prepared can be achieved by Him alone, through you as you walk in the Spirit, pursuing the person of the Lord Jesus Christ and the work prepared by Him for you. For it is written: "...without faith it is impossible to please him: for he that cometh to God must believe that he is, and that he is a rewarder of them that diligently seek him" (Hebrews 11:6).

The treasure of heaven is poured out upon those who press forward, in the blinding light of faith "believe that he is, and that he is a rewarder of them that diligently seek him" (ibid). And most if not all saints believe that in Christ, they have treasure in heaven; for scripture is immanently clear on this priceless, astonishing, extravagant reward. We praise and bless God and sing "Alleluia" that despite our rebellion in Adam, we are brought out of the garden unto the presence of God in the New Jerusalem – the city of the High King! Yet, there is also a treasure open to us on earth...

So what NOW? To apprehend this open treasure, we must go back to where we began. Now we are at the hidden and invisible front itself; where the divine weapons of warfare operate against what is unseen, undercover and kept secret. We come to the deepest corners of the war room of the mind where the Spirit of God breaks forth and the Deceiver whispers worldly wisdom and ways.

Before going on, will you pray together aloud with us?

Jesus, Your word is true. Sometimes I was in darkness, but now I am in the light of the Lord and walk as Your child. You say, I am Your child and that I am also Your sheep. Your word says, "The LORD is my shepherd; I shall not want" (Psalm 23:1). Your word says, "The thief cometh not, but for to steal, and to kill, and to destroy: I am come that they might have life, and that they might have it more abundantly" (John 10:10).

Thank you, Lord for life to the full. In Your Name, the NAME of Jesus I believe what is written and command any unbelief or agreement with the spirit of the world to depart. For in You, believing is seeing. Let Your Word alone, by Your Spirit alone, be in my mind, on my lips and in my heart. May this be so in the NAME of Jesus and to the Glory of the Father in Heaven. Amen.

Are you wondering about this abundant life on earth? Are you longing for this overflowing cup and well-dressed table set in the midst of enemies? Press past yourself and all the hurt and pain and Jesus will meet you there. *"For ye were sometimes darkness, but now are ye light in the Lord: walk as children of light."*

Be confirmed in the Spirit. For His Word and Promise is sealed in scripture, "...your Father knoweth what things ye have need of, before ye ask him" (Matthew 6:8)...

> Therefore I say unto you, Take no thought for your life, what ye shall eat, or what ye shall drink; nor yet for your body, what ye shall put on. Is not the life more than meat, and the body than raiment?....Which of you by taking thought can add one cubit unto his stature? And why take ye thought for raiment? Consider the lilies of the field, how they grow; they toil not, neither do they spin: And yet I say unto you, That even Solomon in all his glory was not arrayed like one of these. Wherefore, if God so clothe the grass of the field, which to day is, and to morrow is cast into the oven, shall he not much more clothe you, O ye of little faith? Therefore take no thought, saying, What shall we eat? or, What shall we drink? or, Wherewithal shall we be clothed? (For after all these things do the Gentiles seek:) for your heavenly Father knoweth that ye have need of all these things. But seek ye first the kingdom of God, and his righteousness; and all these things shall be added unto you. Take therefore no thought for the morrow: for the morrow shall take thought for the things of itself. Sufficient unto the day *is* the evil thereof.
>
> Matthew 6:25-26, 28-30

The reward of God extends beyond the provision of our needs. God extravagantly adorns his creation, even the grasses of the field. Yet they do not spin and toil; they take no thought of what is to be; they do not wonder if God is faithful – or not. They have no mind; therefore in them, there is no battle-front. They simply open when the appointed season comes and the light shines.

Hear the promise of God; you are released to be as the lilies. You are released to glorify God with a pure devotion; you are released from darkness to light; from striving with the devil in the war room of your mind and making your way in the world under its authorities. *"For ye were sometimes darkness, but now are ye light in the Lord: walk as children of light: (For the fruit of the Spirit is in all goodness and righteousness and truth;) Proving what is acceptable unto the Lord."*

The abundant treasure of heaven is Jesus Himself, through Whom you know the Father (John 8:19, 14:7), have the mind of Christ (1 Corinthians 2:16), know the work Christ has prepared for you (Ephesians 2:10), and in Whom you experience the wisdom and power of God as the Holy Spirit dwells in you (1 Corinthians 1:24; John 14:15-16). This is why you may walk in the light of God! For as you are led of the Holy Spirit, you manifest the Light of the World, which is Jesus (John 8:12). Who says, "I am come a light into the world, that whosoever believeth on me should not abide in darkness" (John 12:46).

And here is where we come to the victory of light over the darkness. Here is where we come to the table set before your enemies. Here we come to the victory in the deepest zones of the war room of your mind. For the light of God breaks forth from heaven, through Jesus Christ – upon you. "Wherefore he [God] saith, 'Awake thou that sleepest, and arise from the dead, and Christ shall give thee light" (Ephesians 5:14).

The battle in your war room is covered in the victory of Jesus Christ and sealed by His Blood, in His NAME and by His power. Tomorrow, we will delve farther into what it means to walk in this victory; but for today, receive the gift that God has given you; the provision of heaven on earth:

> For God hath not given us the spirit of fear; but of power, and of love, and of a sound mind. Be not thou therefore ashamed of the testimony of our Lord.
> 2 Timothy 1:7-8a

Will you receive the gift of God to you and in you and for you? Will you accept this gift *"of power, and of love, and of a sound mind?"* (2 Timothy 1:7) Will you walk now in the light of the Kingdom of God, free from the shadow-land of the war-front? Will you be for Christ – all in all? Will you worship and serve Him alone? Will you reprove all darkness and walk in the light of Christ? Will you receive the banquet and cup of victory set in the fields of this world?

Today, we have come through the darkness to the light that illumines the commanding verse of this devotion. Herein lies the recompense of God through the blood of Jesus Christ to those who confess with their lips and believe in their hearts and have been born again of God's Spirit: *"But all things that are reproved are made manifest by the light: for whatsoever doth make manifest is light."*

How will you know? "Walk as a child of the light!" Turn to the Light alone, who is Jesus alone; walking unto the Spirit alone, according to the light of Scripture alone. For God alone has declared victory amidst your enemies with an overflowing cup. God alone has prepared this table for you. All glory, honor and praise to the King Jesus! Amen.

Prayer of Response: War Inside

Please pray aloud with us...

Heavenly Father, You said, "Let there be light," and light shown out of the darkness. Thank You that the light of Jesus has shined in my heart. Thank You that in Christ, I am a new creation; this not of my own doing, but Your gift received in faith. Please shine Your light in me now and bring to my mind those things which I may reprove in the Spirit. In the Name of Jesus, I pray the Holy Spirit penetrates deep and convicts me of sin, righteousness and judgment (John 16:8).

Come Holy Spirit, reprove all that is dark that I may walk in the Light of Jesus. (As the Holy Spirit leads, reprove and take up the confession that is shown).

In the NAME of Jesus I reprove...

In the NAME of Jesus I confess that I believe...

Jesus, You died that I may have life in Your Name. I long to know You, Jesus. I long to shine with Your Light. I long to live for the glory of Your Name, in the freedom You won for me at the cross. I long to walk as a Child of the Light demonstrating all goodness, righteousness and truth. And Your word declares that this longing is fulfilled.

Let me rise up by the power of the Holy Spirit working in me that I may be Your witness with every thought, word, and deed. For it is written: "Now are ye light in the Lord: walk as children of the light." So let it be in me now, and forevermore. So let me prove "what is acceptable unto the Lord" in all that I think in my mind, say with my lips and do with my hands.

I love You, Jesus. I praise You, Jesus. I raise up Your Name, Jesus. And ask all of this for Your Glory alone, according to Scripture alone, by Faith alone, in the hope of Grace alone, through the Holy Spirit alone, in the Name of Jesus. Amen and Alleluia!

Week Seven, Day Two – Strength on the Final

"Wherefore I put thee in remembrance that thou stir up the gift of God, which is in thee by the putting on of my hands. For God hath not given us the spirit of fear; but of power, and of love, and of a sound mind."
2 Timothy 1:6-7

"For all they did cast in of their abundance; but she of her want did cast in all that she had, even all her living."
Mark 12:44

The Lord has carried you through thirty-seven days of "Walking Unto the Spirit;" and you are drawing near to the end of these days. *"Wherefore I put thee in remembrance that thou stir up the gift of God, which is in thee by the putting on of my hands."* As you are walking in the Spirit, let us remember together that at Jesus' baptism the Dove descended and *"...immediately the Spirit driveth him into the wilderness"* (Mark 1:12). Then the Lord pressed into His own 40 days.

Let us also stir up the memory that as Jesus completed these days of prayer and fasting, the Tempter himself came armed with the very accurate words of scripture to shift the Lord's path out of season into a ministry set to a deceptive interpretation and application of scripture. In response Jesus simply spoke the word, and the Enemy departed (Luke 4:1-15). As it was with Jesus, so it has been with us as we have written and completed these "40 Days." So it may also be for you in your season.

372

"Wherefore I put thee in remembrance that thou stir up the gift of God, which is in thee by the putting on of my hands." These "40 Days" have you walked in the faith of Jesus Christ in the gospel of our Lord which, "is the power of God unto salvation to every one that believeth" (Romans 1:16). If you believe, it is promised that as you turn in Christ and leave sins behind; having once waded through the waters of baptism, "ye shall receive the gift of the Holy Ghost" (Acts 2:38b)!

The word of the Lord is true (Psalm 33:4)! So it is that you have been led of the Holy Spirit in this desert season ever deeper toward your calling and destiny in Jesus Christ (Ephesians 4:1); for this was the design and purpose for which the Lord captained the writing of this book. Yet if you are not baptized, or are sensing a press in your spirit toward baptism; do not tarry. For the Son of God Himself received the Holy Spirit as He left the private life for the public life of witnessing unto the Kingdom.

"Put thee in remembrance that thou stir up the gift of God, which is in thee." As you have walked this nearly 40 day journey unto the Spirit, you have willingly followed Jesus. Have you like the Lord Jesus before you, left behind the old and taken up the new during this journey? As you have, the old ways of understanding have passed away, and behold – the new has come (paraphrase, 2 Corinthians 5:17). The spiritual man or woman is guided by the Holy Spirit "into all truth" (John 16:13) in living the gospel-life of being a Spirit-led worker of the Kingdom of God!

As you are washed in the repentance of baptism, filled with the Holy Spirit, and stirred up by His anointing in this desert journey; will you give to the Lord all that is washed, filled and stirred? Or will you go back and give to the Lord only out of your overhead, or your quiet time, or your churchly time away from the real work of life (as the world puts it). Will you die to yourself, take up the Spirit's mantle and give over every living breath to be lived in the power and life of God? Will you acknowledge that God is "the God of the living" (Mark 12:27b); or will you forget the testimony of Scripture and the power of God and walk forward in a fractured life? (Mark 12:24)

"For all they did cast in of their abundance; but she of her want did cast in all that she had, even all her living." Many give unto the Lord Jesus a little portion of the abundance of their life. What about religious rituals, or prayer beads, or spiritual disciplines, or liturgies, or weekly ministries, or religious practices, even the memorizing of scripture verses or the giving of alms, or a life's devotion to the mission field as a witness to Jesus? Even these things for some brothers and sisters may be likened to the giving of the rich; for what is retained is greater than what is given (Mark 12:41-44).

In the spiritual walk, what is asked is not for the giving of part of yourself, or even some of your thoughts, or even 10% of your time, or even a career devoted to the treasure or talents as a tithe unto God. The Lord Jesus is not the Lord only of your increase or your abundance. He is Lord of more than your vocation. *"But she of her want did cast in all that she had, even all her living."*

Jesus is calling you: *"cast in all, even all!"* What does this mean? Take up the gifts that God has given to you, dedicate yourself completely to "living, moving and having your being" in Him (Acts 17:28). Burn like a stirred-up fire; as a living, blazing, lamp of the Holy Spirit of God! *"For God hath not given us the spirit of fear; but of power..."*

> For though we walk in the flesh, we do not war after the flesh: (For the weapons of our warfare are not carnal, but mighty through God to the pulling down of strong holds;) Casting down imaginations, and every high thing that exalteth itself against the knowledge of God, and bringing into captivity every thought to the obedience of Christ.
> 2 Corinthians 10:3b-5

Place your life in the treasury box. Bring "into captivity every thought to the obedience of Christ" (ibid). For scripture confirms you are to live free and clear of fear, cowardice, timidity, and the plethora of worldly or churchly arguments, pretenses, expectations, speculations and presumptions, even to live free of the lusts of the eyes, flesh and the very pride of life (which is each and every independent thought and follow-on word or action), which rises up apart from obedience to Jesus Christ (1 John 2:16-17).

"For God hath not given us the spirit of fear; but of power. Wherefore I put thee in remembrance that thou stir up the gift of God, which is in thee by the putting on of my hands." In dying to

the self and to the world (repentance), and through your confession (baptism); you have received the gifts of God won for the Glory of God by the Blood of Jesus Christ. Therefore, to the Glory of God, let it be said that *"God hath not given **you** the spirit of fear; but of power!"*

How can this be? Jesus *"cast in all, even all!"* The Lord came down from heaven, became man, humbled himself even unto death upon a cross, and gave himself as a sacrifice once and for all that those who received Him may have life in His NAME (Hebrews 10:1-18; Philippians 2:7-11; John 20:31). The Lord has given you new life in Him (Ezekiel 36:26; John 3:5; Romans 6:4, 2 Corinthians 5:17; Ephesians 4:24; Colossians 3:10; 2 Peter 1:4)!

The Lord is not asking you for what He has not already provided to you. The Lord Jesus is not asking you to come to Him by your own power, or through religion, or ritual, or piety, or conservative worldview, or whatever else you might think is a pathway unto Him. He has given all of Himself for you and to you; that you may give all of yourself for Him and to Him. For in losing your life, you find your life – Jesus Christ, the Eternal and Present (Matthew 10:39-40).

> For thus saith the high and lofty One that inhabiteth eternity, whose name is Holy; I dwell in the high and holy place, with him also that is of a contrite and humble spirit, to revive the spirit of the humble, and to revive the heart of the contrite ones.
>
> Isaiah 57:15

The Eternal One by His Blood, has opened heaven and in, by and through the abiding presence of His Holy Spirit, has given a spirit of power! Therefore, you have the power to set down your life; even unto each and every thought, that Jesus might raise it up again. In this the eternal life becomes present now. In this the power of God becomes a present reality. In this, you no longer strive with flesh and blood – even your own (Ephesians 6:12). In this, you become an ambassador of reconciliation and witness to the gospel of Jesus Christ (2 Corinthians 5:18-20). In this you demonstrate the victory of Jesus Christ over all powers, authorities; indeed everything in heaven and on earth and under-the-earth, as you do and say what Jesus does and says through you; "not with enticing words of man's wisdom, but in demonstration of the Spirit and of power" (1 Corinthians 2:4).

For what Jesus Christ has won is yours-in-Him: both salvation unto eternal life and the defeat of the devil (Romans 8:37; 1 John 4:4; 1 John 5:4; Revelation 12:11). For Jesus gave all of His Life for all of your Life. This "Great Exchange" is not for the heavenly life alone; but that the life, light and power of Heaven may break forth through you into this present darkness; into your home, your church, your school, your community, your friends, even unto strangers with whom you connect in daily business...that you may be a witness to the resurrected power of Jesus Christ (Acts 1:8) and others may know He is who He says He is – "not with enticing words of man's wisdom, but in demonstration of the Spirit and of power" (1 Corinthians 2:4).

Yet be warned. The ultimate purpose of Jesus Christ is not to save you, or to defeat the devil. The ultimate purpose of the Lord is to glorify the Name of the Father! If you walk only in the joy of your personal salvation or of your spiritual victory over the devils; you do not have the fullest mind of Jesus Christ. For the great cause for which Jesus died is but served by your salvation and deliverance:

> Now is my soul troubled; and what shall I say? Father, save me from this hour: but for this cause came I unto this hour. Father, glorify thy name. Then came there a voice from heaven, *saying*, I have both glorified *it*, and will glorify *it* again.
>
> John 12:27-28

The gifts of God manifest in accordance to what is written in scripture to the ultimate Glory of God! The spirit of power given to each one of God's witnesses is testified to by Jesus Christ Himself (Acts 1:8; Luke 10:19). And since there is only One Spirit, the manifestation of this power is defined by God, and not by man; for who sits above whom?

Does man as the clay pot declare to the One who brought forth light out of darkness and to Whom all glory belongs; what God means by His word? Or does God as the Potter and Jesus Christ as the Living Word, reveal unto man by the Holy Spirit what God's Word means (Isaiah 45:5-11)? We believe the latter is true; and must be true for anyone whose life is dedicated to glorifying God and worshipping in Spirit and in Truth (John 4:23-24); for it is written "He [God] revealeth the deep and secret things: he knoweth what *is* in the darkness, and the light dwelleth with him" (Daniel 2:22). So let us take God at His Word...

For certainly the power of God is not controlled or directed by any man or woman. For it is the Potter who makes the clay and breathes whatever life or power there is in it – as a gift (James 1:17a). *"God hath...given us the spirit...of power, and of love, and of a sound mind."* A clay vessel remains a clay vessel though there be a treasure within it:

> For we preach not ourselves, but Christ Jesus the Lord; and ourselves your servants for Jesus' sake. For God, who commanded the light to shine out of darkness, hath shined in our hearts, to *give* the light of the knowledge of the glory of God in the face of Jesus Christ. But we have this treasure in earthen vessels, that the excellency of the power may be of God, and not of us.
>
> 2 Corinthians 4:5-7

If any man say that they have power apart from God; so they are. In this case, the glory is misplaced and the vessel of power turns inward on itself – such are the powers of this present darkness (Matthew 12:35). And Jesus is clear that there are both "children of the kingdom" and "children of the wicked one;" and it is in the former in which the light of God shines (Matthew 13:38; 2 Corinthians 4:6). Alleluia *"God hath not given us the spirit of fear!"*

Jesus Himself dwells in you via the Spirit as you walk unto the glory of God, witnessing the gospel in a broken and death-bound world (John 14:26; 1 John 2:20, 27, 4:13). Thereby Jesus teaches those who follow Him to walk in power...

> Verily, verily, I say unto you, He that believeth on me, the works that I do shall he do also; and greater *works* than these shall he do; because I go unto my Father. And whatsoever ye shall ask in my name, that will I do, that the Father may be glorified in the Son. If ye shall ask any thing in my name, I will do *it*.
>
> John 14:12-14

Yes, we are aware that many Christ-followers believe the "greater works" of God were reserved only for the time of the first apostles; indeed, many also believe there is no gift of apostleship outside of the Twelve and the untimely-born Paul. Some even believe that there is no spirit of prophecy or spirit of power alive in the Church as the time for this dispensation has passed.

Each man has the right to his own belief; and since God respects the free will of a man to choose, so do we. We have only our witness to offer. *"Wherefore I put thee in remembrance that thou stir up the gift of God, which is in thee by the putting on of my hands. For God hath not given us the spirit of fear; but of power, and of love, and of a sound mind."*

What is written is True, because God is True (John 17:3). And we have seen the power-filled confirmations of God (Mark 16:20; 1 Corinthians 2:4-5)! The greatest of which is the salvation of souls – to which we will return in a few paragraphs.

In addition to salvation, we can attest first-hand to seeing the supernatural power of God. In Spring 2017, the Lord spoke to

380

my wife's spirit at dusk on a Sunday evening to, "Come to the end of the driveway, for I am passing by." As she stood at the road-edge, she saw the Lord walk over the farm fields before her in the cool of the evening, ahead of a storm, with a blazing light in His Hands and shrouded in a veil of glory! (Habakkuk 3:4)

Our Lord also walks into the midst of the meeting of a group of friends and all there have seen without even blinking; a missing thumb grow anew, mangled joints completely restored, scoliosis removed, knees rebuilt, limbs lengthened, broken-bones healed, autism depart and apnea healed! We have seen countenances of joy restored, marriages restored and the bondage of debt, legalism, depression and fear shattered; and even many more miracles!

And we attest that this power is not of us, but is of God; manifest in our midst by Jesus Christ alone and His Holy Spirit alone according to His Word alone. Who to the Glory of His Name alone sometimes brings angels in our midst. At other times He works through our hands, and those of our very everyday brothers and sisters – that these gospel-works might break forth at the sound of His NAME and glorify His Father who is in Heaven! *"Wherefore I put thee in remembrance that thou stir up the gift of God, which is in thee by the putting on of my hands. For God hath not given us the spirit of fear; but of power..."*

And we are not special evangelists or great apostles...we are simple followers of Jesus Christ witnessing to you from a quiet, wood-heated, antebellum farmhouse in the fields of Ohio. And the hand of the Lord has touched us through the Friends of the Bridegroom here. We are unremarkable and of low estate...indeed, we are as nothing. But our GOD IS who He says He is and does what He says He does! And all of this to the glory of HIS NAME! Alleluia! Alleluia!

> For thus saith the high and lofty One that inhabiteth eternity, whose name is Holy; I dwell in the high and holy place, with him also that is of a contrite and humble spirit, to revive the spirit of the humble, and to revive the heart of the contrite ones.
>
> Isaiah 57:15

Is the watchman-of-your-mind crying out for proof? Photographs, medical reports, and so on? There are plenty of documented miracles. Gently, we confess that it is not our purpose or heart to "prove" miracles are real. This is a devotional work; if you believe you will see miracles, then our own experience is that seeing signs, wonders, and miracles will follow. For in Christ, believing is seeing!

Yet in season, we considered God's Word as True and refused to accept any interpretation apart from what is written:

> Verily, verily, I say unto you, He that believeth on me, the works that I do shall he do also; and greater *works* than these shall he do; because I go unto my Father. And whatsoever ye shall ask in my name, that will I do, that the Father may be glorified in the Son. If ye shall ask any thing in my name, I will do *it*.
>
> John 14:12-14

Believing Jesus at His Word changes everything. Surely the Name of Jesus is not a talisman to be uttered; yet surely at the Name of Jesus, God's power breaks forth through those who are His empty clay jars filled with the treasure of heaven. Those taking all thoughts captive, and in love abiding under the leading hand of the Holy Spirit.

Why do we speak so boldly? Because this has been and is our *belief* and is now our *experience*. As we believed and took up the Word of God as our standard; as we prayed and devoted ourselves to setting all thoughts captive to Christ; as we died through the Spirit to ourselves, fasted and prayed – Jesus fulfilled His Word. Now we *experience* the power of heaven breaking through our emptied and emptying clay vessels *everyday*. The light of God shines into our darkness. And this is not surprising is it? Once again, we turn to what is written:

> For God, who commanded the light to shine out of darkness, hath shined in our hearts, to *give* the light of the knowledge of the glory of God in the face of Jesus Christ. But we have this treasure in earthen vessels, that the excellency of the power may be of God, and not of us.
>
> 2 Corinthians 4:6-7

Surely no manifestation of God's power restoring health or extending limbs can begin to compare to being transformed from spiritual death to new life and seeing the face of Jesus Christ! Though we see Him dimly as in a mirror; yet we know Him and have gone from being alone in the world, to being a temple of God's Holy Spirit; from being conscripted to sin to having liberty

383

in Jesus Christ; from striving to know God via study and exposition, to continually abiding in Him and thereby knowing and experiencing God via the personal and direct revelation of the Holy Spirit! Alleluia! *"Wherefore I put thee in remembrance that thou stir up the gift of God, which is in thee by the putting on of my hands. For God hath not given us the spirit of fear; but of power, and of love, and of a sound mind."*

New birth in Christ is the greatest miracle of all! At the cross Jesus conquered sin and death so with the resurrection power of the Gospel every witness crushes the head of the falling foe and is victorious by the Blood of the Lamb shed at that cross through the word of testimony! The power of the Gospel heals more than an earthly limb...for by the power of God is a spiritual man or woman transferred from bondage to sin and death and born again of water and the Spirit unto God!

And in the whispering and the shouting of the Gospel, the power of God manifests as you glorify God the Father, Jesus Christ and the Holy Spirit in giving the testimony of being lost; then found – of being dead; then alive – of being forsaken; then being loved – of being powerless in the world; to living a life hidden in Christ seated upon heaven's throne.

This is the story of a spiritually dead clay pot, being made spiritually alive as an eternal son or daughter of the Divine God of Heaven who places His Holy Spirit Life in you! *"Wherefore I put thee in remembrance that thou stir up the gift of God, which is in thee by the putting on of my hands. For God hath not given us the spirit of fear; but of power, and of love, and of a sound mind."*

Could it be that your testimony of being born-again in Jesus Christ is the greater work of the gospel? King Jesus came down from Heaven as the Living Son of God (Matthew 1:23), then passed from this eternal life, through the gates of separation from His Father at the cross (Matthew 27:46), to eternal life (Acts 1:9-12). But you were born spiritually dead and separate from God, and through Faith in Christ, have passed from eternal spiritual death and torment, into that which is completely new: eternal life with God!

In giving your testimony of being transformed from spiritual death to spiritual life, are you not testifying to a work Jesus did not himself experience? Are you not testifying to that which is the gift of God and the result of Jesus going to the Father?

Jesus is the Son of God who is with us always until the very end of the age. He has sent power from on high that we might be His witnesses from where we stand unto the very ends of the earth. Those who worship Him, do so in Spirit and in Truth in the twenty-four seven living of life; and this by His hand leading in His Spirit, according to the Father's will and unto His Glory! Surely, "God hath not given us the spirit of fear; but of power, and of love, and of a sound mind."

The spirit of power that God gives glorifies God through extending the work of the cross of Jesus Christ into the here-and-now life. Upon your salvation, you become an adopted child of the Most High God. By the Blood of the Lamb and the word of your testimony, you bring to bear the victory of the cross over the tempter; even the prince of this world who beguiles the nations.

- At the cross, Jesus defeated the foe, "And having spoiled principalities and powers, he made a shew of them openly, triumphing over them in it" (Colossians 2:15).
- In our lives, the victory of the cross is brought to bear as we battle "...against principalities, against powers, against the rulers of the darkness of this world, against spiritual wickedness in high places" (Ephesians 6:12b).

The victory of heaven becomes each believer's own victory, as they walk unto the Holy Spirit and offer themselves, the all of their living, as a clay vessel dedicated to Heaven's Treasure. Therefore what is bound at the cross, is bound. What is loosed at the cross, is loosed. And we may pray, "Thy kingdom come. Thy will be done in earth, as it is in heaven!" (Matthew 6:10) And Jesus' prayer is fulfilled:

> Father, glorify thy name. Then came there a voice from heaven, saying, I have both glorified it, and will glorify it again. The people therefore, that stood by, and heard it, said that it thundered: others said, An angel spake to him. Jesus answered and said, This voice came not because of me, but for your sakes. Now is the judgment of this world: now shall the prince of this world be cast out.
>
> John 12:28-31

For the victory won by Jesus Christ was not to glorify God once and for all time. Nor was it for a certain time or for a few specially anointed people; but to glorify God again and again, through all eternity through all people who believe Jesus and take up His cross.

> Surely he hath borne our griefs, and carried our sorrows: yet we did esteem him stricken, smitten of God, and afflicted...But he was wounded for our transgressions, he was bruised for our iniquities: the chastisement of our peace was upon him; and with his stripes we are healed.
>
> Isaiah 53:4-5

What is bound at the cross by Jesus and loosed through His resurrection and ascension, is yours as a gift of God alone, received of Faith alone, given by Grace alone, to the praise of God alone, by Jesus Christ alone now abiding in us through the Holy Spirit alone (Matthew 18:18). This is the power of the Gospel of Jesus Christ, that you might know Him now and forevermore; and having life in His Name, declare His victory over the darkness. Will you take up the witness-mantle and give all of your living unto God?

For all they did cast in of their abundance;
but she of her want did cast in all that she had, even all her living.

Prayer of Response: Strength on the Final

Please pray aloud with us...

Heavenly Father You said, "Let there be light," and light shown out of the darkness. Thank You that the light of Jesus has shined in my heart. Thank You that in Christ, I am a new creation; this not of my own doing, but Your gift received in faith. Thank You, that by the cross of Jesus Christ and the presence of the Holy Spirit, I need not walk in fear, but may walk in the gifts you give of "a spirit of power, and of love and of a sound mind."

Lord Jesus, You shed your precious blood that I may have life in Your Name. Lord Jesus, Your word says that at Your Name, everything in creation will bow. Lord Jesus, I cry out for Your Holy Spirit to demolish any strongholds within which prevent me from walking fully in the gifts God has given. Please help my unbelief that I may come to an ever-firmer conviction and deeper understanding of walking in the spirit of power given of God.

I pray all this in the Name of Jesus. Amen.

Week Seven, Day Three – Unmingled Love

"Wherefore I put thee in remembrance that thou stir up the gift of God, which is in thee by the putting on of my hands. For God hath not given us the spirit of fear; but of power, and of love, and of a sound mind."
2 Timothy 1:6-7

"Herein is my Father glorified, that ye bear much fruit; so shall ye be my disciples. As the Father hath loved me, so have I loved you: continue ye in my love. If ye keep my commandments, ye shall abide in my love; even as I have kept my Father's commandments, and abide in his love. These things have I spoken unto you, that my joy might remain in you, and that your joy might be full."
John 15:8-11

The Love of God indwelling and compelling the Trinity is promised via the presence of the Holy Spirit unto you, as you abide in and keep Jesus' commandments. Yet the love of man indwelling and compelling the world persecutes those born "after the Spirit" by way of taking on the very same "name." For we do not use one word to describe Love rooted in God and another word for the "love" rooted in the world.

So the root of Love is muddied and covered over with the language, ideals and passions of the world. The confusion of our language begets confusion in what love even is, or does, or does not do. There is not a church or family that is not beset with dealing with the onslaught of worldly love against God's Love. Worldly love is a captivating counterfeit.

389

Wherefore I put thee in remembrance that thou stir up the gift of God...for God hath not given us the spirit of fear; but of power, and of love, and of a sound mind.

The world says it is possible to have many types of love and many objects of love. Even Christians as a matter of expression say that we love our choices, our dreams, our gadgets, our "look," our homes, our dogs, ourselves (indeed self-esteem, which is really self-love, is a trait fostered and encouraged in each one of us), our hobbies, our families, our church, and our God. If pressed, most people would say these are not equivalencies; that though we use one word to describe our dog and our God there are, of course, distinctions within our meaning as we love with different kinds and priorities of love.

Has this breakdown in language which confuses Divine Love and worldly love hijacked the design and heart of our most fundamental relationships? Scripture does warn that a person speaks what is the outflow of the heart (Luke 6:4) and that life and death; blessing and cursing, all come with and through our words (Proverbs 18:21; James 3:10).

To what extent do we rub together human ideas about love, or even religious ideals of love, over God's scriptural witness and the testimony of Jesus Christ Himself? To the extent that such blurring has occurred, the counterfeit love of the world obscures God's Love; which by definition is rooted in God alone and is solely His to define. For "God is love" (1 John 4:8b).

In both the Old and New Testaments we are instructed, "Thou shalt love the Lord thy God with all thy heart, and with all thy soul, and with all thy strength, and with all thy mind; and thy neighbour as thyself" (Luke 10:27; Deuteronomy 6:4-5; Leviticus 19:18). Notably, these are two separate commands in the Old Testament. Hear them separately and you will hear them more clearly:

> Hear, O Israel: The LORD our God is one LORD: And thou shalt love the LORD thy God with all thine heart, and with all thy soul, and with all thy might. And these words, which I command thee this day, shall be in thine heart: And thou shalt teach them diligently unto thy children, and shalt talk of them when thou sittest in thine house, and when thou walkest by the way, and when thou liest down, and when thou risest up. And thou shalt bind them for a sign upon thine hand, and they shall be as frontlets between thine eyes. And thou shalt write them upon the posts of thy house, and on thy gates.
>
> Deuteronomy 6:4-9

> Thou shalt not hate thy brother in thine heart: thou shalt in any wise rebuke thy neighbour, and not suffer sin upon him. Thou shalt not avenge, nor bear any grudge against the children of thy people, but thou shalt love thy neighbour as thyself: I am the LORD.
>
> Leviticus 19:17-18

The teaching and testimony of God is simple and clear: Believers are to love God with all of our being, all of the time, with all people and in all places. Love is to be unmingled as God commands us to give "all" of ourselves and lives in love to Him. The visible evidence of our unmingled love of God is manifest in our extending God's Love to others. We are to love God; then as a matter of loving in God, love others. In this way, love is undivided.

The greatest command to "love God" with "all" our heart, soul, mind and strength, all of the time and wherever we go, is the standard by which the second command is fulfilled. In loving God alone, there is no co-mingling together of worldly priorities or definitions of love or ways of loving. And God reserves unto Himself what the definition and outworking of Love is. St. John summarizes this outworking this way: "Beloved, let us love one another: for love is of God...for God is love" (1 John 4:7a, 8b).

Some call this Love of God; "Radical Love." And it sounds radical. Even Jesus radically shakes up His disciples by pressing them to pursue Him first; before self and above any others. Jesus says, "If any *man* come to me, and hate not his father, and mother, and wife, and children, and brethren, and sisters, yea, and his own life also, he cannot be my disciple" (Luke 14:26).

Wherefore I put thee in remembrance that thou stir up the gift of God...for God hath not given us the spirit of fear; but of power, and of love...

As before, so again grammar is grammar and scripture interprets scripture in these deep matters of Divine Love and its worldly counterfeit. St. John explicitly distinguishes between the love of the world and the Love of the Father and writes: "Love not the world, neither the things that are in the world. If any man love the world, the love of the Father is not in him" (1 John 2:15).

Peeling back the English and looking at the Greek behind "the love of the Father," we find the genitive case – which is the case of possession. We encountered this grammatical construction back in Week Three, Day Two where we saw that the "faith of Jesus Christ" is anchored in and belongs to Christ Himself and is therefore – His own. Later on, in Week Five, Day Five we also saw this possessive form in that the "armour of God" is God's own. Putting on "God's Armour" involves putting on Divine Armour, not a mere similitude or spiritual copy.

In the matters of Divine Love and worldly love, putting on God's Love involves putting on the former, not a mere earthly copy! Consider again this genitive construction translated into the informal possessive: "If any man love the world, the Father's love is not in him" (translation ours, 1 John 2:15b).

Whose Love is not in the man? The Father's. Is the Father the object of love? No, as that is a different form of grammar. The Father is the one in whom Love is kept. Why does "any man love the world?" Because this man is not impelled and compelled by the Father's Love; but is instead captained by worldly love.

To love the world is to be at enmity with God. "That which is born of the flesh is flesh; and that which is born of the Spirit is spirit" (John 3:6). So love in God, is of God. And love which is of man, is of man. "But as then he that was born after the flesh persecuted him that was born after the Spirit, even so it is now" (Galatians 4:29).

Wherefore I put thee in remembrance that thou stir up the gift of God...for God hath not given us the spirit of fear; but of power, and of love....

"God is love" (1 John 4:8)! Praise God! Love is kept in God as "God is love!" And Jesus says to each one of His own, *"As the Father hath loved me, so have I loved you: continue ye in my love."* And so in Christ, through the indwelling presence of the Holy Spirit, you are caught up in this Divine Love for *"God has given us the spirit...of love."*

Can you see the fulfillment of Jesus' words in your life? "They are not of the world, even as I am not of the world" (John 17:16). You yourself are held fast in God's Love. And God's Love is so substantial and essential that we may dwell within this Love! Our Lord promises: *"If ye keep my commandments, ye shall abide in my love; even as I have kept my Father's commandments, and abide in his love."*

Abiding in Love is abiding in God's Love. Therefore, a Believer can walk in One Love alone; which is not a worldly love interpreted to include many loves and sources of love. Worldly love is not kept in God, and therefore is set against God:

> Ye adulterers and adulteresses, know ye not that the friendship of the world is enmity with God? whosoever therefore will be a friend of the world is the enemy of God. Do ye think that the scripture saith in vain, The spirit that dwelleth in us lusteth to envy?
>
> James 4:4-5

Said another way, "No servant can serve two masters: for either he will hate the one, and love the other; or else he will hold to the one, and despise the other" (Luke 16:13). *"If ye keep my commandments, ye shall abide in my love; even as I have kept my Father's commandments, and abide in his love."*

Is the interpreter in your mind rising up to say, how can this be? Everyone knows that the scriptural context for serving two masters is a conversation about money! Let the watchman of your mind hear again the appeal of God through St. John: "Love not the world, neither the things that are in the world. If any man love the world, the love of the Father is not in him" (1 John 2:15).

Money is a created thing in the world, is it not? So are marriages, families, countries, careers, churches and any other thing or person this side of heaven. Jesus says, "He that loveth his life shall lose it; and he that hateth his life in this world shall keep it unto life eternal" (John 12:25). So be careful dear brother or sister with love; "Do ye think that the scripture saith in vain, The spirit that dwelleth in us lusteth to envy?" (James 4:5)

Loving God alone with all of the heart, soul, strength, and mind (Luke 10:27) is a pure devotion to and in God's Abiding Love (John 15:9). Such a man or woman walks in the Father's Love; then through Jesus and by the Holy Spirit, the Father's Love flows through this Christian unto the world.

Can you see the pathway of God's Love? It is always from Him and then through Him and then unto others (John 14:6, 10:9). Walking in the love of God thereby culminates in continuing everywhere in and extending to everyone the Father's Love: *"As the Father hath loved me, so have I loved you: continue ye in my love."*

Here the controversy ends and the joy begins! For so many have been striving to divide their hearts between God and the world! Love cannot be divided, just as God cannot be divided! For God is Love! There is One God! There is One Love! *"If ye keep my commandments, ye shall abide in my love; even as I have kept my Father's commandments, and abide in his love. These things have I spoken unto you, that my joy might remain in you, and that your joy might be full."*

Living in the joy of God's Love has two aspects. First, knowing its substance or source; and second, apprehending its manifestation in Jesus Christ, and by the Holy Spirit – in and through you. The source of Love as we have already seen, is the Triune God. The Love of God is made manifest to you in the Father's sending of His Son and by the Son's death upon the cross:

> And as Moses lifted up the serpent in the wilderness, even so must the Son of man be lifted up: That whosoever believeth in him should not perish, but have eternal life. For God so loved the world, that he gave his only begotten Son.
>
> John 3:14-16a

> Who, being in the form of God, thought it not robbery to be equal with God: But made himself of no reputation, and took upon him the form of a servant, and was made in the likeness of men: And being found in fashion as a man, he

humbled himself, and became obedient unto death, even the death of the cross.

Philippians 2:6-8

The Father's Love manifest in the death of His beloved Son on the altar of the cross. Through the cross, God's love broke the power of sin and death over you, taking darkness captive and delivering you as a son or daughter – no longer of the world – but of glory (Hebrews 2:9-11). *"These things have I spoken unto you, that my joy might remain in you, and that your joy might be full."*

Taking up of the Gospel of Jesus Christ as your own story is nothing less than taking up the Gospel of Love; for God is Love and Jesus is the Son of God. Therefore are you a living manifestation of and testimony to the eternal power and presence of God's Love in the here and now. "If ye were of the world, the world would love his own...but I have chosen you out of the world" (John 15:19).

So the power of Love does not end in Jesus Christ at the altar of the cross, or in the depths of His descent to hell, but ascends in resurrection power to Heaven's Throne – wherein is your life now "hid with Christ" to the glory of God! (Colossians 3:3; Ephesians 1:5-7)

> And the glory which thou gavest me I have given them; that they may be one, even as we are one: I in them, and thou in me, that they may be made perfect in one; and that the world may know that thou hast sent me, and hast loved them, as thou hast loved me.
>
> John 17:22-23

To what end does God give you glory? "...that you may be perfect in one; and that the world may know that thou hast sent me [Jesus]" (ibid, pronoun change ours). Herein God's Love is both eternal and present, manifest both in heaven and in you – on earth, now. That the world may know the Father's Love for and through Jesus; for and through you. *"Herein is my Father glorified, that ye bear much fruit; so shall ye be my disciples."*

Can you now see that the Love of God does not end in the defeat of death, but in the glorious fruitfulness of an ascended life? Can you also see that the power of God broke forth in victory over the power of hell as the Beloved Son, the precious One and Only, emptied Himself upon the uplifted wood altar? As it was with our Lord Jesus Christ, so it also is with you and with us – for "a servant is not greater than his lord. If they have persecuted me, they will also persecute you; if they have kept my saying, they will keep yours also" (John 15:20).

Your taking up of the Gospel of Jesus Christ as your own story is nothing less than emptying yourself and laying down your life. As you love God with all of your heart, soul, mind and strength, your "self" and all of its beloved ones and precious things are also set before the Lord. Here, you die to the old man and worldly love; and are born again unto the Love of God and are kept of God. Here, you bear the love of God to the ones you love and to the world as "...followers of God, as dear children; And you walk in love, as Christ also hath loved you, and hath given himself

398

for you as an offering and a sacrifice to God for a sweetsmelling savour" (Ephesians 5:2 – change in pronouns ours).

So the love of God manifests in your life and you walk in love this side of heaven! This by the now and forever indwelling Holy Spirit of God, through whom we know the Father and the Son:

> And I will pray the Father, and he shall give you another Comforter, that he may abide with you for ever; *Even* the Spirit of truth; whom the world cannot receive, because it seeth him not, neither knoweth him: but ye know him; for he dwelleth with you, and shall be in you.
>
> He that hath my commandments, and keepeth them, he it is that loveth me: and he that loveth me shall be loved of my Father, and I will love him, and will manifest myself to him.
>
> If a man love me, he will keep my words: and my Father will love him, and we will come unto him, and make our abode with him. He that loveth me not keepeth not my sayings: and the word which ye hear is not mine, but the Father's which sent me.
>
> John 14:16-17, 21, 23-24

The Lord is not asking you to Love with a love that He has not already provided to you; for He has provided Himself! The Lord Jesus is not asking you to come to Him by your own power or love according to religious terms, or worldly terms, or even by your own spiritual disciplines or whatever else you might think is a pathway unto Him. He has given Himself as the pathway for you and to you; that you may give all of yourself for Him and to Him.

For in losing your life, you find your life – Jesus Christ, the Eternal and Present.

> For thus saith the high and lofty One that inhabiteth eternity, whose name is Holy; I dwell in the high and holy place, with him also that is of a contrite and humble spirit, to revive the spirit of the humble, and to revive the heart of the contrite ones.
>
> Isaiah 57:15

Having given your life to Jesus; having humbled yourself under the Gospel of Love; you are revived for your God is with you! Thereby you are completely freed from loving as the world loves, to loving as God loves – and this not of your old nature or of your own power – but as God's spiritual gift! For you are indwelled by the Holy Spirit, have the love of God, and abide in Jesus Christ:

> O righteous Father, the world hath not known thee: but I have known thee, and these have known that thou hast sent me. And I have declared unto them thy name, and will declare it: that the love wherewith thou hast loved me may be in them, and I in them.
>
> John 17:25-26

Alleluia! Let us join in the song of St. Paul and take this up as a prayer and song of praise together:

> Blessed be the God and Father of our Lord Jesus Christ, who hath blessed us with all spiritual blessings in heavenly places in Christ: According as he hath chosen us in him before the foundation of the world, that we should be holy and without blame before him in love.

> Having predestinated us unto the adoption of children by Jesus Christ to himself, according to the good pleasure of his will, To the praise of the glory of his grace, wherein he hath made us accepted in the beloved.
>
> Ephesians 1:3-6

Alleluia! Alleluia! Will you let your life be the "Amen" to the Beloved?

Let us keep pressing to even higher ground in the Love of God and take up our spiritual death and spiritual resurrection as a finished matter in the Lord Jesus Christ. Let us stay upon this higher ground and walk in the power of Love all the days of life this side of heaven. *'If ye keep my commandments, ye shall abide in my love; even as I have kept my Father's commandments, and abide in his love. These things have I spoken unto you, that my joy might remain in you, and that your joy might be full."*

For in Christ you are God's Child – and you walk in the fullness and light of God's Love – now and forever! And this not of your own self, but as God's gift. For in dying to self and spiritually taking up the cross, you are brought immediately to Christ and where Christ is – you are, by the power of the Holy Spirit – in Him (John 12:26).

This is why you no longer love according to the world; but according to God. This is why you are not captained by many loves, or divided loves, or languages of love, or cultural pictures of love, or by interpretations of love according to religious traditions or structures, or by the self-fulfilling passions of the heart, soul, mind or body. Even as you put your very self and every beloved

401

person, or lovely created thing of God on the spiritual altar, you commend them – and yourself – to the resurrection power of Jesus Christ! As it is written: *"stir up the gift of God....For God hath not given us the spirit of fear; but of...love."*

For at the cross, you said "I love you" to the High King of Heaven; you forsook life in the world and have been born again as a heavenly man or woman, now grafted as a branch to the vine of God in whose love you live and move and have your being (John 15:5; Acts 17:28). *"Herein is my Father glorified, that ye bear much fruit; so shall ye be my disciples. As the Father hath loved me, so have I loved you: continue ye in my love."*

For whoever believes in Jesus IS rescued from the power of death and brought into eternal life in the abounding and steadfast Love of God (Colossians 1:12-14; Galatians 1:4)! Whoever is born again has received "a spirit of love." For God's Love has shattered sin and death as His Beloved Son chose to give all on the pole of that sacrificial altar (Ephesians 5:1-2).

Loving God "with all thy heart, and with all thy soul, and with all thy strength, and with all thy mind; and thy neighbour as thyself" (Luke 10:27), now takes on its fullest meaning. In Loving God alone you bring all to Christ, and Christ to all, as you abide in His Love and walk in His commandments. For by the gift of the Holy Spirit stirring the new *"spirit of love"* given to you by God, you become the manifestation of God's Love in a lost and dying world.

You become a witness to the cross of Jesus Christ and "walk in love" embodying the gift of eternal life in Jesus Christ; as a "sweetsmelling savour" not yet perfected, but completely fulfilled in you. *"Herein is my Father glorified, that ye bear much fruit; so shall ye be my disciples. As the Father hath loved me, so have I loved you: continue ye in my love. If ye keep my commandments, ye shall abide in my love; even as I have kept my Father's commandments, and abide in his love. These things have I spoken unto you, that my joy might remain in you, and that your joy might be full."*

In this joy, we press unto even higher ground and consider: What spirit of love has God already given? There is but one answer as there is but One Love. It must be that you have received Love from the Father, through the Son, or Jesus would not be commanding all of the branches of the vine to continue on and abide in it. One cannot continue in or abide under something they have not yet received; but only in what they already have been given and taken a hold of.

> Wherefore I put thee in remembrance that thou stir up the gift of God, which is in thee by the putting on of my hands. For God hath not given us the spirit of fear; but of power, and of love, and of a sound mind.
>
> 2 Timothy 1:6-7

403

Prayer of Response: Unmingled Love

Please pray aloud with us...

Heavenly Father, Thank You for loving the world so much that you sent Your Son. I praise and bless You and declare with scripture: "God is love!" Just as You bring life out of death; so You bring love into a broken, dying world. In Christ, I set all I love before You and ask that You gather me to Yourself, that I may take up the Love of God alone.

I take up the prayer of St. Paul, "That Christ may dwell in my heart by faith; that being rooted and grounded in love, I May be able to comprehend with all saints what is the breadth, and length, and depth, and height; And to know the love of Christ, which passeth knowledge, that I might be filled with all the fulness of God" (Ephesians 3:17-19; pronoun change ours).

Thank You that in Christ, I am a new creation. Thank You, that by the cross of Jesus Christ and the presence of the Holy Spirit, I need not walk in fear, but may walk in the gifts You give of "a spirit of power, and of love and of a sound mind." Unto the praise of Your Glorious Grace, in the Name of Jesus alone, by the power of Your Holy Spirit alone, according to Your Word alone. I love You, Triune God and bind myself in Your Love. In Jesus' Name. Amen.

Week Seven, Day Four – Walking in the Spirit

"Wherefore I put thee in remembrance that thou stir up the gift of God, which is in thee by the putting on of my hands. For God hath not given us the spirit of fear; but of power, and of love, and of a sound mind. Be not thou therefore ashamed of the testimony of our Lord..."
2 Timothy 1:7-8

"And we know that the Son of God is come, and hath given us an understanding, that we may know him that is true, and we are in him that is true, even in his Son Jesus Christ. This is the true God, and eternal life."
1 John 5:20

"But the Comforter, which is the Holy Ghost, whom the Father will send in my name, he shall teach you all things, and bring all things to your remembrance, whatsoever I have said unto you."
John 14:26

First the Father came and walked in the cool of the evening with His children (Genesis 3:8). Then in time the Son came, took on flesh and walked morning and evening as the Son of man in the 24/7 doing of life-on-earth (Luke 2:1-20). Then Jesus died, resurrected and ascended unto heaven; and the Holy Spirit was given by the Father, sent of Jesus Christ in His Name – to dwell in the midst of the Children of God forever (John 14:16, 26; John 16:7). We live in the time of the Holy Spirit...

Let us rejoice! Heaven came down in the person of Immanuel and now remains in the person of the Holy Spirit. This Advocate at once indwells the new spirit of your clay-jar temple (1

Corinthians 6:19); intercedes at the Throne of Grace (Romans 8:26); and revives both heart and spirit (Isaiah 57:15; Matthew 3:11; John 3:5). In the beginning, the Father walked in the garden of this world; then later, the Son walked the Holy Land; yet now the Holy Spirit is manifest among us and indwells all who believe the Gospel of Jesus Christ. God is indeed with us (Matthew 28:20)!

The Holy Spirit is not an impersonal force or dynamic wind or silent fire. The Advocate is a person of the Triune God; and it is written that "*he shall teach you all things and bring all things to your remembrance, whatsoever I [Jesus] have said unto you*" (emphasis on pronoun ours). Indeed, it is the presence of the Holy Spirit which has given this 40 Day journey...

> For thus saith the high and lofty One that inhabiteth eternity, whose name is Holy; I dwell in the high and holy place, with him also that is of a contrite and humble spirit, to revive the spirit of the humble, and to revive the heart of the contrite ones.
>
> Isaiah 57:15

God dwells "in the high and holy place" of Heaven, so also He dwells in your temple – in the "Holiest of Holies" of your New Spirit (see Week Five, Day Four). The Great I AM continues His grace, mercy and everlasting love by leaving His Divine Presence in the world. For as the Lord Jesus has prayed to the Father; so the fulfillment is made manifest for us:

> I [Jesus] do not ask for these only, but also for those who will believe in me through their word, that they may all be one, just as you, Father, are in me, and I in you, that they

also may be in us, so that the world may believe that you have sent me.... I in them and you in me, that they may become perfectly one, so that the world may know that you sent me and loved them even as you loved me.

John 17:20-21; 23

Therefore we are not unloved or bereft Children. Our God is with us! This is the gift of God in Jesus Christ: that we may now be reconciled to God and walk in fellowship with Him as beloved children, via the indwelling Holy Spirit who is the Eternal and Present Counselor and Comforter and who by His Presence reveals the "deep things of God" to us (John 14:16, 26; 1 Corinthians 2:10).

"And we know that the Son of God is come, and hath given us an understanding, that we may know him that is true, and we are in him that is true, even in his Son Jesus Christ. This is the true God, and eternal life."

The unchanging power of God's Spirit (Malachi 3:6) as the Eternal and Present Counselor and Comforter manifests God's Faith, Wisdom, and Knowledge in your new spirit. From the meeting table of the new spirit, this gift of God's leading comfort is known by intuition and received in the God-given gift of a sound mind. The gift of God is of a spirit of a sound mind; not a perfected fleshly brain. The gift of God is His Holy Presence continually counseling and comforting us with the knowledge and wisdom of Jesus Christ. *"And we know that the Son of God is come, and hath given us an understanding, that we may know him that is true..."*

> Wherefore gird up the loins of your mind, be sober, and hope to the end for the grace that is to be brought unto you at the revelation of Jesus Christ; As obedient children, not fashioning yourselves according to the former lusts in your ignorance.
>
> 1 Peter 1:13

Pray we may not fashion ourselves in our own ignorance! Grab hold of the practical image given in scripture for the training of your mind. To "gird up the loins" is to gather up the corners of the robe and tuck them into the belt to run, work, train or to fight unhindered.

Praise God as obedient children! For God has given you a mind and the spiritual armor to guard it! For the Belt of Truth is yours, "Stand therefore, having your loins girt about with truth" (Ephesians 6:11-14)!

As you prepare to leave these 40 Days, by the Counsel of God, "gird up the loins of your mind" and tuck every corner of your mind into the Belt of Truth given for you to put on as living armour! Girding your mind is a spiritual act of loving God by giving Him all of your mind, heart, soul and strength by bringing "into captivity every thought to the obedience of Christ" (2 Corinthians 10:5).

And what does it mean to take every thought captive? To tuck every loose end of your thoughts; every unraveling emotion, every fraying hope or fringing belief into Him that is true...Jesus

408

Christ! And this, not of your own effort, but as a matter of receiving in faith what is given in love by our Lord Jesus Christ. *"Wherefore I put thee in remembrance that thou stir up the gift of God..."*

In Christ, your conflicting thoughts and emotions are untangled! In Christ you are free from "fashioning yourselves according to the former lusts in your ignorance" (1 Peter 1:13). In Christ, you are not tripped up by fear of sin or confusing desires. In Christ, you are free from the yoke of your former ways of thinking, living and being for "behold, the old has gone and the new has come" (2 Corinthians 5:17) and *"God hath not given us the spirit of fear; but of power, and of love, and of a sound mind!"*

The Holy Spirit by His very Presence within you has revived your spirit; then by the light of understanding given of Jesus Christ, your mind is renewed and your life transformed (Romans 12:1-2)! Now the inner chamber of your mind, once darkened with sin, is ablaze with the Light of Christ (1 John 1:7; Matthew 5:14)! So it is that you walk in the Light of God as a spiritual man or woman and may now, "Stand fast...in the liberty where with Christ hath made us free, and be not entangled again with the yoke of bondage" (Galatians 5:1).

"Stand fast...and be not entangled" (ibid). As you leave the desert, you need never be entangled in the darkness of ignorance, or confusion, or frayed emotions. You need never be pierced by thorns of faltering belief. You need never be lost in the briers of the cares of the world. For God Himself is the purifying Light of your understanding; and "the light of Israel shall be for a fire, and his Holy One for a flame: and it shall burn and devour his thorns and his briers in one day" (Isaiah 11:17).

Let the blazing Light of the Spirit of God clear the briers and thorns of any habits of thought arising from your "conversation in times past" when you lived "fulfilling the desires of the flesh and of the mind" (Ephesians 2:3). These thoughts and passions, these "cares and riches and pleasures of this life...bring no fruit to perfection" or maturity (Luke 8:14).

For the soundness of a transformed mind is not found in worldly education, purposefulness, thoughtfulness, strength or might. Rather the opposite. The natural mind trained in conformance to the world is held in a yoke of bondage as in a strong hold (Galatians 5:1; Romans 12:1; 2 Corinthians 4:4). Such a mind can become walled up and entangled with worldly or natural presumptions, speculations, arrogant thoughts, and proud arguments which contend against "the knowledge of God" (2 Corinthians 10:5).

Will you lay down the trophies of our modern culture and take up your place *"in him that is true, even in his Son Jesus Christ?"* Will you present your body and your mind as "a living sacrifice, holy, acceptable unto God, which is your reasonable service" (Romans 12:1-2)?

When you are led of the Holy Spirit, you are led of Jesus Christ. Just as a man cannot serve two masters; the mind cannot at once be given over to serving its own natural thoughts and simultaneously bring "into captivity every thought to the obedience of Christ" (2 Corinthians 10:5). The one who attempts this double-thinking is "unstable in all of his ways" and ought not expect to "receive anything of the Lord" (James 1:6-8).

Though double-mindedness is a serious obstacle to perceiving the leading of the Spirit; God has given each Christian what is necessary to prevail even in the hidden world of thoughts; "...because greater is he that is in you, than he that is in the world" (1 John 4:4). And the picture of scripture is of the Holy Spirit as a Dove. King Jesus as your Good Shepherd does not drive you with some spiritual stick into single-mindedness; but instead calls you. For it is written: "A bruised reed shall he not break, and smoking flax shall he not quench" (Matthew 12:20; Isaiah 42:3). What is the smoldering flax, but the dimly burning wick of the Spirit set in the clay-vessel of your body? *"So stir up the gift of God...of a sound mind."*

All that encroaches upon the Spirit and all that presses upon your mind can be consumed as dross by the Refining Fire of the Spirit as your mind is transformed to apprehend and walk in God's will (Romans 12:1-4). For even "the cares of this world, and the deceitfulness of riches, and the lusts of other things entering in," which "choke the word" are tended to in Christ (Mark 4:19).

For as Jesus gave His Life for your life, and His Love for your love: so He sent the Holy Spirit to bear witness through your new spirit; that you may have the "mind of Christ" (Romans 8:16; 1 Corinthians 2:16). By the leading presence and work of the Holy

411

Spirit who knows the mind of God; you may now, "think God's thoughts after Him"!

Before taking up the work of the last steps of these 40 Days unto the Spirit; consider praying aloud for the Holy Spirit to gird your mind and take captive your thoughts in Christ. God loves you and will fulfill the work He has begun in you...

"Dear Heavenly Father, Your words are true. Thank You for sending the Holy Spirit to lead me into all truth! Please let Your Word blaze as a purifying fire through my spirit that I may be free from any spirit of double-mindedness and step into a new purity of mind in and through Jesus Christ. This by the power of Your Holy Spirit and through the gift of a sound mind that You have already given me. Please forgive me of any and all thoughts which were opposed to Your Kingdom. In the Name of Jesus, Amen."

May God's word whisper deeply in your spirit that you may know in your spirit and apprehend by intuition in your mind the gift you have received:

> But Eye hath not seen, nor ear heard, neither have entered into the heart of man, the things which God hath prepared for them that love him.

> But God hath revealed *them* unto us by his Spirit: for the Spirit searcheth all things, yea, the deep things of God. For what man knoweth the things of a man, save the spirit of man which is in him? even so the things of God knoweth no man, but the Spirit of God.

Now we have received, not the spirit of the world, but the spirit which is of God; that we might know the things that are freely given to us of God. Which things also we speak, not in the words which man's wisdom teacheth, but which the Holy Ghost teacheth; comparing spiritual things with spiritual.

But the natural man receiveth not the things of the Spirit of God: for they are foolishness unto him: neither can he know *them*, because they are spiritually discerned.

But he that is spiritual judgeth all things, yet he himself is judged of no man. For who hath known the mind of the Lord, that he may instruct him? But we have the mind of Christ.

1 Corinthians 2:9-16

If you do not instantly sense the Light of God's indwelling Spirit, do not be afraid. For it is better to wait in a time of darkness on the altar of transformation, than to walk in the light of fashioning oneself by human wisdom or reasoning. Be confident that God will meet you and fulfill His word in you (Philippians 1:6).

Who is among you that feareth the LORD, that obeyeth the voice of his servant, that walketh in darkness, and hath no light? let him trust in the name of the LORD, and stay upon his God.

Behold, all ye that kindle a fire, that compass *yourselves* about with sparks: walk in the light of your fire, and in the sparks *that* ye have kindled. This shall ye have of mine hand; ye shall lie down in sorrow.

Isaiah 50:11

As you leave these 40 Days the tempter's primary tactic will be the same with you as it was with Jesus – for you are not above your Master (John 15:18-20). The deceptive powers will work to convince you to take up the word of God, transform yourself, and achieve its ends according to your own means and ends (Luke 4:1-13). Or as God, speaking through Isaiah puts it; to "kindle a fire" and "compass yourselves about" and "walk in the light of your fire" (ibid).

And the world kindles a fire for self-esteem, self-sufficiency, self-awareness, self-improvement, self-discipline, self-direction, self-actualization...and more. Could this whole process focusing on self-development be inadvertently creating a habit of "self-transformation" even in the spiritual life? Pray for the Counselor to strengthen you, for it is written that false and deceitful workers **"transform themselves into apostles of Christ"** even as **"Satan himself is transformed into an angel of light"** (2 Corinthians 11:13-14, emphasis ours).

Be careful to *"stir up the gift of God"* according to the Word of God. *"A spirit...of sound mind"* is not defined, formed or compelled by the world or what is in the world; but finds its spiritual soundness, discretion, judgment, sobriety and discipline in the testimony of our Lord. The gift of a *"spirit...of a sound mind"* does not mean that your natural mind in and of itself has become exalted; rather the opposite. The natural mind must be still; that God may be known (Psalm 46:10). A wonder of spiritual rebirth is that in being still in mind and soul before God, the Lord is exalted

414

not only within you but is also testified to and glorified in the earth (Psalm 46:10-11)!

"A spirit...of sound mind" is the continuing offering of yourself in Christ as a living sacrifice to God with the continual outcome of being able to test or prove the manifest will of God in your life (Romans 12:1-2)! In giving yourself to God, you are no longer giving yourself over to being led by the conforming spirit of the world into self-sufficiency, self-awareness, self-fulfillment, self-discipline or self-whatever. You have laid what is precious of yourself on the altar as a sacrifice of praise; and by faith in Jesus Christ are now transformed by and taught of God (John 6:45). You are not burned to annihilation on this altar; but are a particular clay lamp designed by God for a particular destiny as you hold the burning wick of flax as a light to the world (Matthew 5:14, 12:20). In this your light so shines that all may see the good works that you do and glorify your Father in heaven (Matthew 5:16)!

The Blood of the Lamb has cleansed your clay so your conscience is free from all guilt (Romans 8:33-34). Though you were once a lamp blackened with sin, now may you shine bright as a star in this present darkness (Philippians 2:15b)! For scripture is clear that as you ask Jesus, the Spirit will be given unto you (Luke 11:13); and that as you "Draw nigh to God...he will draw nigh to you" (James 4:8). For God has purified your heart through faith (Acts 15:9). And by "the blood of Christ, who through the eternal Spirit offered himself without spot to God" is your conscience purged "from dead works to serve the living God" (Hebrews 9:14)!

"A spirit...of sound mind" "girds up the mind" in the taking of all stray thoughts, unraveling emotions and or fraying passions of the flesh "into captivity...to the obedience of Christ" (2 Corinthians 10:5). That in loving God with all of your mind, you may put on the Belt of Truth; and by the binding power and presence of Truth, you may walk soundly in the freedom of the revelation of Jesus Christ. Scripture declares that since you are in Christ, you have the understanding of Christ: "The Son of God is come, and hath given you an understanding, that you may know Him that is true, and you are in him that is true, even in...Jesus Christ!" (pronoun change ours).

Stirring up *"a spirit...of sound mind"* is nothing less than putting off the conversations and prayers of the natural, or "old man" and putting on the "new man" "which after God is created in righteousness and true holiness" by the "renewed spirit of your mind" (Ephesians 4:22-24). The "new man" was quickened as you "believe in thine heart" and "confess with thy mouth the Lord Jesus" (Romans 10:9): so now you may with a gift of a sound mind lay aside the conversation and work of the world, go to the secret place of your inner chamber, and "pray at all times in the spirit" (Ephesians 6:18).

Indeed, the spiritual man or woman through prayer arising from the Spirit's intercession (Romans 8:27) takes up and is taken up by:

> ...the word of God [which] is quick, and powerful, and sharper than any twoedged sword, piercing even to the

416

dividing asunder of soul and spirit, and of the joints and marrow, and is a discerner of the thoughts and intents of the heart.

Hebrews 4:12

Thus *"a spirit...of sound mind"* is established in, protected by, and set apart by the Word of God. For only by the Gift of the Father and by the Word of God is the soul and spirit, the deep connecting tissues of man, and matters of the heart divided. For Jesus says: "no man can come unto me [Jesus], except it were given unto him of my Father" (John 6:65).

Only by the Gift of the Father is the flax wick of the Spirit both placed in the lamp and lit! For Jesus also says: "It is the spirit that quickeneth; the flesh profiteth nothing: the words that I speak unto you, they are spirit, and they are life" (John 6:63). So as with your first step of faith in believing in and confessing Jesus; each follow-on step of walking in the Spirit is only by the gift of the Father and by the Word of God.

So becoming a spiritual man or woman is a gift of God given by Grace alone, received through Faith alone in Jesus Christ alone, by the revelation of the Holy Spirit alone, according to Scripture alone – and ALL to the Glory of God alone! Alleluia! God be praised!

So now we have come to what it means to have the gift of *"a spirit...of sound mind;"* yet we have not come to the top of the last desert-mountain! Pray for God's strength to continue pressing toward higher ground! Just as you first received the Word of God and were born of the Spirit and given New Life in Christ; now forever the Holy Spirit indwells, counsels, comforts, guides and teaches you. For it is written:

> Howbeit when he, the Spirit of truth, is come, he will guide you into all truth: for he shall not speak of himself; but whatsoever he shall hear, that shall he speak: and he will shew you things to come. He shall glorify me: for he shall receive of mine, and shall shew it unto you.
>
> John 16:13-14

So having the gift of *"a spirit...of sound mind"* is nothing less than having the gift of the Holy Spirit whispering the revelation of God to you.

After these 40 Days, you may now know that God reveals Himself to you Holy Spirit to spirit, in accordance with the revelation of the Jesus Christ of scripture. As a spiritual man or woman, this revelation is worked out in the unfolding vista of your daily life! What is shared in that inner chamber of your spirit is brought to your mind by intuition – that is, by your spirit taking the instruction of God to cognition. Some describe this process as "knowing, that I know what I know" is from God; or that "what is known of God – is."

In becoming a spiritual man or woman, God does not force Himself upon you and overpower you from heaven. God does not make you an automaton to command this way or that by taking your mind, as that is not love. God gives Himself and asks His Beloved if they will come to Him. Jesus calls you by name and all who would come out are welcomed (John 10:3, 6:37). The Holy

Spirit is thus as a Dove cooing and not some Almighty Drill Sergeant breaking you down and in with force. For why would God give Himself, only to take His Children?

Ask for the living word of God to divide asunder your spirit: from your mind with its thoughts, your soul and its intents, and the flesh of your bones and marrow with their desires (Hebrews 4:12). Ask for the living word of God to be your only yoke; and in so doing, though you retain your personality and are of present mind, embodied soul and sound flesh, you are no longer compelled by their dead works (Matthew 11:30; Galatians 5:1; Hebrews 9:14).

A *"spirit...of a sound mind"* is made manifest as "...we have the mind of Christ" (1 Corinthians 2:16). *"Be not thou therefore ashamed of the testimony of our Lord."* But how? By asking, waiting, and hoping with unwavering "trust in the name of the LORD" that you might "stay upon...God" (Isaiah 50:10b). For scripture is clear that as you ask Jesus, the living water will be given (John 4:10).

As you ask, so shall you receive, by the power of the Holy Spirit! For the "LORD is nigh unto all them that call upon him, to all that call upon him in truth...He will fulfill the desire of them that fear him: he also will hear their cry, and will save them" (Psalm 145:18-19). Indeed, the work is already finished and the veil of the Holiest of Holies has been torn from top to bottom!

Will you be the clay lamp fed by the Eternal Presence of Jesus Christ through the brightly burning wick of the Holy Spirit of the Lord? Will you receive the leading hand of the Holy Spirit already dwelling within you? For your God is with you! He holds you by your right hand and shall guide you with counsel and afterward receive you to glory! (Psalm 73:22-24)

As you walk unto the soundness of mind in the Holy Spirit, in the Love of Jesus Christ by the resurrection power of God; you are translated from being mere sons and daughters of the world to being adopted sons and daughters of glory. Herein do you also share the glory of Jesus Christ; in dying are you raised unto eternal life!

And when does eternal life begin? Now, this side of heaven. For it is written: "And this is life eternal, that they might know thee the only true God, and Jesus Christ, whom thou hast sent" (John 17:3).

Divine Love did not end at the cross, nor is it manifest only in the someday of the New Jerusalem! As the spirit of Truth is perfectly manifested in Jesus Christ, so the Holy Spirit manifests what is of God – to you. With the gift of the spirit of power, and of love and of a disciplined or sound mind, you walk unto the Spirit, and have the keys to manifest the Lord's power, love and sound thinking in your life. And none of this of your own doing, for as it is written, "A man can receive nothing, except it be given him from heaven" (John 3:27).

Now is the day of the Holy Spirit! Now are we come to the end of our 40 Days' Walk; and in Christ by the leading of the Holy Spirit are you to be a heavenly man or heavenly woman. In the

420

storm-front between the world and the Kingdom, as you become less...He will become more (John 3:30).

Yet you may choose to be the clay-lamp of God or to follow the design and purpose of your own mind. You are after all made in God's image with a will to choose the paths of the Spirit or the paths of the world. As we close these *40 Days*, will you choose to die to yourself and be transformed by the renewing of your mind? Or will you take up the life of the old man again with a wink and a nod at the desert?

To the Holy Spirit of God, we commend you and according to scripture, in the Spirit, are praying for all who take up this book:

> For this cause we also, since the day we heard it, do not cease to pray for you, and to desire that ye might be filled with the knowledge of his will in all wisdom and spiritual understanding; That ye might walk worthy of the Lord unto all pleasing, being fruitful in every good work, and increasing in the knowledge of God; Strengthened with all might, according to his glorious power, unto all patience and longsuffering with joyfulness; Giving thanks unto the Father, which hath made us meet to be partakers of the inheritance of the saints in light.
>
> Colossians 1:9-12

Final Response: Walking in the Spirit

Please go back to Colossians 1:9-12 and read it aloud with us...

Then as the Holy Spirit leads, take time to write down what you perceive deep in your spirit as the "walk worthy of the Lord" unto which you are being drawn. Be as specific as you are led to be. In time, God may call you back to this desert highway. If the wilderness time returns, begin again by remembering where you left off.

My Response unto The Spirit

Were you encouraged through this book?

If so, would you comfort, encourage and edify your brothers and sisters in Christ (1 Thessalonians 5:11) by making copies of this book available for them?

Our commission at Valley Springs Institute is to encourage the Church of Jesus Christ and be an instrument in strengthening Faith; that every Believer may take up God's Word and rely upon the Holy Spirit, and that the world may know the Living God who answers prayers and manifests Himself to His People.

If the Spirit leads you to join us in this mission, please reach out via eternalandpresent.author@gmail.com or ValleySpringsInstitute.com.

May we endeavor together in the Spirit, look to Jesus Christ at all times, and magnify God by an unwavering trust in God's Word in much prayer and persevering discipleship.

May the Lord Jesus find Faith in the earth when He returns.

– B.R. MØRK

Made in the USA
Lexington, KY
14 September 2019